A Pocket Guide to Shakespeare's Plays

Kenneth McLeish (1940–1997) was a playwright, translator and the author and/or editor of over eighty books including *The Theatre of Aristophanes*, *The Good Reading Guide*, *Companion to the Arts in the Twentieth Century*, *Myth*, *Key Ideas in Human Thought* and (with Valerie McLeish) *The Listener's Guide to Classical Music*. He has translated work by Aristophanes, Aeschylus, Euripides, Sophocles, Feydeau, Holberg, Ibsen, Labiche and Strindberg. He was a Fellow of the Royal Society of Literature.

Stephen Unwin is Artistic Director of the Rose Theatre in Kingston. He founded English Touring Theatre in 1993, where his Shakespeare productions include *A Midsummer Night's Dream*, *Hamlet*, *Macbeth*, *As You Like It*, *Henry IV, Parts One* and *Two*, *King Lear* and *Romeo and Juliet*. He is the winner of the 2003 Sam Wanamaker Shakespeare Globe Award. He directed Kenneth McLeish's translations of *A Doll's House*, *Hedda Gabler* and *The Master Builder*. He has directed more than fifty theatre and opera productions for the Royal National Theatre, English National Opera, the Royal Opera House, the Royal Court Theatre and many others. His work has been seen at the Donmar Warehouse, the Almeida Theatre and the Old Vic. He has co-written *A Pocket Guide to Ibsen, Chekov and Strindberg* (Faber and Faber), *So You Want to be a Theatre Director?* (Nick Hern Books) and *A Guide to the Plays of Bertolt Brecht* (Methuen).

T0284686

A POCKET GUIDE TO
Shakespeare's Plays

**Kenneth McLeish and
Stephen Unwin**

faber and faber

First published in 1998
by Faber and Faber Limited
The Bindery, 51 Hatton Garden
London EC1N 8HN

Typeset by RefineCatch Limited, Bungay, Suffolk
Printed and bound in Great Britain by CPI Group (UK) Ltd,
Croydon, CR0 4YY

A CIP record for this book
is available from the British Library

ISBN 978-0-57123-745-6

Printed and bound in the UK on FSC® certified paper in line with our continuing
commitment to ethical business practices, sustainability and the environment.
For further information see faber.co.uk/environmental-policy

Contents

'In Nature's infinite book of secrecy / A little I can read'

Soothsayer, *Antony and Cleopatra*

Introduction

William Shakespeare lived for fifty-two years (1564–1616). He spent some twenty-five of them (c.1588–1613) working as a dramatist and actor in London, living in lodgings while he maintained his home and family in Stratford-on-Avon. In the early part of his career, he may have spent the summer months (when the theatres were open) in London, returning to Stratford during the winter and on the frequent occasions when plague closed the theatres. (His poems *Venus and Adonis* and *The Rape of Lucrece* were written in 1592–3, during a particularly lengthy period of this kind.) He was a shareholder in the company as well as writer and performer, and he used his considerable earnings from drama to buy property in Stratford, where he was thought of more as a respected burgher and family man than a member of the ragtag-and-bobtail theatrical profession.

During Shakespeare's life there was a shift from the relative prosperity of the early years of Queen Elizabeth's long reign (1558–1603), through the problematic, quasi-imperial rule of her later years, to the more introverted, machiavellian and unpopular style of James I. The temper of the Court was a matter of importance. London was a small community, and far more than in modern times, its political and mercantile élite was affected by the day-to-day enthusiasms, prejudices, intrigues and scandals of the monarch and Court circle. Loss of favour could be sudden – as when Elizabeth turned against her former favourite Essex, provoking him to rebellion – and punishment could be arbitrary – as when James I held Ralegh in the Tower for sixteen years merely on suspicion of conspiracy. People travelling up-river to performances of *Romeo and Juliet* or *Hamlet* might well have been uneasily conscious of the Traitors' Gate of the Tower and the heads impaled on spikes beyond it. In the arts, although patronage could be lavish – for example, Shakespeare's company regularly played at Court and had a fashionable following – royal censorship forbade explicit political or religious controversy and any depiction of contemporary figures.

In Shakespeare's year, the two or three Court performances may have been the most glittering occasions, but he earned his bread and butter in the public theatres. In open-air venues such as the Globe (which his company built in 1599), the season ran from May to September. In indoor venues such as the Blackfriars (which they also used from 1608 onwards), plays could be performed at any time. In the public theatres, greater licence was tolerated than at Court, particularly from such stars as Will Kemp (the leading comedian of Shakespeare's company until 1599). New scenes were inserted to accommodate the comics and Kemp regularly ended shows with an impromptu solo turn, dancing and improvising topical repartee. City Fathers criticized the theatres as centres of sedition, and Puritans muttered about profanity, but the stage community and its audience affected not to notice.

The public theatres had a large and mixed audience. Prices at the Globe ranged from one penny (groundlings, standing) to sixpence (gallery seats in the 'Lords' Rooms' upstairs). The full theatre may have held as many as 3000 people, though numbers were probably often fewer. The Blackfriars was smaller and more exclusive; its prices were up to five times higher. There is debate about just how socially mixed the spectators really were – for example, were the 'groundlings' merely the London poor or a loose group of students, apprentices and other impoverished but aspirant play-lovers? Spectators probably came from a wider social circle than those of today, but the spectrum may not have been as broad as romantic image has it.

Performances at the Globe took place on a large stage with two doors and no scenery. At the Blackfriars, the stage-area was at one end of a long room and candlelit, but the layout was similar. Props and costumes were elaborate: the clothes, for example, were often donated by rich patrons. There were no directors or designers, and actors worked not from full scripts but from their cues.

As we read or see Shakespeare's plays today, it is easy to think that they must have had a self-conscious aesthetic: the nature of monarchy and development of nationhood in the histories, or the huge ethical and moral themes discoverable in the tragedies. Although what we know of contemporary performance suggests that the emphasis may have been far more pragmatic – on the characters, their relationships, the words they spoke and the action of the story (a fact with implications for modern production practice) – such themes can hardly have escaped more thoughtful spectators. The extraordinary intellectual vitality and fluency of late Elizabethan and Jacobean theatre made it an ideal medium not only to reflect the dynamic movement of a society in rapid change, but also, perhaps, to articulate and contribute to those changes.

Shakespeare's England was a place not of the sunny stability often claimed for it, but of self-questioning, crisis and conflict. During his lifetime, older ways of wealth-creation began to be displaced by the growth of early capitalism. In the last quarter of Elizabeth's reign, new trade-routes were opened up, and London became a commercial and financial centre on a level with Amsterdam, Antwerp and other major European ports. This expansion was accompanied by developments in industry and a growing interest in scientific, technological and geographical discovery, much of it inspired by the need to streamline production and find new markets.

Intellectual radicalism was one of the most remarkable features of the new merchant class to which Shakespeare himself belonged, and as his plays testify, it spread from trade-centred matters to every aspect of human endeavour. In contrast to the growing inflexibility and hierarchism of medieval European thought, the intellectual boundaries of Shakespeare's world were expanding at an exponential rate.

This expansion included new scepticism about both established religious beliefs and long-held traditions. In England, the period began with the displacement of Roman Catholicism by Protestantism, and the intellectual aftershocks of this revolution were felt throughout Shakespeare's life. Using the language of the recently-translated English Bible, all kinds of groups and individuals began questioning the old, divine-right stratification of society and proposing images of both a differently distributed economy and a newly constructed moral law. These new energies, and the contradictions between them and the old order, are incessant themes in Shakespeare's plays.

For Shakespeare and his audience, not the least change was the evolution of England (still not Britain) as a nation-state and of London as its capital. The centralizing of power from regional lords to the Court in London, and the self-confidence and innovative thinking engendered by ever-expanding contact with the non-European world, encouraged a growing sense of 'England' and 'Englishness'. Focus on the capital was increased at the end of the sixteenth century by deforestation, enclosure of common land by rich landowners and a series of poor harvests, leading to a rural discontent which penetrated even Shakespeare's Arcadia, and to the arrival in London of people from all over the country: part of the melting-pot which provided his theatre audience.

Although new thinking and the new age brought significant improvements in the quality of most people's lives, it remains true that the practicalities of Shakespeare's London left much to be desired by modern standards. Life expectancy was some years shorter than today, disease was rife, rule was authoritarian and harsh, and even such basics as comfort and protection from the elements were unpredictable, especially for the poor.

All these trends and realities are the stuff of Shakespeare's work. His plays live not merely for the dazzle of the language – hardly a word is lazily used – or the dynamism and fascination of the story-telling, but for the way he roots profound moral, ethical and spiritual matters in every-day reality. Even in his most fantastical plays, real people, with all their contradictions, are placed in specific and meticulously-realized social worlds. Although some of the detail is now dead, the authenticity of those characters and those worlds remains: the plays provide images of truth. By constantly developing dramatic and dialectical opposites, Shakespeare creates the illusion of life stretching out in every direction.

'Poetic', 'learned' and 'witty' passages in the plays are not pasted on, but spring from the characters' own feelings at each moment. In real life, people move in an instant from wit to lyricism, from cleverness to banality – and that naturalness is echoed in Shakespeare's texts and helps to 'create' his characters. In the richness of his human insight, even the most extreme experiences have an ordinary mortal basis. The connection is made, and explored, between our most intimate dreams and the demands and rewards of the practical world at large. Above all others, this is the quality which speaks to generation after generation, to people of every nationality, and which guarantees the life in his plays and their continuing resonance. He is more than just his fame.

Out of the mountain of writings on Shakespeare, we would like to recommend three books in particular, which develop or chime with ideas put forward in these pages. Andrew Gurr's *The Shakespearean Stage* (C.U.P., 3rd edn, 1992) and Peter Thomson's *Shakespeare's Professional Career* (C.U.P., 1992) are accessible and vivid discussions of Shakespeare as a working dramatist. Ted Hughes's *Shakespeare and the Goddess of Complete Being* (Faber and Faber, 1993) is enthralling criticism, a poet musing on a poet and offering new insights in every sentence.

Kenneth McLeish, Stephen Unwin, 1997

Authors' note

In the quotations, we have used the minimum of punctuation, just enough to make the meaning clear. Similarly, we have not described every character, but concentrated our space on those we thought most significant. A more detailed view of the characters is given in Kenneth McLeish's *Shakespeare's Characters A–Z* (1984).

There is much disagreement about the precise dates and order of Shakespeare's plays. We have decided to set them in approximate chronological groupings of Early, Middle 1, Middle 2 and Late, with the Death of Queen Elizabeth and the Coronation of James I providing a useful midpoint. In compiling this sequence, we have drawn on Charles Boyce's *Encyclopaedia of Shakespeare* (Facts on File, 2nd edn, 1997).

Approximate Chronology of the Plays

The Early Plays (1588–96)

The Two Gentlemen of Verona
The Taming of the Shrew
The Comedy of Errors
Henry VI, Parts I, II and III

King John
Titus Andronicus
Richard III

The Middle Plays 1 (1596–1603: Elizabethan)

The Merchant of Venice
A Midsummer Night's Dream
Love's Labour's Lost
Richard II
Henry IV, Parts I and II
The Merry Wives of Windsor
Romeo and Juliet

Much Ado About Nothing
Henry V
As You Like It
Julius Caesar
Twelfth Night
Hamlet

The Middle Plays 2 (1603–7: Jacobean)

Troilus and Cressida
Othello
Measure for Measure
King Lear

All's Well That Ends Well
Macbeth
Antony and Cleopatra
Coriolanus

The Late Plays (1607–13)

Pericles
Timon of Athens
The Winter's Tale
The Tempest

Cymbeline
The Two Noble Kinsmen
Henry VIII

All's Well That Ends Well

 Source

Giovanni Boccaccio, *The Decameron*.

 Story of the play

Helena, daughter of a famous physician, has since her father's death been the ward of the Countess of Roussillon. She is in love with the Countess's snobbish son Bertram. Hearing that the King is sick and has said that whoever cures him can name their reward, she gives him a healing potion and asks him to order Bertram to marry her. Immediately after the wedding, Bertram leaves for war in Italy with his friend Parolles. He writes a letter to Helena saying that if she wants him to accept her as his wife, she must first get a ring from his finger and become pregnant with his child – conditions which he thinks will never be fulfilled. Helena disguises herself as a pilgrim and goes to Florence, where she intends to find Bertram or become a nun. She lodges with the same widow as Bertram, and makes friends with Diana, the widow's daughter. Bertram is trying to seduce Diana, and the women conspire to outwit him. Helena takes Diana's place in Bertram's bed, sleeps with him and takes his ring.

Having (as he thinks) succeeded with Diana, and hearing that Helena has died in France, Bertram now plans to return home. (He is delayed by two officers, the brothers Dumain, who trick Parolles into showing Bertram that he is not the honest, loyal friend he thought he was.) Back in France, Bertram makes plans to marry the daughter of Lord Lafeu. But at the last moment Diana appears, waving a ring (not Bertram's ring, but one the French king earlier gave Helena) and claiming that he promised to marry her and then deserted her. Bertram angrily denies this, and Diana is about to be arrested when Helena comes in, wearing Bertram's own ring and pregnant with his child. The conditions of the letter have been exactly fulfilled, and he has no choice but to accept her as his wife.

🖙 Characters

King of France	Reynaldo, *a steward*
Duke of Florence	Lavache, *a clown*
Countess of Roussillon	Widow of Florence
Bertram, *her son*	Diana, *her daughter*
Helena, *her protégée*	Violenta *and* Mariana, *her*
Parolles, *a follower of Bertram*	*neighbours*
Dumain *and* Dumain, *French*	Gentle Astringer, Lords,
captains	Officers, Page, Servants,
Lafeu, *an old lord*	Soldiers

HELENA On the page, Helena can seem single-minded and unscrupulous. She is determined to make Bertram her husband, and keep him, whether he wants it or not. She manoeuvres the King of France into forcing Bertram to marry her; when her new husband escapes to Italy she follows him (and is quite prepared to enter a nunnery and die if her quest fails); she sleeps with him and fulfils his conditions by a trick which is, on the face of it, as heartless as anything he does or says to her.

None the less, although Helena's actions can seem hard and scheming, her actual nature belies them entirely. She is radiantly beautiful – Lafeu says that she could 'quicken a rock, and make you dance canary / With sprightly fire and motion' – and she is loved by everyone she meets (except Bertram). With the Countess she is loving and dutiful; with Diana and the Widow she is warm and friendly; in the last act she appears like a *deus ex machina* from ancient tragedy, to unknot the complications (Bertram is about to have Diana arrested on a trumped-up charge) and bring about the happy ending. All the play's poise and radiance are hers, and when her torments of love and sexual desire for Bertram are finally resolved, her happiness warms our hearts.

BERTRAM The Count of Roussillon is young, and seems both pompous and arrogant. He is easy meat for the flatterer Parolles –

and then jumps at the chance of humiliating him. Forced to marry a girl he does not love, he sulks, runs away and lays down impossible conditions. He seduces Diana with utter unconcern, and then, when she confronts him, flatly and indignantly denies it. Faced with proof that his marriage conditions have been exactly fulfilled, he gives way with what sounds like total lack of understanding of the real issues. Emotionally, Bertram is as immature as Claudio in *Much Ado About Nothing* – and the reasons are either that, like Claudio, the part was played on Shakespeare's stage by an actor only barely in his teens, or that Bertram is deliberately made ungracious to contrast with Helena's outgoing radiance. For all her winsomeness, she is unscrupulous in getting what she wants; so he, for all his churlishness, is an innocent ripe for education (at her hands) in the manners of the world and the ways of love.

PAROLLES Parolles' name means 'words', and appropriately, he is a master phrase-maker. (For example, when Bertram asks whether or not he should go to Italy, Parolles answers, 'To the wars, my boy, to the wars! / He wears his honour in a box unseen / That hugs his kicky-wicket here at home / Spending his manly marrow in her arms / Which should sustain the bound and high current / Of Mars' fiery steed . . .') He is a confidence trickster, a toady and a liar, ever alert for his own advantage, and has no scruples whatever. Tricked by the Dumain brothers into thinking that he has been captured by the enemy, he eagerly offers to save his own skin by betraying both the city of Florence and his own young master.

In his day Parolles was seen as a kind of cut-price Falstaff, and he is still sometimes played that way, pulling at the audience's affection. But he replaces Falstaff's moral, rueful self-awareness with a kind of icy cockiness, and is aptly described (by the First Lord) as 'a most notable coward, an infinite and endless liar, an hourly promise-breaker, the owner of no one good quality . . .' In the play's complex moral world he contributes cynicism, deviousness and compromise – and it is part of Shakespeare's plan that because of his liveliness as a character, he all but tips the balance.

DUMAIN AND DUMAIN The Dumain brothers were probably played by two of Shakespeare's comedians, working as a group with a colleague who played Parolles. Their specialities are physical bustle and spectacular verbal gibberish ('Throca movosus, cargo, cargo'; 'Biblibindo chicurmurco'), and the trick they play on Parolles (persuading him that they are the enemy and – in Bertram's hearing – conning him into betraying all the war-dispositions of his own side) has a crucial function in the play's moral articulation. At a moment when we might begin to doubt the probity of Helena's motives or methods in pursuing Bertram, the brothers draw attention away from her and focus it on Parolles, a figure of true immorality and deviousness, and then give him a splendid comedy comeuppance.

DIANA The daughter of the Widow of Florence is named after the hunting goddess in ancient myth. She is a courageous young woman, and the relationship between Diana, her mother and Helena is particularly interesting: three women unite, finding together the power they need to bring down Bertram and deal with him, the power each lacks individually. In this relationship, Diana and Helena help each other (Diana consenting to the 'bed trick'; Helena rescuing Diana in the French court): this united front against the world is common in Shakespeare's young men, but rare among his women.

LAVACHE Lavache, jester of the former Count of Roussillon, is now aged and dependent on the goodwill of Bertram, the new Count, and the Countess, Bertram's mother. This hardly helps his temper. Lavache is a bitter Jacobean clown who sees only hellfire and disaster, a superannuated comedian whose humour (or perhaps ill-humour) sours every conversation he takes part in. Part of the paradox of his character, and of his presence in the play, is the extraordinary patience and kindness he evokes in others.

LAFEU This ceremonious old lord, from the same generation as the King of France, the Countess of Roussillon and the jester Lavache, was a friend of Bertram's father, and now tries to take his place. He warns Bertram (unavailingly) against Parolles, and is loving towards Helena (the Countess's ward), scornful of the young grandees who refuse to court her because she is 'of lower birth'. His name suggests that once he was fiery and impassioned, but by now this has dwindled to a kind of dear-old-man sentimentality. (For example, in the trial-scene when Bertram agrees to accept Helena, triggering the happy ending, Lavache bursts out, 'Mine eyes smell onions: I shall weep anon' – a line whose combination of pathos and bathos is worthy of Shallow himself.)

COUNTESS OF ROUSSILLON Bertram's mother is a matriarch, brisk (for example with Lafeu) but businesslike. However, her love for Helena is sincere and moving: her requests that Helena call her 'mother' are not mere ceremony.

KING OF FRANCE The King, as a character, belongs almost entirely to fairy tale. His fatal illness, his calm acceptance when it is miraculously cured, his worldly-wise serenity and absolute authority in the trial scene – all splendidly set off the seething emotions and moral equivocations of the other characters in this complex play.

☞ About the play

The atmosphere of this subtle, haunting play is sometimes described as Chekhovian, blending melancholy stoicism with powerful emotional and social realism. As with Chekhov's plays, its underlying points seem to be that comedy and tragedy are entwined in human life, and that although happiness is ultimately possible, even certain, it is achieved unexpectedly and as if by default. However destructive and obsessive human character may be, it still has positive potential; at some time in the future, when we least expect it, 'briars shall have leaves as well as thorns / And be as sweet as sharp'.

This Chekhovian mood is only one dimension of the play. In a way characteristic of Shakespeare's 'bitter comedies' (the others are *Troilus and Cressida* and *Measure for Measure*), *All's Well That Ends Well* draws ideas from several different genres, deconstructing or ironizing them in the process. For example, at its heart is the story, common in romance, of an orphan girl in love with a rich young boy who does not love her. Shakespeare adds to this a motif from fairy tale, Helena's magic curing of the king – and then twists them together to pose a plot-problem of a new and psychologically vexing kind, realistic and outside the realms of either romance or fairy tale: What happens when the tables are turned and the rich young boy is handed to the orphan girl as prize? At first he rejects her, and the play seems simply to be ringing changes on the same old fairy-tale dilemma.

But then the genre changes again, and something emerges which is almost like Brechtian epic theatre. Senseless militarism, with its peacock vanity and rough-house *machismo* (powerfully embodied in the Parolles scenes) is contrasted with a triangle of three unhappy, struggling women: Helena, embarked on a pilgrimage which she imagines will lead only to a nunnery and then to death; Diana, dealing with the contrast between doubting her own worth and the fact that men find her attractive; Diana's widowed mother, coping with the indignities and constraints of poverty. When they defeat Bertram by tricking him they are playing by his rules, but their goal is more profound than anything he could contrive. There is a significant difference between their 'bed trick' and the one in *Measure for Measure*. In *Measure for Measure*, Mariana takes Isabella's place so that the central character can avoid sex; in this play the opposite is the case, a fact that allows Shakespeare to reiterate another of the themes implicit in all his comedies, the positive value of female sexuality.

In the play's last scene the various genres overlap and merge. Realism, magic, fairy tale, romance, the counterpointing of ideas in epic theatre, all converge to produce an answer to the riddle posed at the start of the action, a happy ending which has been reached only because the two main characters have changed. In the course of the action, Helena has taken on some of Bertram's qualities, and now he reveals the possibility that he might take on some of hers. His recognition that he has been at fault is a small moment in terms of lines but enormous in the meaning of the play. 'O pardon!' he says, and then, in answer to Helena's question 'Will you be mine, now you are doubly won?', 'If she, my liege, can make me know this clearly, / I'll love her dearly, ever, ever, dearly.'

The lines can sound like platitude, but in human terms the truth they embody has been reached by a difficult and painful journey, and is irrevocable.

In performance

Although there are no accounts of performances of *All's Well That Ends Well* in Shakespeare's time, references to a play called *Monsieur Paroles* both suggest that the piece was known and also hint at the reason. Parolles continued to be its main drawing-power in the seventeenth century, when it was also tricked out with songs and dances to make it sunnier and more fanciful than Shakespeare's original. In the nineteenth century the play (which works better on stage than in the study) fell foul both of scholars objecting to what they considered its unconvincing dramaturgy (they found the ending flat and silly) and of the censor (who found it immoral). Even in the twentieth century it remained one of Shakespeare's least-performed works, despite a handful of memorable productions and outstanding performances by (among others) Laurence Olivier (Parolles), Edith Evans and Peggy Ashcroft (the Countess), Ernest Milton and Alec Guinness (the King of France) and Catherine Lacey and Irene Worth (Helena).

> HELENA   I think not on my father
> And these great tears grace his remembrance more
> Than those I shed for him. What was he like?
> I have forgot him. My imagination
> Carries no favour in it but Bertram's.
> I am undone. There is no living, none
> If Bertram be away. Twere all one
> That I should love a bright particular star
> And think to wed it, he is so above me.
> In his bright radiance and collateral light
> Must I be confronted, not in his sphere.
> Th'ambition in my love thus plagues itself:
> The hind that would be mated by the lion
> Must die for love. [I, i]

Antony and Cleopatra

☞ Sources

Plutarch, *Lives*. Act Five, focused almost exclusively on Cleopatra, owes debts to the tragedy *Cleopatra* (1594) by Samuel Daniels – who repaid the compliment in 1607 by revising his own play in the light of Shakespeare's.

☞ Story of the play

Following the assassination of Julius Caesar and the deaths of Brutus, Cassius and the other conspirators, Antony shares rule of Rome with Lepidus and Octavius, Caesar's nephew. Their power is challenged by the young Pompey, son of Caesar's former rival, and the need for unity is great between them. However, Antony has fallen in love with Cleopatra, queen of Egypt and Caesar's former mistress, a woman fourteen years his junior. She hides her true feelings and it is never clear whether she shares his passion or is merely using the love-affair to ensure the safety of her people and her country.

When Octavius and Lepidus accuse Antony of neglecting his duties, he quarrels with them, and the dissension grows until he abandons Rome entirely, sides with Pompey and crowns himself and Cleopatra joint rulers of the Eastern provinces of the Republic. Octavius gathers the Roman fleet to fight Antony and Cleopatra's joined forces at Actium. The two sides are evenly matched, but at the last moment Cleopatra turns her ships and sails away. Antony follows and is defeated.

Enobarbus, hitherto Antony's devoted lieutenant, defects to Octavius. Antony is defeated in a land battle after the Egyptians once more flee. Antony blames Cleopatra, who responds by hiding in her Monument and sending him a message that she is dead. Thinking that both his career and his love are ended, Antony falls on his sword, is carried to the Monument and dies in Cleopatra's arms. Rather than be captured and enslaved by the Romans,

Cleopatra kills herself (by taking a poisonous snake hidden in a basket of figs and letting it bite her breast). Octavius orders that the lovers be buried together, commenting that 'no grave upon the earth shall clip in it / A pair so famous.'

Characters

ROMANS

Mark Antony, Octavius Caesar, M. Aemilius Lepidus, *joint rulers of Rome*

Sextus Pompeius

Domitius Enobarbus, *Antony's second-in-command*

Canidius, Demetrius, Dercetas, Eros, Philo, Scarus, Silius, Ventidius, *followers or allies of Antony*

Agrippa, Dolabella, Gallus, Maecenas, Proculeius, Taurus, Thyreus, *followers of Caesar*

Menas, Menecrates, Varrius, *followers of Pompey*

Euphronius, *an ambassador*

Octavia, *Octavius's sister, married to Antony*

EGYPTIANS

Cleopatra

Charmian, Iras, *her maids*

Alexas, Diomedes, Mardian, Seleucus, Soothsayer

Clown

Attendants, Messengers, Officers, Soldiers

ANTONY Ancient Roman writers claimed that the virtues which made the city great included an all-conquering sense of duty and a refusal to accept moral and ethical compromise. Antony's love-affair flouted this code. His failure was not so much that he ran to the bed of an exotic foreigner – many Romans, including Aeneas, the founder of the nation, and Antony's mentor Julius Caesar, did precisely the same – but that when he did so, he deliberately put second his duty to his country and his moral integrity. His failure was not of character but of principle, and all the more unforgivable for that.

By contrast, Shakespeare makes Antony's obsession part of a general tragic flaw, the division in his nature between self-control and self-indulgence, and his inability to resolve it. Like Lear, Antony replaces the reality of power with magnificent but self-indulgent and arrogant display. Lear, however, is changed by events, as his suffering gives him true dignity and moral substance. Antony is denied such tragic dignity, and his attempted suicide – as the result of the last of a long series of tricks played by Cleopatra, when she sends false word that she is dead – seems not so much noble as exhausted and pathetic.

It is at this point, as Antony is taken into the Monument and dies in Cleopatra's arms, that Shakespeare at last allows him dignity. The power of his love transforms not only his own passing from the world, but also Cleopatra and the Romans who find his body. It is as if the shell of his imperfections has been peeled from him; his epitaphs from Cleopatra and from Octavius reveal the truth of the man within: 'The crown o' the earth doth melt . . . / . . . there is nothing left remarkable beneath the visiting moon'; 'The death of Antony / Is not a single doom: in the name lay / A moiety of the world.'

CLEOPATRA   Like Lady Macbeth (a part written perhaps at the same time, perhaps for the same actor), Cleopatra is a complex, layered creation, and from the start Shakespeare invests the role with irony. We are constantly reminded that we are watching a performance, and one which teeters on the edge of danger. The boy was even able to carry off explicit references to his own performance (for example, in Act Five, 'I shall see / Some squeaking Cleopatra boy my greatness / I' th' posture of a whore') and, in a very Lady Macbeth-like comment, to ask (about the asp) 'Dost thou not see my baby at my breast, / That sucks the nurse asleep?'

Irony in performance articulates ambiguity in the character itself. For most of the play, Cleopatra plays a dangerous, exhilarating and self-admiring role, flirting with one of the most powerful men in the world, mocking him, leading him on, playing games with him. It is never clear – perhaps even to herself – whether she truly loves Antony, or is manipulating their relationship for her own personal and political ends.

Then, in Act Five, Shakespeare caps all this – and offers the actor the part's greatest challenge and reward – by transforming Cleopatra's flirting into true love, and giving her a mystical apprehension of her own destiny. Antony's death shows her the reality of existence, of her own nature and of relationships. She moves, with a self-awareness which is now moving as well as theatrical, to her own consummation in death, the ending which has from the very start (ironically) underlain her entire affair with the Romans, and perhaps her life.

OCTAVIUS CAESAR Octavius, Julius Caesar's nephew (and later, after the events of this play, the Emperor Augustus), is brave, loyal, noble, politically skilled and a fine commander. He has little time for emotion, and the aloofness which is one of the main components of his public success also makes him seem formal and brisk in private. His coolness is in striking contrast to the hot-headedness of Antony and Cleopatra, and not unexpectedly wins the day.

ENOBARBUS A blunt soldier, Enobarbus is at first as over-whelmed by Cleopatra and all she stands for as his friend Antony ('The barge she sat on, like a burnished throne / Burned on the water. The poop was beaten gold . . .'). But later, saddened at the way Antony is putting Egypt first and Rome second, he leaves his service, returns to Octavius and is part of the army which defeats Antony. He knows that his decision was right (' 'Tis better playing with a lion's whelp / Than with an old one dying'), but it tears the heart out of him ('I am alone the villain of the earth'), and he dies of grief.

CHARMIAN AND IRAS Cleopatra's maids are charming, happy in their work and have a salty wit: Charmian, for example, claims that her ambition is 'to be married to three kings in a forenoon, and widow them all'. Events destroy them. In the Monument, Iras dresses Cleopatra for death and then, heart-broken, dies herself. Charmian closes Cleopatra's eyes ('Now boast thee Death, in thy possession lies / A lass unparalleled. Downy windows, close . . .'), puts the snake to her own bosom and dies beside her mistress.

CLOWN The Clown comes to town from the countryside with a basket of figs containing a snake ('the pretty worm of Nilus . . . / That kills and pains not'), delivers it to Cleopatra with a string of garrulous remarks about 'worms' and their feeding, devils, death and women, and is hustled offstage. His short scene (a single page) comes straight after Cleopatra's announcement to her maids that she is determined to die with honour, in her 'best attires', and dazzlingly focuses tension on the coming suicide.

SOOTHSAYER Cleopatra's maids flirt with the Soothsayer, asking him to tell their fortunes and then responding with joky ambitions of their own. Later, the Soothsayer reminds Antony of the character differences between him and Octavius ('Thy demon, that's thy spirit which keeps thee, is / Noble, courageous, high, unmatchable / Where Caesar's is not. But near him thy angel / Becomes a fear as being o'erpower'd . . .') and warns him to 'Make space enough between you'. Antony refuses to listen, with fatal results.

MESSENGER At one point Cleopatra claims to have sent 'twenty several messengers' after Antony. We see only a few of them onstage, but each of these has real character. One of them brings Cleopatra news that Antony has married Octavia, and is slapped, 'haled up and down' and only just escapes being stabbed dead for his trouble. Prudently, in his next scene he finds several faults to report in her (she is boring, 'dwarfish', has 'a low forehead' and is older than Cleopatra), and is rewarded with gold.

☞ *About the play*

Antony and Cleopatra is one of a group of plays (the others are *Othello*, *King Lear*, *Macbeth* and *Timon of Athens*) written over the same period and exploring the same basic theme: what happens when a 'great' and 'noble' mind gives way under the stress of private feeling. Plutarch, Shakespeare's main source, saw Antony very much in this light, as the epitome of ancient Roman virtue corrupted by private vice and the excess and exoticism of an alien culture. Shakespeare enriched Plutarch to provide a double-headed tragedy, his two protagonists exemplifying different kinds of 'greatness' and 'private vice', but destroyed in the same way, by the conflict between the two.

The play's construction mirrors this theme. At one level it is dark and intimate, exploring the 'fatal attraction' of individual human sexuality and locating it in the mysterious world of ancient

Egypt. But it is also public, examining an equally fatal division in political style and substance. The subversive force of sex threatens Rome itself, and the Republic must subordinate that energy if its power is to be maintained. The destinies of individual and state impinge on one another – a favourite Shakespearean idea, carried over from his history plays of the previous decade. They are inseparable, and one or the other must accommodate or be destroyed.

Tensions between individual will and the political world's spiralling complexities permeate the play. Antony declares that he is prepared, for Cleopatra's sake, to 'let Rome in Tiber melt, and the wide arch / Of the ranged Empire fall', but the realities of Roman politics are such that he finds it impossible to abandon his responsibilities; it is as if the clash between Rome and Egypt were inscribed in his soul. He is aware of the threat his love poses to the stability of the Republic, and his upbringing and military career (as Julius Caesar's lieutenant) have instilled in him the duty Rome needs from its leaders. All this comes hard up against his infatuation, not just with Cleopatra but with the exotic world she represents. Unable to resolve the conflict, and aware that he is fighting a battle which can never be won, he accepts the fact like the soldier he is: 'The next time I do fight / I'll make Death love me, for I will contend / Even with his pestilent scythe.'

In a similar way, for all the regal magnificence and power in which Cleopatra is draped (and drapes herself) she is also human: obsessive, vain, driven by destabilizing sexuality, impulsive and haunted by Death. Antony's sure political instincts and soldierly honesty (the 'Roman-ness' in him) are matched by her quickfire intelligence and calculated unpredictability (the 'Egyptian-ness' in her), but she is knocked off-balance by exactly the same irrational forces as he is: love, and then a growing and overwhelming sense of her own disastrous destiny.

Other characters also embody the play's main conflict. Enobarbus is Antony without the flair: in love with love but not a lover, detached, eventually unable to balance his duty to Rome with his admiration for Antony his master, and dourly, self-hatingly choosing Rome. Octavius sacrifices Octavia, his unfortunate sister, on the altar of *realpolitik* in a humiliating non-marriage to Antony – a deed which tinges all his subsequent political success and the lessons he learns about life as the play proceeds. Iras and Charmian, full of libidinous merriment and energy, go the opposite way from Enobarbus, following their beloved mistress to the pit of Death. And framing all such private accommodations and tragedies are the politics and realities of the wider world, embodied in Lepidus, Agrippa, Maecenas and the other grandees, Pompey and his cut-throats, and dozens of vividly-drawn soldiers, messengers and servants: the bustling continuum of the world in which Antony and Cleopatra move, and on which their personal tragedy makes so much impact.

In performance

Richard Burbage played Antony at the first production, the only known performance until 1849 of Shakespeare's unadulterated text. (In the interim it was replaced by Dryden's derivative *All for Love* (1678), or by versions cannibalizing both plays.) Real appreciation of the play dates from the twentieth century, when it has attracted performers of the calibre of Constance Collier, Edith Evans, Margaret Rawlings, Peggy Ashcroft and Barbara Jefford (Cleopatra), and Laurence Olivier, Michael Redgrave, Christopher Plummer, Alan Howard and Michael Gambon (Antony). Charlton Heston directed himself in a 1972 film.

PHILO
Take but good note and you shall see in him
The triple pillar of the world transformed
Into a strumpet's fool. [I, i]

As You Like It

☞ Source

Thomas Lodge's novel *Rosalynde*, made over as romantic satire by Shakespeare's addition of such characters as Jaques and Touchstone.

☞ Story of the play

Oliver, the elder son of Sir Roland de Boys, wants to inherit all Sir Roland's property, and when his younger brother Orlando grows up and demands his share, he arranges for him to fight a professional wrestler, Charles, and for Charles to kill him. The match takes place at the court of Duke Frederick, who has usurped the power of *his* brother ('Duke Senior') and banished him to the Forest of Arden together with his courtiers, including the gloomily philosophical lord Jaques.

Orlando survives the wrestling match and escapes with his servant Adam to join Duke Senior in the forest. Duke Frederick sends Oliver into the forest to find him. At the wrestling match, Orlando has fallen in love with Rosalind, the daughter of Duke Senior, and she with him. Duke Frederick, afraid that Rosalind's popularity with the people will remind them of her father, exiles her as well, and she too escapes to the forest, disguised as a boy ('Ganymede') and accompanied by her friend Celia (Duke Frederick's daughter) and the court jester, Touchstone. Orlando meets her, takes her for a boy and tells her of his love for Rosalind. Thinking herself safe in her disguise, she suggests that he ease his love-sickness by paying court to her as if she were Rosalind.

The forest's other occupants are country people. The shepherd Silvius loves Phebe, but Phebe will have nothing to do with him: she has fallen in love with 'Ganymede'. Touchstone seduces the goatherd Audrey. Orlando saves Oliver's life and the brothers are reconciled. 'Ganymede' tells Orlando that she will bring Rosalind to marry him, and at the ceremony reveals her true identity. Phebe, at first broken-hearted, is reconciled with Silvius. Duke Frederick repents, restores his brother's power and vows to retreat to a monastery. The four pairs of lovers (Rosalind and Orlando, Celia and Oliver, Phebe and Silvius, Touchstone and Audrey) are happily united, and the only person who remains unchanged is Jaques, who follows Duke Frederick into the monastery.

☞ *Characters*

Duke Senior	Audrey, *goatherd*
Rosalind, *his daughter*	Sir Oliver Martext
Duke Frederick	Charles (*wrestler*); William;
Celia, *his daughter*	Denis, Adam (*Oliver's servants*);
Oliver, Orlando, *brothers*	Jacques (*brother of Oliver and*
Jaques	*Orlando*); Amiens, Le Beau
Touchstone, *jester*	(*lords*); Hymen; Lords, Pages,
Corin, Silvius, Phebe, *shepherds*	Singers

ROSALIND *As You Like It* begins in emotional winter and ends in spring – and Rosalind's character reflects that change. At the start of the play, depressed by her situation (her father, Duke Senior, has been banished by her uncle), she makes the resolute if emotionally frozen decision to 'forget the condition of her estate' by 'devising sports' and, specifically, to make herself fall in love with the first young man she sees (Orlando, as it happens, at the wrestling match; but it could have been anyone). Soon afterwards she herself is banished, and she reacts by disguising herself as a boy and going with her friend Celia to live in the forest.

Arden works its magic on Rosalind, as on everyone else. She discovers that Orlando is in love with her, as she with him – and only the boy's disguise she wears comes between them. What was once protection becomes a torment, and her attempts to find the right moment and way to reveal her true identity are the play's emotional heart. The love she once pretended, now real, irradiates the action.

ORLANDO At the start of the play Orlando seems little more than a standard, hot-headed adolescent hero. He complains to

Adam that he has been unjustly treated throughout his growing-up, is sulky with his brother (*Oliver*: 'Now sir, what make you here?' *Orlando*: 'Nothing: I am not taught to make anything'), takes on a pointless wrestling match in a spirit of bravado, and when he finds that Oliver is still plotting to kill him, rushes impetuously off to exile.

However, the Forest of Arden soon works its magic, and Orlando changes before our eyes. His agreement with the disguised Rosalind (to practise courting on her) begins as a game but deepens into affection, witty friendship, and finally to a love which is at first yearning (he still thinks she is a boy) and is then gloriously fulfilled. The happy ending is classically romantic, but the growth in Orlando's character, matching that in Rosalind's, gives it emotional depth and substance.

JAQUES In Ben Jonson's *Every Man in His Humour* (in which Shakespeare acted in 1598), the people are not 'characters' but 'humours': rage, dullwittedness, affability and so on. In *As You Like It* (probably planned at the same time), Jaques is another such 'humour': melancholy.

Jaques is an intellectual dandy, prepared to analyse every situation and derive what exquisite lessons he can from them. (The 'seven ages' speech is typical.) If no other subject offers itself, he turns his attention on himself. For example, he tells us that his melancholy is 'neither the scholar's melancholy, which is emulation; nor the musician's, which is fantastical; nor the courtier's, which is proud; nor the soldier's, which is ambitious; nor the lawyer's, which is politic; nor the lady's, which is nice; nor the lover's, which is all these; but it is a melancholy of mine own compounded of many simples, extracted from many objects and indeed the sundry contemplation of my travels, in which my often rumination wraps me in a most humorous sadness'. He is a striking portrait of an Elizabethan intellectual, and at the end of the play he goes into a monastery, self-absorbed to the last, to see what the monks can teach him.

TOUCHSTONE Touchstone is a self-made man who has made his way at court and picked up the manners and mannerisms of his social superiors. It is social comedy with an acid edge to dump such a sophisticate in a forest, and watch him first patronize the rustics (to Corin the shepherd: '[It is a] simple sin in you, to bring the ewes and the rams together, and to offer to get your living by the copulation of cattle . . .') and then fall in love with a sweet but exasperating goatherd ('Bear your body more seemingly, Audrey').

CELIA Sometimes a small part can steal the show. This tends to happen with Celia, Duke Frederick's gentle daughter who goes into exile because her friend Rosalind asks her. Throughout the coming-and-going in the forest, she supports Rosalind, helping her games with Orlando and standing up for him when Rosalind seems to be bullying him. Warmth of character suddenly blossoms into sparkiness at the end of the play, when she suddenly announces that she is in love with Orlando's brother Oliver and means to marry him.

☞ About the play

When Hymen, god of weddings, arrives to resolve all complications at the end of Act Five, he is confronted by couples representing four very different social classes and sexual principles.

Touchstone and Audrey articulate one of the play's key contrasts, between court artificiality and the warmth and naturalness of country life. Their relationship is an attraction of opposites. They are 'in lust' with one another, and their journey from emptiness to fulfilment embodies the moral movement of the action, towards that union and resolution which, as Hymen says, causes '. . . mirth in Heaven / When earthly things made even / Atone together.'

The second couple, the shepherds Phebe and Silvius, though drawn from the stock of pastoral poetry and romance, are characterized like prototypes of the self-taught, working-class characters from D.H. Lawrence. They suffer all the agonies of unrequited love, Silvius for Phebe and Phebe for 'Ganymede' – and anyone familiar with the conventions recognizes at once that they were meant for one another.

The third couple is Celia and Oliver, daughter and son of two upper-class, warring families. Love, in their world, is a key element in political negotiation, and their union will involve their families as much as it does themselves. Their romance is a matter of diplomacy and formality as well as of the heart, and Shakespeare enlivens it with a structured series of miracles (escape to the forest, rescue from the beast, love at first sight, sudden conversion to goodness) to bring it to the point where Hymen descends from the skies and blesses them, for all the world like a monarch ratifying a treaty long-prepared by underlings.

The fourth couple, Rosalind and Orlando, an orphan and a rejected younger son, are part of an emerging radical group (almost middle-class). Theirs is a new, individualistic version of love, in which true feelings are all-important, the woman's negotiating stance is essential and the notion of personal truth is constantly pursued.

The formal patterning of this ending is extraordinary. But it is not sterile, symmetry for its own sake (as in Lodge's original novel). It involves a new and radical vision of how to organize society. After the cruelty of the play's opening court scenes (in which an elder son abuses his younger brother, physical combat is used to cause humiliation and hurt, and a ruler exercises arbitrary power), the protagonists make their way into the forest (that is, escape Nurture for Nature) – and their initial response is negative. Duke Senior valiantly tries to find 'sermons in stones', but it is only when the miracle of human charity is dramatized, when the significantly-named Old Adam nearly starves to death and his plight forces Orlando to face up to his own terrors and confront Duke Senior and his followers, that the basis of a decent future can be glimpsed. Jaques' 'seven ages of Man' speech draws up a brilliant diagram of human experience. But the individual's story can be understood only within a social structure. Even Jaques himself, that cynical individualist, functions only in terms of the society around him. Without the ironical framework of Arden, his ruminations would be no more than empty brilliance.

Acts Three and Four resemble a series of dialogues touching on a whole range of subjects: they are almost an Elizabethan guide to witty conversation. And Shakespeare's point is that such discussions are only possible after – and because of – what has happened up until now, with the arrival of a new moral universe. Without such a civilizing factor, life can be led only *in extremis*, in the wintriest conditions. But now, the main topic of discourse is the all-embracing one of love, and it is in these two acts that the four couples discover the true natures of their proposed loved ones and are eventually able to face Hymen. Appropriately for a play in which a character is named Touchstone, the process it shows of self-discovery and burgeoning relationships parallels the method of scientific research being developed at the time: hypothesis leading to experiment leading to conclusion. (In the 1590s Francis Bacon was already working to assess and codify, by logical, 'scientific' methods, all human knowledge until his time.) As so often, Shakespeare took ideas from the air around him (in this case, the vogue for pastoral romance and the quest for scientific rigour) and transmuted them to gold.

At the centre of all this is Rosalind: witty, full of heart, moral, driven, confused, the Goddess of Love reincarnated in an ordinary English girl. Her scepticism about the accepted conventions of love makes her question the very meaning of the word: 'The poor world is almost six thousand years old, and in all this time there was not any man died in his own person, *videlicet* in a love cause . . . Men have died from time to time and worms have eaten them, but not for love'. She knows that when romantic conventions are swept away, and despite such checks as death, the cruelty of the world and the agonies of the social order, love itself is unfailing and irresistible. This is the truth she must tell Orlando, the truth to which we must all surrender: as the page boys sing in Act Five, we must 'take the present time' and 'love the spring'.

☞ In performance

As You Like It opened the new Globe Theatre in 1599. Although there is no other surviving evidence, the fact that four plays of the time (*The Merry Wives of Windsor*, *Much Ado About Nothing*, *As You Like It* and *Twelfth Night*) all have female leading parts of a similar type may suggest a boy actor of particular ability, for whom Shakespeare wrote parts of ascending challenge and reward as he grew older.

The play fell out of favour in the seventeenth century, and was at first revived in the eighteenth century in a rewritten version incorporating scenes and songs from almost every other Shakespeare comedy and even from some of his tragedies. The true text was not restored until 1740 (in a production for which Arne wrote his well-known settings of the songs), and from then on *As You Like It* has been one of Shakespeare's most popular comedies. Every actress of note has played Rosalind, from Peg Woffington in the 1750s to Peggy Ashcroft two centuries later, and including Mrs Kendal, Athene Seyler, Edith Evans, Katharine Hepburn, Vanessa Redgrave and Maggie Smith.

Curiosities include a production with surrealist designs by Salvador Dalí and three all-male productions: in 1920 at the Central YMCA, in 1967 at the Royal National Theatre and in 1992 by the touring company Cheek By Jowl.

ROSALIND O how full of briars is this workaday world. [I, iii]

ROSALIND Come, woo me, woo me, for now I am in a holiday humour and like enough to consent. [IV, i]

ROSALIND Men are like April when they woo, December when they wed. Maids are May when they are maids, but the sky changes when they are wives. [IV, i]

The Comedy of Errors

☞ Sources

Shakespeare multiply expanded Plautus' comedy *Menaechmi*. The scene where Dromio of Syracuse compares the body of Nell the kitchen-maid to the sphere of the world contains ideas from accounts of Drake's recent voyages to the Spanish Main, and also parodies an erotic poem of John Donne, a law student when the play was performed at the Inns of Court in 1594.

☞ Story of the play

Egeon, a merchant of Syracuse, lost his wife, one of his twin sons and one of their twin servants in a shipwreck many years before, and is wandering from town to search for them. In Ephesus he falls foul of a law stating that any Syracusan caught in Ephesus must pay a fine within twenty-four hours or be executed. Unknown to Egeon, his son Antipholus of Syracuse and Antipholus' servant Dromio of Syracuse are also in Ephesus. Like Egeon, they are unaware that their twins Antipholus of Ephesus and Dromio of Ephesus now live, and prosper, there.

The play becomes literally a comedy of errors, as both Antipholus and Dromio are mistaken for their brothers. The Syracusans are startled but not surprised, because they know that Ephesus is famous for wizards, ghosts and shape-changers. Antipholus of Syracuse is greeted by strangers and given jewels in the street. Invited to dinner by a woman he's never met (in fact his brother's wife Adriana), he falls in love with her sister Luciana (much to Adriana's annoyance, as she thinks he is her husband). Antipholus of Ephesus is barred from his own house and refused a gold chain he has ordered for his wife, on the grounds that the goldsmith gave it to 'him' earlier. The two Dromios are beaten for disobeying orders which were actually given to their twins.

Eventually the goldsmith has Antipholus of Ephesus arrested for debt and tackled as a lunatic (by Pinch, the quack-doctor). Egeon and Antipholus of Syracuse seek refuge in the same Abbey – and Egeon recognizes his son, and the Abbess as his long-lost wife. They hurry to the Duke, the families are reunited, Antipholus of Syracuse promises to marry Luciana, and all ends happily.

☞ Characters

Solinus, *Duke of Ephesus*
Egeon, *a merchant from Syracuse*
Antipholus *of Syracuse, his son*
Antipholus *of Ephesus, his twin*
Dromio *of Syracuse, servant of*
   Antipholus of Syracuse
Dromio *of Ephesus, his twin,*
   servant of Antipholus of Ephesus
Adriana, *wife of Antipholus of*
   Ephesus

Luciana, *her sister*
Luce, *Adriana's servant*
Balthazar, *a merchant*
Angelo, *a goldsmith*
Pinch, *a quack doctor*
Abbess, Courtesan, Gaoler,
   Merchants, Officers

ANTIPHOLUS OF SYRACUSE An innocent young man, engaged on what he sees almost as a Homeric quest (to find his long-lost brother), Antipholus is none too happy, in Ephesus, to become the butt of what he takes to be ghosts and wizards. But he is gifted with healthy opportunism, a sweet nature and a delight in taking things as they come, and for all his wariness of the supernatural, these qualities carry him through all the mistaken identities and surprises to a happy ending.

ANTIPHOLUS OF EPHESUS An ambitious young merchant, street-wise and upwardly mobile, he is completely baffled when people keep claiming he is someone else, or an impostor. Convinced that the whole thing is a string of malicious practical jokes, he becomes angrier and angrier. However, he is not the stock farce blusterer, but a man discomfited, thrown out of his element, and this gives him humanity. He thought he had his world under control, and when it is turned upside-down, he has no cure for it but rage.

ADRIANA Adriana is a self-assured young woman who shares all the values and interests of her upwardly-mobile husband, Antipholus of Ephesus. Secure in her position in society, and happy in the home of which she is mistress, she is not best pleased when the chain of mistaken identities begins. Like her husband, she takes them for practical jokes, and reacts sharply – particularly when she thinks that 'her' Antipholus is proposing a love-affair to her own sister Luciana. But even in the height of her anger, she reveals that she is still in love with Antipholus ('My heart prays for him, even though my tongue do curse'), and this is a major factor in the joy of the play's last scene, when all the farcical complications are unravelled.

LUCIANA Luciana is no less bewildered than her sister Adriana when the man she takes for her brother-in-law announces that he is in love with her and proposes marriage. But she is innocent, spirited and determined, more conventional than her sister and a good match for the 'other' Antipholus. Their compatibility is a small but important strand in the tapestry of pleasures which makes up this happiest of plays.

DROMIO OF SYRACUSE Dromio has grown up with 'his' Antipholus, and they are more like friends than servant and master. Antipholus calls him 'a trusty villain . . . that very oft / When I am dull with care and melancholy / Lightens my humour with his merry jests', and they spend their time in sparky discussions about nothing (which countries the parts of fat Nell's body look like, or whether hairy men are more cheerful than bald men). Not even numerous beating (by the 'wrong' Antipholus) make Dromio lose his cheerfulness, and he reacts to what he takes to be supernatural events with ironical delight rather than terror: when his master is arrested he says 'A devil in an everlasting garment hath him . . . A fiend, a fairy, pitiless and rough . . .'

DROMIO OF EPHESUS This Dromio is harder-edged and more cynical than his twin, and his tongue is sharper. Well used to his self-absorbed and irritable master Antipholus of Ephesus, he cannot resist cheeky answers even when he knows they will end in beatings. When Antipholus asks him about a sum of money he was to take to the bank: 'Where are those thousand marks you had of me?', he answers (knowing nothing about it), 'I have some marks of yours upon my pate / Some of my mistress' marks upon my shoulder / But not a thousand marks between you both'. He is fiercely urban.

ABBESS At first, the Abbess is stiff and dignified, almost to the point of parody. But when she recognizes her husband and long-lost sons, she melts into joy and humanity. This is a movement from two dimensions to human warmth which is characteristic of the way Shakespeare expands and explodes the boundaries of farce in this play.

PINCH Pinch is the quack doctor whom Adriana hires to exor-cize the spirits she thinks are driving her husband mad. He speaks only a dozen lines, but they are so obviously fake – 'I charge thee, Satan, hous'd within this man / To yield possession to my holy prayers / And to thy state of darkness hie thee straight . . .' – that they earn him an instant beating.

☞ *About the play*

This miniature masterpiece, Shakespeare's shortest play, enriches its source at every point it touches. The original is a straight-forward farce about a man whose long-lost twin arrives in town and is mistaken for him. By a simple stroke, giving the twin brothers twin servants, Shakespeare multiplies the possibilities of confusion many times, and then plays every conceivable variation on the basic gag. At this level, *The Comedy of Errors* is a firework show of social panic, slapstick violence and surreal misunder-standing – and it is funniest in the theatre when played entirely seriously. Too often the play is regarded as an excuse for alien comic invention; the fun in Shakespeare's scheme is in the way his characters react with increasing panic and violence to the confusion which engulfs them.

Comic invention is not, however, Shakespeare's main enrich-ment of his material. He deepens the characterization with fine language and by focusing not only on incident but also on relationships, particularly between husbands and wives, and servants and employers. Crucially, by framing the action with Egeon's (ultimately successful) search for his long-lost son, Shakespeare adds an element of quest which suffuses all the misunderstandings with emotional desperation – and then, by letting his powerful and unstoppable comic mechanism loose on characters already unsure about their own identity, he both amuses us with preposterous antics and explores the predicaments of believable people caught in situations which make them question both their individuality and their sanity.

In the closing scene, Shakespeare bathes the discovery of self and the reuniting of long-lost relatives with a radiance well outside the usual realms of farce, creating a mood in which magic, faith and wonder seem as inevitable as the air we breathe. His Ephesus is a mythic location – ancient cult-centre of the Mother Goddess; burial place of the Virgin Mary – which enshrines the most mysterious elements of religious faith. In the first scene, the lonely traveller Egeon is to be executed for what seem to be cruel and arbitrary reasons. In the end, through the intervention of the Abbess, he is not merely reunited with his long-lost family, but triumphs over death.

These two different worlds, transcendental and real, are embodied in the characters. Antipholus of Ephesus is the very picture of the harrassed *bourgeois* flailing in situations he neither understands nor controls. Locked out of his own house, pressurized by creditors he has already paid, railed at by a wife who thinks that he is being unfaithful, he reacts with violence, escalating in proportion with his bewilderment, until by the time he confronts and attacks the conjuror Pinch, his cherished identity as an urban sophisticate has fallen apart all round him. Similarly, Antipholus of Syracuse reacts entirely plausibly to the world of myth and mystery. He is full of anxiety about the witchcraft for which he has heard Ephesus is famous, is terrified of the 'siren's call', presumes that a courtesan is the 'Devil's dam', and is so wrapped up in his search for his long-lost brother that he loses everything he had when his ship sailed into harbour.

The two servants – whose role is absolutely central – straddle the play's twin worlds. On the realistic level they are Renaissance equivalents of the long-suffering, resourceful slaves of Roman comedy, a match for their masters in all but social status. On the mythic level Dromio of Syracuse is his master's companion in a long epic voyage, a kind of sweet and charming version of Sancho Panza, while Dromio of Ephesus is compared to an ass, the beast which bore Jesus into Jerusalem on Palm Sunday. At the end of the play, when the two worlds come together and the halves of human identity are miraculously united, the servants symbolize this by joining hands and leaving the stage together. As Dromio of Syracuse puts it, 'We came into the world like brother and brother / And now let's go hand in hand, not one before another.'

🖝 In performance

The first known performance, on December 28 1594, formed part of end-of-term revels by the law students of Gray's Inn in London, an event so riotous that many 'senior gentlemen' went home in disgust. In the next three centuries the play was revived infrequently, but in the twentieth-century it came back into its own, being played sometimes as part of a double bill (with *The Bells* in 1924, with *Titus Andronicus* in 1957) and sometimes 'straight' (for example Tim Supple's admired RSC production of 1996). Adaptations include two sprightly musicals, by Frederick Reynolds in 1819 and by Rodgers and Hart (*The Boys from Syracuse*) in 1938.

ANTIPHOLUS OF SYRACUSE
I to the world am like a drop of water
That in the ocean seeks another drop
Who falling there to find his fellow forth
Unseen, inquisitive, confounds himself.
So I to find a mother and a brother
In quest of them, unhappy, lose myself. [I, ii]

Coriolanus

👉 Sources

Plutarch, *Lives*; Livy, *History of Rome*.

👉 Story of the play

There is conflict in Rome between the starving citizens and the aristocrats who hold all the power. The citizens are helped by one lord (Menenius), who encourages them to join together for the general good. Menenius' arrogant friend Caius Marcius, by contrast, despises both them and the officials (Sicinius, Brutus and the other tribunes) appointed by the senate to speak for them. (Sicinius and Brutus are as outspoken about their loathing for Caius Marcius as he is about them.)

Caius Marcius, an outstanding soldier, wins a victory almost single-handed at Corioli against the Volscians. The Roman senate honours him with the surname Coriolanus, and he is promised the consulship if he will only humble himself to beg the citizens' 'voices' in his support. He does this reluctantly, making his distaste quite obvious, and Sicinius and Brutus seize their chance to turn the people against him, saying that he refused to allocate them free grain on the grounds that they were fickle and brainless and did not deserve to be fed. There is almost a riot in the Forum, Coriolanus rounds once more on the people and is exiled.

Rejected by Rome, Coriolanus goes to Antium, where the Volscian forces are regrouping, and asks Aufidius, their commander, to accept him as an ally or to kill him. Aufidius offers him command of the Volscian army, and Coriolanus agrees to lead them against Rome. He becomes a successful and popular general, and Aufidius grows ever more jealous and starts looking for reasons to accuse him of treachery.

The Volscians lay siege to Rome, and Coriolanus's friends go to beg him to spare the city. They fail. Coriolanus's mother

Volumnia, his wife Virgilia and his young son Marcus make a second appeal, Virgilia's tearful pleading balanced by Volumnia's reminder to her son of his aristocratic duty. This appeal succeeds. Coriolanus signs a treaty and draws his Volscian soldiers back to Antium. Aufidius accuses him of treachery, the two men quarrel and Aufidius's men murder Coriolanus. Only now, with Coriolanus dead at his feet, does Aufidius (ironically or otherwise) proclaim his nobility and order him a 'noble memory'.

Characters

ROMANS
Caius Marcius (*later* **Coriolanus**)
Volumnia, *his mother*
Virgilia, *his wife*
Valeria, *her friend*
Young Marcius, *Coriolanus's son*
Menenius Agrippa, *Coriolanus's friend*
Cominius, *consul*
Lartius, *general*
Sicinius, Brutus, *tribunes*

Nicanor

VOLSCIANS
Tullus Aufidius
His Lieutenant
Adrian
Aedifes, Attendants, Citizen of Antium, Citizens of Rome, Conspirators, Guards, Herald, Lictors, Messengers, Senators, Servants, Soldiers

CORIOLANUS In the nineteenth century, many critics and actors saw Coriolanus as a kind of giant among pygmies, a hero too grand to be accommodated by the age he lived in. Later ages, in particular those of Kafka, Sartre and Camus, tended to think of him as an outcast, a man at war with himself and unable to decide what he is or what he wants, let alone relate it to the society around him. There are hints of both interpretations in the text, but Coriolanus is a simpler character than either would suggest.

The Coriolanus that Shakespeare created is a heroic soldier whose success has frozen his character. Since birth he has been encouraged to think of himself as invincible, and the play shows what happens when he is confronted with his own hollowness and forced to seek accommodation with other people. At first, he believes that the simple fact of his existence is enough, that he has a divine right to the authority he claims. That authority, and the self-esteem which arises from it, lead him to arrogance, political ineptness, humiliation, separation from his family and an unheroic death. He is a lonely colossus, and is toppled by lesser mortals; but Shakespeare is more interested in the psychology of his inner hollowness, and in the despairing efforts he makes to come to terms with it.

CITIZENS In a famous simile, Menenius compares Rome to parts of a human body – and Shakespeare characterizes the citizens as if they were a single, multi-voiced organism, but endlessly changing shape and focus. They are the complex mass of ordinary people, passionately arguing contradictory positions. In the scene just before Coriolanus begs their 'voices' for his consulship, eight separate individuals speak, notably the hot-headed First Citizen and the sarcastic Second and Third Citizens. When Brecht reworked the play for the Berliner Ensemble in the 1950s, he concentrated on the way the 'many-headed' mob forms itself into a single revolutionary group; in Shakespeare they are more amorphous, a continuum of discontent which helps to create the unstable, volatile atmosphere of this unsettling play.

AUFIDIUS At the start of the play, Coriolanus's Volscian rival and friend/enemy seems almost like his twin, sharing both his military genius and his scorn for the common people. They spar on the battlefield more like intimates than enemies. But the difference between them is crucial. Coriolanus is precisely the man he seems to be, while Aufidius is playing a game, dissembling his true feelings. As Lartius has already explained to Coriolanus, 'Of all things upon the earth he hate[s] / Your person most; that he would pawn his fortunes / To hopeless restitution, so he might / Be call'd your vanquisher'. That Aufidius can play this part, and Coriolanus can ignore it, is typical of them both.

Later in the play, Aufidius begins, Iago-like, specifically to plot Coriolanus's downfall, and once again Coriolanus is too wretched, or too wrapped up in old-fashioned codes of honour, to take due heed. The result for him is sordid murder – and for Aufidius, a closing speech of deepest irony ('My rage is gone', it begins, 'And I am struck with sorrow') which closes the play not with pomp or honour but in a symphony of discords.

VOLUMNIA Coriolanus's relationship with his mother is central to his make-up. As soon as Volumnia speaks of her ruling passion – 'Anger's my meat; I sup upon myself' – we see where Coriolanus's spirit came from. Unlike her son, Volumnia knows how to control her temper and use it 'to better vantage'. But there is still no compromise in her, and it is when he cannot deal with that fact in the intercession scene that Coriolanus's spirit is finally broken.

MENENIUS Coriolanus's old friend is a kind of honest broker, constantly trying to patch up quarrels. He urges the citizens not to fight the senate and the senate to support the citizens. He tries to stop the brawl in the Forum after Coriolanus hurls insults at the crowd. When Coriolanus leads the Volscians against Rome, he goes to his camp to beg him to reconsider.

Menenius is a well-meaning old man, wiser after the events than in preventing trouble in the first place. Apart from Virgilia, he is the only person in the play who truly loves Coriolanus – a fact which sets into high relief the cruel scene where he is mocked and jostled by Volscian sentries outside the walls of Rome, and then is spurned by his idol, apparently out of hand. (He says to Coriolanus, 'The glorious gods sit in hourly synod about thy particular prosperity, and love thee no worse than thy old father Menenius does . . .'; Coriolanus says to him, 'My affairs / Are servanted to others . . . Therefore, be gone'.) As often in Shakespeare, this savagely comic scene comes just before the climactic moment in the entire action, and focuses attention on a specific moral weakness in the protagonist just before that person takes the irrevocable step which will lead to disaster. (Here, Coriolanus goes on to hear, and yield to, the intercessions of his wife and mother.)

BRUTUS AND SICINIUS The 'bald tribunes' who champion the ordinary citizens of Rome against Coriolanus are men of very different characters. Brutus is quiet-spoken but open about his own insincerity: 'Now we have shown our power / Let us seem humbler after it was done / Than when it was a-doing . . .' Sicinius is an elderly rabble-rouser. Coriolanus calls him an 'old goat' and a 'tongue o' the common mouth', and Volumnia proudly tells him that her son 'hath struck more blows for Rome / Than thou hast spoken words'. In the brawl scene he urges the citizens to throw Coriolanus from the Tarpeian Rock, and when he is overruled and banishment is substituted, he tells the Guards to 'follow him . . . with all despite' and 'give him deserved vexation'.

ADRIAN AND NICANOR In one of the 'common-people' scenes which so enrich Shakespeare's plays, Adrian and Nicanor meet and chat on the road between Rome and Antium, the Volscian command-centre. They are fellow-professionals in the same business, and share news and comments before going arm in arm to the nearest pub for supper. What makes this scene especially notable is that Adrian and Nicanor are spies, Adrian for the Volscians and Nicanor for the Romans, and their conversation, as well as the pleasure of hearing the banter between two old friends, gives us a worm's-eye view of the tortured politics and manoeuvrings of their social superiors. The placing of the scene is ironical and pointed: it occurs just before Coriolanus arrives, disguised, to meet Aufidius and defect from Rome. His anguish, and the conflict between patriotism and arrogance which engenders it, come in sharp contrast to the political agnosticism of Adrian and Nicanor, who are more interested in good company and comfortable beds than the importance or otherwise of the news they carry.

☞ About the play

Like its companion-pieces *Antony and Cleopatra* and *Timon of Athens*, *Coriolanus* is about an individual whose personal obsession (in Coriolanus's case, with honour) turns him in on himself, makes him unable to function in the wider world and finally destroys him. The play is political – set in the same kind of dangerous, volatile Rome as *Julius Caesar* some eight years earlier – but its heart is personal tragedy, the story of a man with military genius but no other talents, destroyed by his inability to compromise.

Shakespeare seems to have been uneasy with, or sceptical about, the psychological effects of the qualities required for military glory. In his long gallery of soldier-leaders, only Henry V has a full and rounded personality – and we are shown every detail of the effort of acquiring and keeping it. Bolingbroke's triumph turns to ashes in his mouth when he causes the death of Richard. Macbeth's military success fuels his embition and leads to the collapse of his ethical integrity. Antony is corrupted by his taste for luxury, Othello by proud jealousy, Lear by a kind of arrogant innocence about the world. In *Troilus and Cressida*, both Greek and Trojan heroes are defeated by the sheer relentlessness of a war which none of their bravado can foreshorten. In this company, Coriolanus epitomizes the kind of leader who has never had to compromise, never had to consider even the existence of political arts. He gets what he wants because of who he is – and when this fails to work as well in peacetime as on the battlefield, when instead of enemies to kill there are opponents to convince, his self-esteem collapses and his tragic fall begins. As in so many plays, as in the lives of so many of his rulers, Shakespeare's point is that rank is nothing in itself without attention to its moral and human obligations.

A second main theme, examined in a way equalled in no other Shakespeare play, is the nature of the upbringing which caused this ice to form in Coriolanus's soul. We see his mother Volumnia encouraging Marcus, his small son, to bloodthirstiness (the boy tears butterflies apart with his teeth), and we realize that, in the same way, she has always approved of nothing in her son but the code of honour. Coriolanus's battle-wounds are the only badges of honour he needs to win respect. Pliability and empathy are not 'antic Roman virtues'. When, in the intercession scene, Coriolanus refuses to give up his revenge against the city and people who have (he thinks) betrayed him, Volumnia bluntly and devastatingly replies that attacking his country is the same thing as trampling on his own mother's womb, and proceeds to an aria of sarcastic shame at his desecration of his name and honour which leaves him, literally, speechless: the stage direction says that he '[holds] her by the hand a time, silent'. When he does find words, they are a torrent of broken, emotional entreaties to Aufidius to agree that in the same circumstances he, too, would yield. This is not the Coriolanus of old, and not the proud military ruler. His giving way may be a kind of redemption (if we think of him as a moral human being), but it leaves him nowhere to go as a character except onward to his death.

With attention so tightly focused on Coriolanus, his mother and his friend/enemy Aufidius, the inner lives of other characters have less importance, and they are sketched rather than fully drawn. Minor characters, by contrast, are created with all Shakespeare's skill at showing a whole person in a handful of lines. The play's background is a many-headed mutter of servants, officials, sentries, messengers, conspirators and, most vociferous of all, citizens of Rome. Their fire and bustle make a striking contrast with the ice in Coriolanus's soul and the freezing moral dilemmas he is compelled to face.

☞ In performance

Although never one of Shakespeare's most popular plays, *Coriolanus* has stayed firmly in the repertoire since Richard Burbage created the leading role. Actors who have had success with it include John Philip Kemble and Sarah Siddons, Charles Macready (whose production was revived no fewer than twenty times), Edwin Forrest, Laurence Olivier, Sybil Thorndike, Steven Berkoff and Nicol Williamson. The play has proved highly susceptible to revision, usually for political reasons. At the time of the Jacobite uprisings, for example, Coriolanus was made English and Aufidius Scottish, and after the Second World War Coriolanus regularly became a prototype Hitler. In 1953 Bertolt Brecht's Marxist revision focused on the citizens, and in 1973 John Osborne reworked the play as *A Place Calling Itself Rome*, a modern-dress study in political expediency and tyranny.

> CORIOLANUS   Oh mother, mother
> What have you done? Behold the heavens do ope
> The gods look down, and this unnatural scene
> They laugh at. [V, iii]

Cymbeline

☞ Sources

Giovanni Boccaccio, *The Decameron*; an anonymous Dutch story, *Frederyke of Jennen*; an anonymous stage romance, *The Rare Triumphs of Love and Fortune*. The historical details, such as they are, come from Raphael Holinshed, *Chronicles*.

☞ Story of the play

Cymbeline, King of England, has three children. His sons Guiderius and Arviragus have been brought up in exile in Wales. Egged on by his scheming second wife, he plans to marry off his daughter Imogen to his doltish stepson Cloten. But Imogen instead marries Posthumus Leonatus, and Cymbeline banishes him to Italy.

In Rome, Posthumus boasts to Iachimo of Imogen's beauty and fidelity, and Iachimo bets that he can go to England and seduce her. In England, he tells Imogen that her husband is unfaithful, then hides in a trunk in her bedroom, creeps out when she is asleep, notes down details of her furnishings and her appearance and takes this evidence and her bracelet back to Rome.

Posthumus vows to punish Imogen. The Roman general Lucius is mounting an expedition to attack England, and Posthumus sends his servant Pisanio with him, instructing him to kill Imogen. Pisanio, however, struck by Imogen's beauty, tells her the truth, and she disguises herself as a boy ('Fidele') and escapes to Wales, where she meets up with Guiderius and Arviragus, not knowing that they are her long-lost brothers.

Imogen falls ill, and takes a potion given her long ago by her wicked stepmother, which puts her in a sleep like death. Cloten, who knew of her flight to Wales, has disguised himself as Posthumus and followed her, intending to rape her, but Guiderius intercepts him, cuts off his head and lays the decapitated body beside her on the bier. Imogen awakes and, seeing the corpse in Posthumus' clothes, takes it to be her husband.

Posthumus himself has by now returned to England, disguised as a peasant. He is captured by the Romans, but before they can execute him they are defeated by the English army (led by Cymbeline) and the Welsh guerrillas. The last act of the play is an enormous untangling of all the loose ends, as Cymbeline recognizes his long-lost sons, Iachimo confesses, Posthumus and Imogen are reunited and everyone except Cloten and the wicked queen (who has died of apoplexy) lives happily every afterwards.

☞ Characters

Cymbeline, *King of Britain*
Imogen, *his daughter*
Queen, *his second wife*
Cloten, *her son*
Posthumus Leonatus, *secretly married to Imogen*
Belarius, *a lord banished to Wales*
Arviragus, Guiderius, *known as his sons Polydore and Cadwal, but actually Cymbeline's long-lost sons*
Iachimo, Philario, *Italian friends of Posthumus*
Caius Lucius, *Roman general*

Helen, Pisanio, *servants*
Cornelius, *a doctor*
Philharmonus, *a soothsayer*
Jupiter (*in Posthumus' vision*)
Apparitions (*of Posthumus' father, mother and brothers, dead in the wars*), **Attendants, Captains, Gaolers, Gentlemen** (*one Dutch, one French, one Spanish, the others British*), **Ladies, Lords, Musicians, Officers, Senators, Soldiers**

CYMBELINE Cymbeline is named after a real historical character: he was an enemy of Rome, and father of Caratacus, who all but defeated the might of the Roman army in the first-century AD. But the name, and the fact that England in the play is attacked by Rome, are the only details taken from actual history. Shakespeare's Cymbeline is a king from fairy tale. He has exiled his legitimate sons, married a scheming second wife, plans that his beautiful daughter should marry the queen's oafish offspring, and when she chooses another husband he packs her into exile.

Although Shakespeare leaves these melodramatic events intact, he deepens Cymbeline's character, making him a kind of holy innocent, a man (like Henry VI) bemused by his own life, reactive rather than proactive – and then allows him a kind of redemption at the end, when despite the complete tangle his ineptness has caused for himself and all around him, he is set free (again, by others' actions) and given the beautiful gift of a second chance at his own life, a second opportunity for happiness.

IMOGEN Imogen (or Innogen), Cymbeline's daughter, is a blend of the beautiful princess of fairy tale and the practical but emotionally confused young heroines Shakespeare created in such comedies as *Twelfth Night* or *As You Like It*. Everyone who sees her falls in love with her: even Iachimo, on the brink of raping her, cannot bring himself to touch her. She is trapped in the circumstances of fairy tale, dressing as a boy and going into exile, drinking a magic potion and waking from the sleep it induces to find (as she thinks) her beloved husband's headless corpse beside her. The unknotting of the plot is a series of equally unlikely revelations. But throughout it all, her goodness, determination, experience of grief, humanity and very real heroism shine through, as if from a different kind of story altogether, and carry the play far beyond the realms of fairy tale.

POSTHUMUS LEONATUS At the start of the play Posthumus is an orphan from a fairy-tale. He falls in love with a princess, marries her, is banished from his beloved and trapped into a foolish wager by a conman – the sequence of events is brisk, and what happens to him is more important than any character he shows. But from the moment when Iachimo returns and convinces him that Imogen is unfaithful, he becomes a human character before our eyes. He is still trapped in hectic and headlong action – he sends a servant to kill his beloved, then disguises himself and rushes off in hot pursuit, fights in a battle, is captured, sees visions, is sentenced to death and almost instantly reprieved – but his reactions are not wooden but intensely passionate and persuasive, as if he were a real person trapped in a storybook. His reunion with Imogen, and the ecstasies it provokes of mingled remorse and love, are among the most plausible and touching moments in the play.

IACHIMO Iachimo is a relative of Iago in *Othello* (a diminutive version of whose name he bears, as it were 'Jack' instead of 'John'). He is Shakespeare's version of that popular character in Elizabethan and Jacobean drama, the 'Machiavel'. This person, named after the real-life Niccolò Macchiavelli (although the name was probably pronounced 'make-evil', relating the character to the Devil), was a callous, self-delighting plotter who revealed his intentions in gloating soliloquies to the audience but whom none of the other characters suspected of wickedness until it was too late to stop what was happening or deflect it.

In *Othello*, Shakespeare used the 'Machiavel' character, and the irony it brings to the entire action of the play, for tragic ends. In *Cymbeline* he softens and blurs the edges to fit a different kind of story. In the early scenes, Iachimo's villainy is so double-dyed that it is almost comic – as is his physical action, for example his pepperiness with Posthumus in Rome or his jack-in-a-box appearance from the trunk in Imogen's bedroom. Then, when he is captured and revealed, instead of gloating and snarling as a true 'Machiavel' would do, he changes character completely, admits what he has done and begs forgiveness. This is very like what happens with Borachio in *Much Ado About Nothing* (from about ten years earlier; perhaps played by the same actor?), and the effect both is vital for the play's romantic happy ending and adds depth and realism to Iachimo's own character.

CLOTEN The part of Cymbeline's stepson, as doltish as the name implies, was played by Robert Armin, the leading comedian of Shakespeare's company at the time. Armin had a standup solo act as a dimwitted yokel, and may have partly imported it into performances of this play, even improvising some of the dialogue. (Some say that Cloten's verse lines are probably by Shakespeare, the prose lines by Armin.) In the versions of the story Shakespeare used as sources, Imogen's evil step-brother is no more than the standard glowering youth of all romantic fairy tale; casting Armin in the part must have completely changed its weight in the theatre, and helped the feeling of a kaleidoscopic whirl of varied entertainment so characteristic of this play.

LORDS The Lords play company comedy with Cloten in the same way as the Dumain Brothers do with Parolles in *All's Well That Ends Well* or Audrey and Sir Oliver Martext do with Touchstone in *As You Like It*. The fool Cloten is the centre of the scenes, the First Lord pretends ironical sympathy and the Second Lord points up Cloten's idiocy to the audience. (*Cloten*: 'Was there ever a man had such luck? When I kissed the jack, upon an up-cast to be hit away! I had a hundred pound on't – and then a whoreson jackanapes must take me up for swearing . . .' *First Lord*: 'What got he by that? You broke his pate with your bowl.' *Second Lord, aside*: 'If his wit had been like him that broke it, it would have all run out.') It is significant that their disrespect is towards the heir to the throne.

☞ About the play

Cymbeline is a notoriously difficult play. For all its romance form and fairy-tale motifs, it is rich in psychological and political detail, a sophisticated metaphorical drama whose underlying meaning must be decoded if it is not to seem lumbering or twee. Its verse, lacking the passages of soaring genius that elsewhere make Shakespeare's work so accessible, is charged with condensed, gestural power, full of abbreviation, quick cuts and exclamations.

At the play's heart are two different versions of what a court can be: the corrupt, cruel and incompetent one which rules in London, or the warm-hearted but secret court-in-exile in Wales. *Cymbeline* shows how new moral and political values can rise from the ashes of a corrupt and wasted society. It offers an almost mystical vision of the peace and unity that can follow social change – and does so, partly, by cloaking its political themes in the consolations of romance.

Shakespeare's central concern is the idea of a Britain derived from the antique societies which preceded it: not only those of ancient Rome (as opposed to decadent Papist Italy), but also the Celtic world on the fringes of the Anglo-Saxon heartland – an evolutionary process of geographical and psychological bonding whose validity the play constantly examines. In one of the boldest strokes of metaphor in the play, Shakespeare takes a romantic heroine, Imogen, and makes her story symbolize the entire journey of the nation's soul. The play's driving narrative is her heroic struggle against the corruption which arises from both the decaying old world (symbolized by Cymbeline) and the equally suspect 'new' Italian aesthetic (symbolized by Iachimo). Her journey, literal and metaphorical, takes her through private grief, a flight in disguise to confront the ancient past, the illusion of her own death, the death (or apparent death) of her loved one, and her eventual rebirth into happiness and fulfilment.

Cymbeline is presented as blind to the secret court (which symbolizes the truth of his country), foolish and powerless, exactly the king Britain doesn't need. Cloten, the king's stepson, is the parody of a decayed royal prince, and his final appearance, as a headless corpse disguised as the spouse of the soul of Britain, is a perfect (dis)embodiment of his intended role in the headless body politic. Posthumus belongs to a new class in Jacobean Britain: self-made men judged not by their birth but by their actions. He undergoes every trial with fortitude, and is finally reunited with his destiny, Imogen the soul of Britain.

The last scene of the play is one of the most mysterious and beautiful things Shakespeare ever wrote. In quick succession he brings together all the divergent elements of his complex plot. The queen's death, the defeat of Rome, Iachimo's confession and pardon, the reunion of Posthumus and Imogen, the revelation of the whereabouts of Cymbeline's true sons and the explanation of Jupiter's message all lead to the same conclusion: the vision of a Britain which is both the natural heir of the classical world and (bypassing Papist Italy) a moral, independent and peaceful land in its own right.

Ironically, the use of the romantic form in which Shakespeare dresses all these political metaphors can make them less, not more, meaningful. The histories tell their political messages more explicitly; the tragedies offer a more perfect form for presenting the darkest, most terrible truths about the human race. *Cymbeline* is an ambitious, but perhaps a misguided, masterpiece.

☛ *In performance*

In 1682, Thomas d'Urfey adapted *Cymbeline* as *The Injured Princess*, or *The Fatal Wager*, an extravaganza which kicked the original from the stage for seventy years, until Colley Cibber and David Garrick revived Shakespeare's text. Since then, the play has been revived regularly if not frequently, usually focused on the role of Imogen. Actresses who have made their mark in the part include Sarah Siddons (who performed with Garrick and then with her brother John Philip Kemble), Helen Faucit and Ellen Terry in the nineteenth century (Terry playing against Henry Irving), and in the twentieth century Sybil Thorndike, Peggy Ashcroft, Vanessa Redgrave, Judi Dench and Geraldine Page. Bernard Shaw was underwhelmed by the play (in Irving's production), describing it as 'stagy trash of the lowest melodramatic order' and commenting 'With the single exception of Homer, there is no eminent writer, not even Sir Walter Scott, whom I can despise so entirely as I despise Shakespeare when I measure my mind against his'; forty years later, in *Cymbeline Refinished*, he wrote a new Act Five, replacing Shakespeare with his own ironic twists and turns.

IMOGEN

But soft no bedfellow. O Gods and Goddesses
These flowers are like the pleasures of the world
This bloody man like the care on't. I hope I dream
For so I thought I was a cavekeeper
And cook to honest creatures. But 'tis not so
'Twas but a bolt of nothing, shot of nothing
Which the brain makes of fumes. Our very eyes
Are sometimes like our judgements, blind. Good faith
I tremble still with fear. But if there be
Yet left in heaven as small a drop of pity
As a wren's eye, feared gods, a part of it.
The dream's here still. [IV, ii]

Hamlet, Prince of Denmark

☞ Sources

Shakespeare may have based *Hamlet* on an anonymous play, popu-
lar in the 1590s and now lost. The original story was published in
Saxo's thirteenth-century *History of Denmark* and in François de
Belleforest, *Tragic Stories*.

☞ Story of the play

All is not well in Denmark. On the royal battlements at night, the
ghost of the old king is seen but refuses to say anything. In the
throne-room, Prince Hamlet (the old king's son) is disgusted by
Claudius (the new king and Hamlet's uncle) and queen Gertrude
(Hamlet's mother and Claudius' wife) refusing to mourn. He goes
to the battlements, where the ghost says that Claudius murdered
him by pouring poison in his ear. Hamlet vows revenge.

To test Claudius's guilt, Hamlet pretends to be mad (to the distress of his beloved Ophelia). Hamlet arranges for a company of
visiting actors to perform a play re-enacting his father's murder,
and Claudius's violent reaction convinces Hamlet of his guilt. He
finds Claudius praying, but cannot bring himself to murder him.
Hamlet visits his mother in her room, and accuses her of complicity (egged on by the ghost, which he alone can see). Hearing a
noise behind a wall-hanging, he stabs his sword through the
material and kills Polonius, Ophelia's father and chief minister of
state.

Claudius sends Hamlet to England, and arranges for him to
be killed there. But Hamlet escapes and returns to Denmark,
getting his two friends Rosencrantz and Guildenstern killed in
the process. Also newly home is Ophelia's brother Laertes, who
has been studying in Paris. Furious to avenge his sister's grief-
stricken madness and his father's murder, Laertes fights Hamlet at
Ophelia's grave and challenges him to a duel before the court.

Claudius suggests that he use a poisoned sword, and provides a drink of poisoned wine in case this fails.

At the beginning of the duel, the swords are switched so that Hamlet has the poisoned blade. Gertrude drinks a toast to Hamlet, using the poisoned wine. Laertes and Hamlet wound each other. Laertes dies of the poison, and Hamlet stabs Claudius and forces him to drink the rest of the poisoned wine before he, too, dies in the arms of his friend Horatio. The Norwegian prince Fortinbras arrives with soldiers, to take command in Denmark.

☞ *Characters*

Hamlet, *Prince of Denmark*
Claudius, *the King, his uncle*
Gertrude, *the Queen, his mother*
Ghost *of Hamlet's father*
Polonius, *Lord Chamberlain*
Laertes, *Polonius' son*
Ophelia, *Polonius' daughter*
Horatio, *Hamlet's friend*
Guildenstern, Osric,
   Rosencrantz, *courtiers*

Fortinbras, *Prince of Norway*
Gravediggers
Courtiers and soldiers including
   Barnardo, Cornelius,
   Francisco, Marcellus,
   Reynaldo *and* **Voltemand;**
   Norwegian Captain *and*
   soldiers; **English Ambassadors;**
   Gentleman; Priest

HAMLET Two things above all determine Hamlet's character: his rank as prince and his quicksilver intellect. He is the rising and most dazzling star of the Danish court. He feels that he is a man of destiny whose duty is to put right the 'rottenness' in Denmark, and his curse is that this makes demands on his temperament for which it is unsuited. He is convinced that action is essential, both practically (to avenge his father's murder) and morally (to cure the corruption which it symbolizes). But his talent is for thought, not action, and before he can choose any particular course, much less put it into practice, something new happens and he has to reassess the situation.

When Laurence Olivier filmed *Hamlet* in 1948, glib publicity spoke of 'the tragedy of a man who cannot make up his mind'. Hamlet (the character) is subtler. Trapped in a situation which he cannot control and which escalates wildly and bloodily even as he struggles to understand it, he keeps thinking and feeling his way towards solutions – or at least ways to make the choices ahead more simple – and then finds that they make things worse, not better. It is not that he can't make up his mind, more that the dazzling mental and emotional agility which has served him so well in his university studies has no bearing at all on real danger and the deviousness and callousness of lesser men.

CLAUDIUS In private, Claudius appears tormented by guilt for his brother's murder. Early in the play, he suddenly turns and cries, as much to himself as to the audience, 'The harlot's cheek, beautied with plastering art / Is not more ugly to the thing that helps it / Than is my deed to my most painted word . . .', and later, praying alone, he seems to be gazing into a black pit of self-loathing: 'O wretched state! O bosom black as death! / O limed soul that, struggling to be free / Art more engag'd . . .'

Such anguish suggests a man destroyed by moral compromise. Claudius has committed a crime for which there is no redemption. He is just as much trapped in tragedy as Hamlet, though for different reasons. It is also open to question whether he is a better king, a more pragmatic and effective politician than the brother he killed. Only Hamlet describes him as a monster.

None the less, and whatever Claudius's motives and feelings may be, Shakespeare leaves us in no doubt about the villainy of his actual deeds. He has killed his brother; he plots to have Hamlet murdered, once by Rosencrantz and Guildenstern, once by Laertes with a poisoned sword; he presides over the duel with a regal joviality which masks his plans and the poison he has prepared. In short, Shakespeare soaks the part with irony, and whether Claudius is the melodramatic villain Hamlet claims he is, or a tragic and self-lacerating figure, performing his own life to hide the emptiness within, he remains equivocal from first to last.

GERTRUDE Gertrude is tormented by weakness and sexual guilt. In both public and private she affects a kind of frosty disdain which masks her true feelings (for example, that she prefers her new lover Claudius to her dead husband Hamlet senior). She is a secretive and reactive figure, and her death in the final scene appropriately comes not from planning but by accident, when she drinks the poisoned wine prepared for Hamlet. In the context of the scene, the cathartic blood-letting which has been long postponed but which is the only possible outcome of the moral and ethical tangle of the action, the irrelevance of this death to the main issue symbolizes Gertrude's entire character and her tragedy.

POLONIUS Polonius is a man whose life has been devoted to court service. He is a wily, able politician, trusted and respected even by those (like Gertrude) who find him long-winded and boring.

Polonius' blind spot is Ophelia, the daughter he loves equally, if not more than, his political position. He is convinced of the possibility of uniting his two obsessions in a single action by marrying Ophelia to the rising young prince of Denmark, but is driven almost to distraction by the need to protect her, at almost any cost, from Hamlet's malaise. He loses his political sure-footedness and begins plotting with the King and Queen to spy on Hamlet – and the results are pathetic and futile, when he lurks behind a wall-hanging and is stabbed to death. His grotesque death is both (morally) a tragic waste of the qualities he used to have and (dramatically) the start of the play's unstoppable surge towards catastrophe.

OPHELIA Everyone treats Ophelia as if she were not so much a person as a cipher. Polonius and Laertes harangue her like a child in a schoolroom. Hamlet shouts at her like a madman, ignoring her distress and implying that she is a whore. When Gertrude talks of her suicide, it is as if she were describing a picture rather than the actual death of someone real. The lines she speaks and the songs she sings (in the mad scene) are as wide-eyed as they are touching.

Ophelia's strength, and her tragedy, are that she has grown up in one of the most secretive and dangerous places in Europe (the Danish court), and been untouched by it. Surrounded by machination and murder, she has remained a shining light of purity. Ophelia dotes on her father, her brother, and the prince she is to marry, however much they all ignore her, and it is hardly surprising that when her entire world collapses round her, she falls into madness and suicide. In the rottenness of Denmark, innocence is no protection.

FIRST PLAYER Shakespeare may have played this part himself (it is often doubled with the Ghost), and the player's scenes are full of good nature, affability, and an absolute determination not to make a professional compromise – he may add Hamlet's new material to his script and listen to the prince's amateur ideas on how to act, but he makes no changes at all to his usual barnstorming style. All this may be partly a theatrical in-joke at the expense of 'our bending author' or some senior member of his company, but it also throws light on the fact that almost everyone else at court, with the possible exceptions of Ophelia and Horatio, is also giving a 'performance'.

About the play

Hamlet is one of Shakespeare's most experimental works. Superficially, it revels in every trick of the melodramatic 'revenge tragedies' popular at the time: a ghost, a graveyard, madness, love spurned, poison, a duel. But Shakespeare was also concerned to show his hero's mind and character, both in dialogue and in soliloquies revealing Hamlet's tormented private thoughts. These psychological and philosophical glimpses reveal a person on the rack, and Shakespeare explores them not in high poetry – *Hamlet* is one of the plainest-spoken of his tragedies – but in a kind of racing, philosophical rhetoric which encourages us not just to observe Hamlet's plight but to relate it to ourselves.

In days when English audiences still expected 'tragedies' to be high-flown and bombastic, set in exotic Middle Eastern or Mediterranean locations and swaggering and gory in almost equal proportions (Marlowe's *The Jew of Malta* is an example), *Hamlet*'s innovations included a northern European setting, a large number of contemporary references, and above all a 'hero' who lacked all the usual heroic traits. Hamlet is good at fighting but is no warrior; he knows about love but is no Romeo; he broods on his father's murder but is famously slow to take revenge.

Unlike the larger-than-life protagonists of earlier tragedy who are the playthings of fate, Hamlet is a philosophical and political thinker in true Renaissance style: one who sees through the surfaces of the world and understands how badly it is organized, who feels the pain caused by cruelty and despairs at it, but whose 'resolution is sicklied o'er with the pale cast of thought' to such an extent that he is almost literally paralysed when it comes to action. Strikingly, he also foreshadows the radical puritanism which was to revolutionize English thought half a century later, in the time of Cromwell. He judges people not by rank or status but by the quality of their actions. He is unsure about female sexuality and rages against the abuse of patriarchy. Above all, he considers 'too deeply' and urges himself and his contemporaries towards a purgative catastrophe of which they can have little apprehension.

Hamlet's struggle with the society he lives in brings him up against some of the most profound truths of human experience: the fragility and sadness of love, the futility of violence, the transitory nature of life and an intimation of the great 'undiscovered country' in which social order is confounded and aspirations perish. None the less, the play is philosophically open-ended. Its issues are discussed but never resolved, one reason for its endless popularity with thinking readers and spectators. The action brings us face to face with what we feel to be true in our deepest hearts, but it never points morals or pre-empts our further, private thoughts – and this, coupled with Hamlet's apparent honesty about the workings of his mind and soul, makes him seem a person of almost infinite complexity and possibility. He can be explained in any way we choose – one reason, perhaps, why so many people treat him less as a character in a play than as a mirror of themselves.

☞ In performance

Hamlet has not always been treated with the respect we show it today. In the 1750s, David Garrick gave it a happy ending. At the end of the nineteenth century, W.S. Gilbert's *Rosencrantz and Guildenstern*, anticipating Tom Stoppard, sent up the whole idea of Shakespeare, Ghosts and Moody Danes. Twentieth-century updatings include Maurice Evans' 1950s *GI Hamlet* (in which Hamlet is a soldier suffering from 'postwar blues') and Melissa Murray's feminist *Ophelia* (1972).

Hamlet films begin with three notable silent versions, one starring Sarah Bernhardt, another led by Johnston Forbes-Robertson – one of the greatest Hamlets of his day – and the third featuring the Danish actress Asta Nielsen. Later came Laurence Olivier's 'thinking-athlete' account of 1948 (notable for his peroxide-blond hair and the way he reshaped the text), Innokenti Smoktunovsky's acclaimed 1960s Russian version, a US Western (*Johnny Hamlet*, 1972) and a respectable, if Ruritania-set, Kenneth Branagh version (1997).

The enormous list of actors who have enhanced their reputations in *Hamlet* includes both John Kemble and his sister Sarah Siddons in the eighteenth century; Edwin Booth and Forbes-Robertson in the nineteenth century; and in the twentieth century John Gielgud (famous for his mellifluous way with the verse), Richard Burton (sexily heroic), David Warner (in 1960s student-protest mode) and Jonathan Pryce (almost a casebook study of mental illness, and famous for the way the Ghost was inside him, in his mind, and he had to vomit it out before our eyes).

> HAMLET What a piece of work is a man! How noble in reason,
> how infinite in faculty, in form and moving how express
> and admirable, in action how like an angel, in apprehension
> how like a god – the beauty of the world, the paragon of
> animals! And yet to me what is this quintessence of dust?
> Man delights not me – no, nor woman neither, though by
> your smiling you seem to say so. [II, iii]

Henry IV, Parts I and II

👉 Sources

Raphael Holinshed, *Chronicles*; Anon, *The Famous Victories of Henry V*.

👉 Story of the plays

Richard II shows the events which precede *Henry IV* in historical sequence: Bolingbroke's leadership of the rebellion against Richard and his accession as Henry IV. In *Henry IV Part I* the new King is himself faced with rebellions in Wales (led by Glendower), Scotland (led by Douglas) and Northumberland (led by Hotspur). He is too ill to take much part in the fighting himself: eaten by the guilt he feels for Richard's death, and depressed by the contrast between the noble, dignified Hotspur and his own son Hal, Prince of Wales, who (as his father sees it) is wasting his energies with a group of rogues from the Boar's Head Tavern in Eastcheap, led by the fat knight Falstaff. The relationship between Falstaff and Hal (who is learning from it his true moral and royal nature) is the heart of the play, and in Act Five, at the battle of Shrewsbury, Hal shows his mettle by leading his father's army and killing Hotspur.

In *Part II*, Hal's brother Lancaster takes up the fight against the rebels (now led by Northumberland and the Archbishop of York), while Hal gradually begins to separate himself from Falstaff. Falstaff, threatened with arrest for debt, goes to Gloucestershire to recruit an army and join the royalists, and stays with his garrulous old friend Justice Shallow. In Yorkshire, Lancaster tricks the rebels into laying down their arms, and then arrests them. By this time, King Henry is on his deathbed, still tormented by doubts about Hal's suitability to succeed him. He falls asleep, and Hal takes up the crown; when Henry awakes, he persuades him at last that his ways have changed and he is fit to rule. Henry dies, and Hal makes his peace with his old enemy the Lord Chief Justice, agreeing to uphold the rule of law. On his way to be crowned king, he is accosted by Falstaff (who has hurried from Gloucestershire in hopes of high office), and rejects him. The past is dead; England is reborn under a new kind of king, and its glory will be restored by the war which Hal is going to fight in France (and which is the subject of the next play in sequence, *Henry V*).

Characters

AT COURT
King Henry IV
Henry, Prince of Wales
Prince John of Lancaster
Westmoreland
Blunt
in Part II only
Clarence, Gloucester
Warwick, Kent, Surrey
Lord Chief Justice
Gower, Harcourt

REBELS
Earl of Northumberland
Harry Percy ('Hotspur')
Archbishop of York
Lady Percy, *Hotspur's wife*
in Part I only
Worcester
Douglas
Owen Glendower
Mortimer (Earl of March)
Vernon
Glendower's Wife
in Part II only
Lords Bardolph, Hastings, Mowbray
Coleville, Falconbridge; Blunt
Lady Northumberland
Travers, Morton

FROM THE BOAR'S HEAD TAVERN
Sir John Falstaff
Mistress Quickly
Bardolph
Peto
Poins
Francis, *the drawer*
in Part I only
Chamberlain
Gadshill
in Part II only
Pistol
Doll Tearsheet
Falstaff's page

IN GLOUCESTERSHIRE
(Part II only)
Justice Shallow
Justice Silence
Davy
Bullcalf, Feeble, Mouldy, Shadow, Wart, *recruits*

OTHERS
Lords, Ladies, Officers, Soldiers, Messengers, Musicians
in Part I only
Carriers, Travellers, Sherriff
in Part II only
Beadles, Drawer, Fang, Grooms, Rumour *as prologue*; Second Porter, Snare

PRINCE HENRY Falstaff and the others take Hal for one of themselves: a carefree, hedonistic prankster whose royal position is no more than something to joke about, akin to Bardolph's red nose or Falstaff's belly. But we know (because Hal tells us in a soliloquy) that he is merely playing a role, that he will 'uphold / The unyoked humour of [their] idleness' only for a while and will one day 'throw off' this 'loose behaviour'. This knowledge gives an edge of irony not only to such episodes as the Gadshill scenes (when he and Poins disguise themselves and trick Falstaff), but also to Hal's relationship with his father the King and the court, who believe that the role he is playing is his true character, and refuse to accept his assurances that he is in fact loving, patriotic and royal.

In *Part I* Hal's relationship with Falstaff begins like that of son and father, but by the beginning of *Part II* Hal's growth towards maturity has pulled them apart. In *Part I* his role in the civil war (where he defeated Hotspur) seemed, at least in part, to be an interruption to his 'merry days' with Falstaff and others. In *Part II*, state affairs, his relationship with his real father and his imminent succession are in the forefront of his mind, and increasingly, he seems to belong to a different age and sensibility from his Boar's Head companions. In the end, assuming at last the mantle of the leader he has become, he rejects Falstaff in a single peremptory phrase ('I know thee not, old man'). We weep to hear it, but in fact it was prefigured very much earlier, from the moment in *Part I* when Falstaff (playing the part of Hal) said to Hal (playing the part of the king) 'Banish Peto, banish Bardolph, banish Poins, but for sweet Jack Falstaff, kind Jack Falstaff, true Jack Falstaff . . . banish not him thy Harry's company . . .', and Hal replied 'I do, I will'.

HENRY IV One of the play's main preoccupations is the way moral self-awareness and growth are essential for the psychological and political health of both a monarch and his country. Henry, who as Bolingbroke in *Richard II* was a pragmatic, nononsense commander, is now sick, insecure and brooding. His country is torn apart by civil war, he feels personal guilt for the death of Richard, his predecessor, and his son and the heir to the throne is (so he thinks) entirely unsuitable to rule. He continually speaks of a crusade to the Holy Land which will redeem both him and his country.

Henry's soul-sickness is essential for the action. We see, as he does not, that Hal's association with Falstaff and the others is temporary, that he is daily learning the qualities he will need as king. In *Part II* he begins to take the reins of power from his father, and when they are finally reconciled (in the scene after Hal, thinking his sleeping father dead, tries on the crown), Henry is released, metaphorically and psychologically, from the burdens he has borne throughout his reign.

FALSTAFF In *The Famous Victories of Henry V*, one of Shakespeare's sources, unruly prince Hal is shown roistering with a group of drunks, thieves and conmen led by Sir John Oldcastle, a corrupt and ruined aristocrat. Shakespeare took over this idea in *Henry IV*, but developed it to show the prince growing away from the indiscipline of his youth and gradually learning how to take on the burdens and duties of his royal position. In the new scheme, the tavern also stands for the unruly, self-indulgent England under the rule of Henry IV: an England which will find new vigour and purpose once Hal becomes King. In such a scheme, most of Hal's acquaintances (Poins, Pistol, Mistress Quickly and the others) are notable more for vitality than for morality. Their leader is Falstaff (originally 'Oldcastle', but renamed after objections from descendants of the real Oldcastle, an early Protestant martyr).

The character of the bluff, amoral braggart is a staple of comedy, dating back to such figures as Dionysus in ancient Greece or the Lord of Misrule in medieval English Christmas entertainments. These characters, however, are two-dimensional: walking obsessions with food, drink and a good time, cheerful, anarchic and uncomplicated. Falstaff shares all these qualities, but adds a rueful self-awareness, a feeling that he knows the kind of life he leads, has weighed its pleasures against the moral compromises required and made a deliberate and self-defining choice. At times,

Shakespeare shows this in a dark light, at others he gives Falstaff a kind of perverse moral authority which is not affected even by his willingness to prey on both aristocratic equals (for example Shallow) and social inferiors (for example the recruits in *Part II*). Falstaff's awareness of his own moral and financial bankruptcy, and of the obsolescence of his kind and class, gives the part an over-riding melancholy, the vulnerability of real humanity. Thanks to his complex, subtle personality, and his superb way with words, he steals the play.

However, at the end of *Part II*, Falstaff, and any spectator seduced by him, is dealt a hammer-blow by Shakespeare. Dreaming of power and wealth, Falstaff goes to the new King for preferment, and is dismissed. The Old Adam is discarded; new values rule.

THE REBELS Hotspur, the pivotal figure in the revolt in *Part I*, is regarded by King Henry as having all the princely qualities his own heir lacks. Unlike Hal, however, Hotspur is an aristocrat from a glowing tapestry: heroic, brave, witty and truthful but with little depth or sophistication. He is all honour, all chivalric code; he has no need, as Hal does, to understand human failing in others or transcend it in himself; in short, he lacks the qualities which Hal is learning and practising. In a world which is discovering subtlety and compromise, Hotspur is an attractive anachronism; he belongs not so much with Hal, harbinger of the future, as with that other figure from the past which England is now discarding: Falstaff.

Northumberland, Hotspur's father, supported King Henry (then Bolingbroke) in his war against Richard II. But he has a prickly dignity, and is persuaded by Hotspur to rebel because of an insult to their family. At the start of *Part II*, when he hears of Hotspur's death, he has perhaps his finest dramatic moment, when he tries to steel himself not to mourn. He takes over the rebellion, but soon retires to watch events from Scotland and fades from the play.

Worcester, Hotspur's uncle, is a sophisticated politician interested in ends, but in neither the means nor the individual human beings needed to bring them about. One of the cleverest and most devious people opposed to King Henry, he plays diplomatic games with the royalists (designed to protect his own position if they win), and is captured and executed, unmourned, at Shrewsbury.

Other rebels are more broadly characterized. Douglas and Glendower are fire and rant respectively. The Archbishop of York is a hypocritical figurehead. The finest small part is that of Lady Percy, Hotspur's loving and sparky wife, whose grief at his death and the waste of war is one of the play's most moving scenes.

AT THE BOAR'S HEAD TAVERN The landlady, Mistress Quickly, is involved in a love/hate relationship with Falstaff. In *Part II* she tries to make him pay the money he owes her, only to be mocked or wheedled into lending more. Like everyone else in Falstaff's circle, she has splendid liveliness of language, particularly when she is angry. Doll Tearsheet, the whore, has an equally sharp tongue. For example, she rounds on Pistol (who has been imprudent enough to come between her and Falstaff) with 'Away, you cut-purse rascal, you filthy bung, away! By this wine, I'll thrust my knife in your mouldy chaps if you play the saucy cuttle with me. Away, you bottle-ale rascal, you basket-hilt stale juggler, you'. Bardolph is a leathery ex-soldier, notable for his warty face and bulbous nose. He is ruined by drink, and for most of the play is too sozzled to play anything but second fiddle to others. Pistol, another ex-soldier, is possibly a former actor (with a line in bombastic language to prove it). Poins, a Court servant, is the confidant not of Falstaff but of Hal. His humour is cynical and somewhat cruel, and he incites Hal, among other things, to rob the others at Gadshill, and later to disguise himself as a drawer and hear what Falstaff really thinks of him.

LORD CHIEF JUSTICE The Lord Chief Justice, senior law officer of England, spars with Falstaff and loses each bout – and our delight is like seeing a pompous teacher cheeked by a clever schoolboy. But the Justice comes into his own at the end of *Part II*, when the new King Henry shows that he bears him no malice for arresting him earlier, and agrees that the new reign will be subject to the rule of law. It is then the Chief Justice's duty to banish Falstaff from Court – and he relishes it.

SHALLOW Shallow is an old Justice of the Peace, a former lawyer (and before that the merriest of students) who now grows apples in Gloucestershire. Falstaff, an old acquaintance, visits him and tries to cheat him of some money. But Shallow is too full of chirpy reminiscence even to notice. 'Jesu, Jesu, the mad days I have spent!' he cries, and his happiness takes us briefly into an Edenic vision of rural England.

🖐 About the plays

The central character of *Henry IV* is not Henry, Hal or Falstaff, but England itself: the plays describe nothing less than the struggle for the country's soul. This takes place on three separate planes. First, the struggle for a geographically unified nation is enacted in the Welsh and Northern rebellions which rage through both plays. Second is the struggle for the country's wealth: the plays show a largely corrupt upper class robbing the 'common-wealth' for their own greed, corrupting the working class in the process and largely ignoring the middle class whose values are soon to be victorious. Third, the struggle for the nation's soul is embodied in the contest for the next King's moral integrity, and is enacted in the dramatic triangle of Hal, his father the king, and his surrogate father and dysfunctional moral tutor Falstaff. The three planes of struggle overlap and interconnect, and their interaction adds dynamism and focus to the panorama of English life which the plays present.

As so often with Shakespeare's history plays, the vivid dramatic foreground is backlit by a Biblical motif: the related tales of the fall of Adam and Cain's life after he murders Abel. The King (who as Bolingbroke was responsible for the death of his predecessor and 'near brother' Richard II) has ever afterwards been tormented by guilt and condemned to live, as he feels, under the 'murderer's mark', the mark of Cain. He is also Adam exiled from the Garden of Eden, the paradise of Edward II's England, and he is fated never to reach the Holy Land and redemption: his dream of dying in Jerusalem is realized only ironically, in a room called Jerusalem in the Palace of Westminster.

Henry's guilt colours the action and meaning of both plays, and Shakespeare uses it to articulate a theme which recurs in most of his histories: that there is often conflict between an individual's personal psychological needs and the broader political picture, and this conflict leads to tragedy. In terms of Henry's political project, the modernization and centralization of England, his 'murder' (as he perceives it) of Richard II is presented as having been tragically necessary. His wish to expiate it, to wipe away both his and his nation's guilt by a crusade to the Holy Land, is a solution to psychological yearning but not political need. In terms of state-craft, the modernization of England involves, first, the pacification and absorption of alternative cultures (particularly those of Wales and the North), and second, dealing with the corrupt and degenerate warlord-aristocracy which is a last hangover from the age of feudalism.

In *Part I*, the rebellion is led by Harry Percy (Hotspur), and is an affair of singleminded honour and integrity, an ironical parallel to the rebellion in *Richard II* which put Bolingbroke on the throne in the first place. Shakespeare also parallels the two men's characters. Like the Bolingbroke of *Richard II*, Hotspur is heroic, quick, brave, witty and honest; his tragedy lies in the old adage that the brightest and best die first. In *Part II*, by contrast, the rebellion of the Archbishop of York and his followers is presented as self-seeking, grotesque and futile. Unlike the impassioned and stalwart Douglas and Glendower who fought alongside Hotspur, York's supporters are the shadowy lords Bardolph, Hastings and Mowbray and the unlucky Coleville of the Dale (who has the ignominy of being so impressed with Falstaff's rumoured reputation that he surrenders to him). Their revolt is an unheroic mess, right down to the point when the rebels are brutally tricked by the young Adonis, Lancaster. This treachery, and the rebels' opportunism and cynicism, are part of the overwhelmingly melancholic mood of the second play.

Another component of Henry's misery is his anxiety about the suitability for rule of the Prince of Wales. If a king does anything right, it must be the preservation and continuity of the monarchy itself, and Hal's mixing with the wrong sort does not bode well. Once again, however, Henry is letting private obsession blur his understanding of what is really happening. Shakespeare presents us with a new concept of the education of a monarch, far removed from the manly exploits and training in political cunning of feudal times (attributes demonstrated by Hotspur in *Part I* and Lancaster in *Part II*). Hal's 'slumming it' is shown to be an essential prerequisite for the common touch he is to exhibit to such good effect as Henry V. Hamlet-like, he has a playful, experimental side to his nature, and uses everything at his disposal to gain a clearer idea of who he is and of what he is capable. He announces to the audience, in plain terms, that his quest to discover the truth involves playing a long game: '. . . herein will I imitate the Sun / Who doth permit the base contagious clouds / To smother up his beauty from the world / That when he please again to be himself / Being wanted, he may more be wondered at / By breaking through the foul and ugly mists / Of vapours that did seem to strangle him.' This self-awareness on his part, and ironical knowledge on ours, is crucial. King Henry's apprehensions are misplaced and the 'modern' monarch which Hal will become, thanks to his journey of discovery, will finally redeem England and resolve its disunity in a way his father could never do.

Despite all of the pain and struggle, at the heart of these plays is the spirit of comedy, embodied in the gigantic role of Falstaff. He is Adam expelled from the Garden, the embodiment of the fleshliness of Man, the sinner, the weak and frail human being – and it is precisely this aspect of life, its vulnerability, vulgarity and warmth, which Hal must learn and which Falstaff is uniquely qualified to teach him. In terms of the plays' morality and psychology, Falstaff is a 'modern' character, complex and ironic. But – and this is one of the wellsprings of the part's humanity, not the least component of its appeal – in terms of their ethics and politics he is entirely and gloriously equivocal: a member of the old ruling class, corrupt, lazy and seductive all at once. With Hal he may be a moral tutor in a topsy-turvy world, but in his relationship with the world at large he is either a parasite (as with Mistress Quickly or the lords he gulls on the battlefield) or himself the host for parasites (Bardolph, Poins and the others). He continually uses his unfailing inventiveness and verbal dexterity to postpone the judgement that inevitably awaits him – a directly opposite process to that of Hal's other 'father and tutor' Henry, who is morosely and ineluctably drawn to pursue a judgement which eternally eludes him. Shakespeare clinches his underlying metaphor of the Lost Eden by granting Falstaff a kind of redemption. As the expelled Adam, he is allowed to enter a new, secular Paradise, the 'merry England' which Henry has so longed to create but never lives to see, symbolized by the apple-orchards of Gloucestershire.

It is an important part of the dramatic method of the plays, underlining the moral vigour of the 'new' England as compared with the old, that whereas Henry, his courtiers and those who rebel against him are depicted as magnificent but sterile lay-figures, everyone in Falstaff's circle is richly and roundly characterized: Bardolph, Pistol, Shallow, Mistress Quickly, the yokels drafted into Falstaff's army, and the grooms, carriers, waiters, barmen and other working people, depicted with a kind of social and domestic realism which before had appeared only sporadically in drama, in sunbursts of 'ordinary' character in the midst of the more solemn main action of the Mystery Plays.

☞ In performance

Queen Elizabeth I began the tradition of preferring Falstaff to all other characters, liking him so much that she commanded a sequel (*The Merry Wives of Windsor*). In 1622 the plays were conflated into a single piece (and retitled *Sir John Falstaff*), a tradition revived by Orson Welles in his 1966 film *Chimes at Midnight* and by Joan Littlewood for the Edinburgh Festival in 1974.

Famous Falstaffs begin with Shakespeare's colleague Will Kemp, continue with the Restoration actor Thomas Betterton, James Henry Hackett (who played it every year from 1828 to 1871, ageing and thickening into the part year after year), Herbert Beer-bohm Tree (self-indulgent) and in the twentieth century Maurice

Evans, Brewster Mason and Robert Stephens. Four actors were particularly praised for playing Falstaff 'without padding', a tribute as much to comic presence as physical girth: 'Bellower' Quinn in the 1730s, Stephen Kemble a century later, Roy Byford in the 1920s and John Goodman in 1981. The most praised of all Falstaffs were Orson Welles in the film and Ralph Richardson in a 1945 production also featuring Olivier as Hotspur (in *Part I*) and Shallow (in *Part II*).

That 1945 production also saw a fascinating 'take' on the question of Hotspur's stammering. In 1914, Matheson Lang had seized on the description of Hotspur as 'thick of speech' to mean that he stammered, and the tradition lingered: a prime example of character plastered on to a role rather than drawn out from inside it. In 1945 Olivier combined this tradition with Hotspur's dying line 'Thou art dust / And food for – ' to make Hotspur have trouble with his 'w's.

> FALSTAFF Honour pricks me on. Yea, but how if honour
> prick me off when I come on? How then? Can honour
> set-to a leg? No. Or an arm? No. Or take away the grief of
> a wound? No. Honour hath no skill in surgery then? No.
> What is honour? A word. What is that word, honour? Air.
> A trim reckoning. Who hath it? He that died o' Wednesday.
> Doth he feel it? No. Doth he hear it? No. It is sensible,
> then? Yea, to the dead. But will it not live with the living?
> No. Why? Detraction will not suffer it. Therefore I'll none
> of it. Honour is a mere scutcheon, and so ends my
> catechism. [Part I, V, i]

> SHALLOW How a yoke of bullocks at Stamford fair?
> SILENCE By my troth I was not there.
> SHALLOW Death is certain. Is old Double of your town living
> yet?
> SILENCE Dead, sir.
> SHALLOW Jesu, Jesu, dead! 'A drew a good bow; and dead! 'A
> shot a fine shoot. John o' Gaunt loved him well, and betted
> much money on his head. Dead! [Part II, III, ii]

Henry V

☞ Sources

Raphael Holinshed, *Chronicles*; Edward Hall, *The Union of the Two Noble and Illustrious Families of Lancaster and York*; a number of anonymous biographies of Henry, including *Deeds of King Henry V of England*, written by a man who served at Agincourt.

☞ Story of the play

In a prologue, the Chorus asks the audience to make up for the limitations of the theatre by imagining the bustling scenes the actors describe. We then hear that Henry has reformed his giddy ways, and he announces to a supercilious French ambassador (who has brought him a bag of tennis balls from the Dauphin of France) that he intends to fight for the English lands won by his forebears in France. The Chorus describes the fleet preparing to sail from Southampton, and warns that three lords are plotting against Henry. The King arrests the lords and sails. In the Boar's Head Tavern, Mistress Quickly tells Nym, Bardolph, Pistol and the boy Robin of Falstaff's death, and they decide to seek their fortunes as soldiers in France.

The Chorus announces the siege of Harfleur. We see the battle, and in particular the part played in it by the English, Scots, Irish and Welsh captains (brave) and by Nym, Bardolph and Pistol (not brave). Although Henry wins, his army is so weakened that, with winter approaching, he plans to return home – until the French send a message inviting surrender, and he announces instead that he is marching on Calais.

On the night before the battle of Agincourt, Henry, in disguise, visits his soldiers round their campfires. He quarrels with Williams, a common soldier, who challenges him to a fight after the battle. The French lords, meanwhile, gamble on the number of prisoners each will take. The battle is fought and won; during the fighting, Robin is treacherously killed with the other boys guarding the baggage. Henry resolves his quarrel with Williams.

After another brief Chorus, we see the aftermath of Agincourt. First, the contrast is made between bravery and cowardice among the ordinary soldiers (when Fluellen meets the braggart Pistol and forces him to eat his leek for disparaging the Welsh nation), and then Henry arranges peace with France and proposes marriage to princess Katharine, whom we have previously seen shyly learning English from her maid.

👉 Characters

ON THE ENGLISH SIDE
King Henry
Gloucester, Bedford, *his brothers*
Exeter, *his uncle*
York, *his cousin*
Lords Cambridge, Salisbury, Scroop, Warwick, Westmoreland
Archbishop of Canterbury
Bishop of Ely
Sir Thomas Gray
Sir Thomas Erpingham
Captains Fluellen, Gower, Jamy, Macmorris
Privates Bates, Court, Williams
Mistress Quickly
Bardolph, Nym, Pistol, Boy (*Robin*)

ON THE FRENCH SIDE
King Charles
Queen Isabel
Princess Katharine
The Dauphin (Lewis)
Constable *of France*
Dukes of Berri, Bourbon, Bretagne, Burgundy and Orléans
Lords Rambures, Grandpré
Mountjoy, *a herald*
Le Fer
Ambassador
Governor of Harfleur
Alice, *Katharine's maid*
Attendants, Chorus, Citizens, Messengers, Soldiers

CHORUS The Chorus speaks a Prologue and Epilogue and introduces each act. He sets up an ironical contrast between the modest realism of the theatrical means available and the grandeur and magnificence of the story the actors have to show us. There is a constant awareness of the power of his rhetoric: typical lines are 'O do but think / You stand upon the rivage and behold / A city on th' inconstant billows dancing / For so appears this fleet majestical / Holding due course to Harfleur. Follow! Follow! . . .'

(of the English fleet sailing for France) or 'From camp to camp through the foul womb of night / The hum of either army stilly sounds . . .' (of the night before Agincourt). The Epilogue is a formal sonnet, and the effect is to set a kind of seal on what we have seen, to round it off with a final flourish as one might sign a painting – pulling the focus right back from the intimate, raucous and realistic version of history which the scenes of the main action have presented.

HENRY In *Henry V*, Henry is no longer the carefree Hal who once caroused with Falstaff and the others. He has put aside his former life and grown into his role as a new kind of king: heroic, secure in his divine right but also self-aware and politically pragmatic. Shakespeare shows his quality in two brisk scenes at the beginning of the play: his reception of the French ambassador who brings the Dauphin's tennis balls, and his decisive response to the Lords' conspiracy at Southampton (paralleled later in the play when he refuses to pardon Bardolph, his old drinking-partner, for stealing from a church). An explicit contrast is also made between the languor and artificiality of the French military command and Henry's common-touch heroics at the siege of Harfleur ('Once more unto the breach, dear friends') and at Agincourt (the Crispin's Day speech).

Shakespeare humanizes Henry by showing him as a person with ordinary feelings and impulses, for example with Williams and the other soldiers on the night before Agincourt and in the Act Five scene when he woos Princess Katharine. Henry ends the first scene with a soliloquy to the audience (his only such utterance in the play), talking of the nature of kingship and human vulnerability. In the wooing scene, the role he plays (of a gauche, tongue-tied lover) partly serves to put Katharine at her ease, but also makes ironically explicit the difference between the office he holds and the ordinary man he is. In short, the play shows him progressively developing a new sense of self and a new kind of regal discourse, unbombastic but moving, rooted in experience yet inspirational – and they are the keys to his success.

FLUELLEN At one level, Fluellen is a figure of fun: a fiery, prickly patriot with an amazing gift for mangling the English language. But he is also sincere, honourable and brave. Henry treats him with respect, and after the battle is won, Shakespeare allows him genuine dignity, in the scene where he refuses to fight Williams and presses him, with warm-hearted, uncomplicated kindness, to take a shilling: 'It is with a good will; I can tell you, it will serve you to mend your shoes. Come, wherefore should you be so pashful? Your shoes is not so good. 'Tis a good shilling I warrant you, or I will change it.'

KATHARINE In history, Katherine was nineteen when she married Henry. In the play she is a child, and in Shakespeare's company was probably played by a boy as young as eight or nine. She has only two scenes, but her charm, innocence and pretty way, first with French and then (in the wooing scene) with broken English, can steal the show. The portrait is so convincing that one wonders whether Shakespeare's Katharine was an accomplished actor at such a young age, or genuinely French.

COMMON SOLDIERS On the night before Agincourt, Henry, disguised, joins three soldiers round their campfire, and they discuss whether or not the King understands the feelings of ordinary citizens. Two of the soldiers, Court and Bates, are minimally characterized. But the third man, Williams, expresses himself with fire and eloquence. The scene's dramatic purpose is to lead up to Henry's great soliloquy before the battle ('What have kings that privates have not too / Save ceremony, save general ceremony . . . ?'); Williams's obstinate independence of mind is central to the meaning of the play.

FOUR CAPTAINS Macmorris (Irish), Gower (English), Jamy (Scots) and Fluellen (Welsh) have one scene together, in which Macmorris and Fluellen argue about the respective bravery of the Irish and Welsh, and the others try to keep the peace. Macmorris and Jamy are there chiefly for 'funny-accent' comedy, but the other two are more deeply drawn. Fluellen's bardic irascibility and salt-of-the-earth honesty are put to serious dramatic use later in the action. Gower is a career officer, proud of his profession and with all a regular soldier's scorn for such fly-by-nights as Pistol: 'Why, 'tis a gull, a fool, a rogue, that now and then goes to the wars, to grace himself at his return into London under the form of a soldier . . .'

FRENCH NOBLES The elders are serious: King Charles (ageing and inadequate); Queen Isabel; the princes Burgundy and Bourbon; the Constable (brave and sincere); the dignified herald Mountjoy. The younger lords, led by the Dauphin, are popinjays: the Ambassador (who sneeringly delivers the Dauphin's present of tennis balls to Henry); Berri; Bretagne; foppish Orléans; the fire-eater Grandpré; haughty Rambures.

ENGLISH NOBLES The English nobles, far less characterized than their French counterparts, include the King's bluff uncle Exeter; old Sir Thomas Erpingham (who lets Henry disguise himself in his cloak on the eve of Agincourt); dry-as-dust Canterbury and Ely; milords Clarence, Gloucester, Salisbury, Warwick and Westmoreland.

FROM THE BOAR'S HEAD TAVERN Shakespeare brings into the play Henry's companions from *Henry IV* and *The Merry Wives of Windsor*, using them not to provide light relief but to show how far Henry has travelled from his Falstaffian youth, and magnificently darkening their characters. Mistress Quickly, overwhelmed by her feeling that the death of her beloved Falstaff marks the end of an era, dies of grief. Bardolph and Nym are hanged; the Boy is murdered. Pistol brags his way round the battlefield, then, hearing that his wife (Mistress Quickly) has died, announces that he will go home and live by thieving.

☞ *About the play*

Henry V is a central part of Shakespeare's project, spread over a dozen plays, to describe in mythical terms the birth of modern England. From *Henry VI* to *Henry VIII*, from *King John* to *Richard II*, from *Richard III* to *King Lear*, from *Cymbeline* to

Henry IV, he produced not so much a tapestry of his country's history as a set of stories and instances refracting aspects of its deepest character. The sequence is not systematic (in the manner of his main source, Holinshed's *Chronicles*); each play draws general themes and ideas from specific historical events in the way Greek tragedians used ancient myth.

The principal subject of *Henry V* is not Henry's psychological growth or the politics and tactics of his reign, but war: its misery and attraction, heroism and terrors, and the idealism and cynicism of those involved in it. Attitudes to the play over the years have largely depended on current views of war. In Elizabethan and Victorian times, when conquest was regarded as a fulfilment of national destiny and an assertion of national identity, pomp and ceremony rode high. In more recent years, when ideas of imperial duty and 'just wars' have lost authority, the play has been quarried for irony and parodies of the patriotic and military impulse.

From the start of the action, Shakespeare's Chorus sets a tone which embraces both these alternatives. He admits that the theatre's technical means are limited and despairs of doing justice to his theme, while at the same time filling our ears with nimble and magnificent effects. In acknowledging the sober limits of illusion, the Chorus points us instead towards an equally sober and carefully focused analysis of reality.

One example makes the point. In *Henry IV Part II*, Henry's father advises him to 'busy giddy minds / with foreign quarrels'. At the start of *Henry V*, Canterbury and Ely encourage just such a war. Their declared purpose is that Henry should reclaim lands which are his by right of succession; their undeclared purpose (of which an earlier scene has made the audience aware) is to take the government's eye off the Church's riches. The young King then trumps this dubious politicking by making a genuine moral point, a warning about the inevitable loss of life in a war with France.

Henry's war-leadership is remarkable less for strategic skill than for dazzling rhetoric. It is almost as if, facing such odds, the English need something which transcends brute fighting-skills: Shakespeare's language at its most sinewy and most overwhelming. Speeches such as 'Once more into the breach, dear friends' are pieces of superb manipulation, tools to inspire their audience. In *Henry V* it is not just King and nation but the English language itself which is refined by experience and comes out stronger.

The presence, in the new world which Henry is forging, of Bardolph, Nym, Pistol and the Boy on the one hand, and on the other of Gower, Fluellen, Williams and the other ordinary soldiers, is crucial. Unlike the preening French, figures from a gorgeous tapestry, these are the common people rarely given individuality in 'true' history books (at least until the twentieth century): those who do the fighting and the dying. Their 'reality' infuses the whole play, humanizes the politics and the military tactics, and is a main contributor to the mythic self-image of England and the English which Shakespeare was constructing and which has lasted ever since.

In performance

Henry V was popular in Shakespeare's lifetime, then vanished almost entirely for 200 years. It came into its own in the nineteenth century, often (for example in Charles Kean's 1859 production) as a grandiose patriotic spectacle, basing set-piece scenes (such as the siege of Harfleur or the battle of Agincourt) on epic paintings and providing work for 200 extras grouped in 'living portraits' behind gauze curtains. Twentieth-century actors and directors, inspired by the revulsion which followed the 1914–18 war, turned this tradition inside out, exploring the play's darknesses and ironies. Then, in 1938, Ivor Novello mounted a jingoistic production in London, and in 1944 Olivier made his magnificent, flag-waving film. In the 1970s Alan Howard played Henry in a sequence of the 'tetralogy' in which he also played Richard II and Prince Hal, and in the 1980s, on stage and film, Kenneth Branagh made Henry a kind of quizzical, tortured god-king.

Henry VI, Parts I, II and III

👉 Sources

Raphael Holinshed, *Chronicles*; Edward Hall, *The Union of the Two Noble and Illustrious Families of Lancaster and York*.

👉 Story of the plays

Part I. On the death of Henry V, his son is only nine months old. Factions at court, led by the Duke of Gloucester and the Cardinal of Winchester, quarrel for political control. The Earl of Somerset and the Duke of York set up rival factions (named after their respective emblems, the red rose of Lancaster and the white rose of York). Meanwhile, in France, the English army is fighting to keep the gains made by Henry V decades before. Its principal adversary is La Pucelle (Joan of Arc). Peace is not made until La Pucelle is captured and executed and Henry (now adult) marries the French princess, Margaret of Anjou (who unknown to him, is having an affair with his ambassador the Earl of Suffolk).

Part II. The Wars of the Roses continue. Margaret and Suffolk plot against Gloucester, claiming that his wife consorts with witches. Suffolk is executed for Gloucester's murder. The Duke of York plots against Henry, first encouraging a people's revolt led by Jack Cade of Kent, and then taking the field himself. At the Battle of St Albans, York's son Richard (the future Richard III) kills Gloucester, and the Yorkists have won the day.

Part III. Henry agrees that the Yorkists can succeed him, providing that he can rule so long as he lives. This decision disinherits his own son Edward Prince of Wales, and Queen Margaret now goes to war against the Yorkists, defeats them and executes York. York's sons Edward, Clarence and Richard raise another army, but quarrel among themselves when Edward (the eldest) prefers Lady Grey to the French bride his brothers find him for political reasons. Warwick, their chief supporter, defects to the king's side, but even so, the royalists are defeated. Henry and the Prince of Wales are murdered, and Queen Margaret banished. But although the Yorkists now rule, and Edward the eldest is king, the brothers are still at one another's throats – the situation which bridges the end of this trilogy and the beginning of the next play in sequence, *Richard III*.

Characters

PART I

King Henry
Exeter, *his great-uncle*
Gloucester, Bedford, *his uncles*
Bishop of Winchester
Duke of York
Earls of Cambridge, March, Salisbury, Somerset, Warwick
Lord Talbot
John Talbot, *his son*
Sir John Fastolfe, Sir William Lucy, Sir William Glansdale, Sir Thomas Gargrave
Lord Mayor of London
Woodville, *lieutenant of the Tower*
Vernon, *Yorkist*
Bassett, *Lancastrian*

IN FRANCE

Charles, Dauphin (*later king*)
Joan la Pucelle
Shepherd, *her father*
Reignier, *Duke of Anjou*
Margaret, *his daughter*
Dukes of Alençon, Burgundy
Bastard of Orléans
Governor of Paris
Master-Gunner of Orléans
His Son
General *at Bordeaux*
Countess of Auvergne

Attendants, Fiends, Herald, Lawyer, Legate, Messengers, Officers, Porter, Servants, Soldiers, Watchmen

PART II

King Henry
Queen Margaret
Duke of Gloucester
Duchess of Gloucester
Cardinal Beaufort, *Bishop of Winchester*
Duke of York
Edward, Richard, *his sons*
Dukes of Buckingham, Suffolk, Somerset
Lord Clifford
Young Clifford, *his son*
Earl of Salisbury
Earl of Warwick, *his son*
Lords Say, Scales
Sir Humphrey Stafford
William Stafford, *his brother*
Sir John Stanley, Sir William Vaux
Jack Cade, *rebel*
George Bevis, John Holland, Dick the Butcher, Smith the Weaver, Michael, *his followers*
Alexander Iden, *Kentish gentleman*

Whitmore, *pirate*
Margery Jourdain, *witch*
Roger Bolingbroke, *conjurer (ie medium)*
Saunder Simpcox, *impostor (ie conman)*
Mistress Simpcox, *his wife*
Thomas Horner, *armourer*
Peter, *his man*
Clerk of Chatham
Mayor of St Albans
John Hume, John Southwell, *priests*
Aldermen, Apprentices, Attendants, Beadle, Citizens, Falconers, Gentlemen (*in gaol with Suffolk*), Matthew Gough, Guards, Herald, Ladies, Lieutenant, Lords, Master's Mate, Messengers, Officers, Petitioners, Sherriff, Shipmaster, Soldiers, Spirit

PART III

King Henry
Queen Margaret
Edward, *Prince of Wales*
King Louis XIV *of France*

Dukes of Exeter, Norfolk, Somerset, York
Earls of Hastings, Oxford, Northumberland, Pembroke, Richmond, Warwick, Westmoreland
Lords Clifford, Hastings, Stafford
York's sons Edward (*later Edward IV*), Edmund, George (*later Duke of Clarence*), Richard (*later Duke of Gloucester and Richard III*)
Marquess of Montague
Sir John Montgomery, Sir John Mortimer, Sir Hugh Mortimer, Sir John Somerville, Sir William Stanley
Lady Grey, *later Edward's queen*
Lord Rivers, *her brother*
Bona, *sister of the Queen of France*
Son that has killed his father
Father that has killed his son
Attendants, Huntsman, Keepers, Lieutenant of the Tower, Mayor of York, Messengers, Nobleman, Soldiers, Tutor, Watchmen

HENRY Henry is handicapped from the start. He comes to the throne at only six months of age. Throughout his childhood, he is sidelined while powerful rivals use the regency to jostle for supremacy. He tries to settle the war with France by marrying a French princess, only to find her conducting affairs and plunging enthusiastically into the English dynastic struggle. None the less, he is a good, moral man (for example, in *Part II* he is willing to discuss terms with Cade rather than let 'so many simple souls perish by the sword'), and this gives his failure, each time, a dimension which is tragic rather than merely pitiful. When he is stripped of all he has and imprisoned in *Part III*, Shakespeare enhances his moral dignity by the power of language (the scenes are a kind of preview of the banishment scenes in *Richard II* some ten years later), setting him apart from the unscrupulous thuggery of almost every other person of rank in England.

MARGARET Spread over four plays (the *Henry VI* trilogy and *Richard III*), the role of Margaret is one of Shakespeare's most elaborate and striking creations. We first meet her in *Part I*, as an ostensibly innocent young princess courted on behalf of his king by Suffolk, and flirting with him almost as Beatrice does with Benedick in *Much Ado About Nothing*. In *Part II* she is a devious, powerful and mature woman, plotting against Gloucester, manipulating politics through her lover Suffolk and rounding spectacularly on Henry when he has him executed. In *Part III* she is like a vengeful Fury, raging at Henry, her followers and her enemies and insulting the captured York (in the scene with the paper crown). Then, in the battle-scenes – by which time she is in her fifties – Shakespeare suddenly lets patriotism flood her character and motivate her rage, a *coup de théâtre* which overturns everything we know of her and throws the machinations of her enemies the Yorkists into even sharper focus.

WARWICK In *Part I*, Warwick is too young to play a significant part in war or political discussion, to show any of the consummate qualities which later earned him the nickname 'kingmaker'. He has few lines, and is merely one among many young lords who support the Yorkists. In *Part II*, he is a rising star but still tends to behave like an over-eager puppy, plotting energetically for Gloucester against Somerset and and raging about the battlefield of St Albans, slicing every enemy in sight, but prevented by York just in time to save him from disaster when he challenges someone who far outmatches him (Clifford). In *Part III* he comes into his own at last as a mature, experienced statesman, speaking for York, advising his sons, arranging Edward's coronation and leaving for France to arrange a marriage which will consolidate their royal position. At this point his master betrays him, choosing a wife of his own (Lady Grey) and leaving Warwick, as politician, high and dry. Warwick deserts to the Lancastrians, but the heart has gone out of him, and his decline is a sequence of tragic futility: his supporters are killed or drift away, and he himself, having refused the pardon offered him by Edward, is forced to fight his former protégés and is wounded, dragged out of the centre of events (a highly symbolic moment) and killed.

YORK In performance, the trilogy is sometimes trimmed and shaped to highlight York, playing him as a twisted villain throughout, as if he were a kind of prototype of his son Richard (the future Richard III). This gives edge to his quarrels with Henry and to his sulky fury when Margaret mocks him with the paper crown in *Part III*. But the interpretation distorts Shakespeare's dramatic plan. In this, York is one of a number of conspirators and warlords of equal stature. All are morally flawed, and none is more or less admirable than the others. York may stand out only because of the flamboyance of what he says and does, but he is by no means the trilogy's chief villain.

BISHOP OF WINCHESTER (*Parts I and II*) The quarrel between Gloucester and Winchester starts the trilogy spinning with furious rivalry, words flying like knives and heads being broken in every street. The ambitious, worldly Winchester, bastard son of John of Gaunt, typifies the Elizabethan notion that all Catholic prelates were devious and destructive – and his suggestion, later in *Part I*, that the infant Henry be kidnapped for political advantage does nothing to dissipate this impression. In *Part II* he has risen to the rank of Cardinal (Beaufort), but is still at Gloucester's throat, enthusiastically joining in the plot to topple him. After this, however, his part diminishes, and he is last seen on his deathbed, full of self-lacerating repentance.

GLOUCESTER (*Parts I and II*) In *Part I*, Gloucester, the king's uncle, is differentiated from the other lords jockeying for position chiefly by his spectacular rudeness to his political rival Winchester. In *Part II*, a generation later, he has become the elder statesman who has united the kingdom – and whom every other lord is determined to topple. He seems invincible, because of both his rank and his grandly-stated, no-nonsense patriotism. But then they find a flaw in him – his love for his wife – and use it to prise his life apart.

The tragic irony is that Gloucester falls not because of evil intentions or personal wickedness, but because of a 'good' moral feeling, true love. His scenes with his wife, and his penitence just before he is murdered, are among the high points of *Part II*, and the fact that the country slides irrevocably into civil war so soon after his death is a clear symbol of the qualities of nobility and honour for which he stood and which his compatriots so clearly lack.

SUFFOLK (*Parts I and II*) For most of his time in the plays, Suffolk is presented as an uncomplicated villain, snarling at the Yorkists, seducing the King's young bride so that he can use her to influence the King, bringing down the Duke of Gloucester by bribing fake witches to discredit his wife, and hiring assassins to murder Gloucester. He comes to a suitably bad end, arrested, banished, captured by pirates and then murdered on a beach by a one-eyed ruffian (Whitmore) who turns out to be a true patriot as well as a pirate. But Suffolk's character is more than such lip-smacking melodrama. Shakespeare shows him falling in love with the queen he has seduced, tender and passionate – and heart-broken when he is torn from her. Even such a man, in such an equivocal and self-engineered situation, is capable of 'true' moral feeling – a theme which might, in a more mature single play, have been more fully developed than the intriguing glimpses we are given here.

LA PUCELLE (*Part I*) Only the English characters in the play take Joan of Arc (Jeanne la Pucelle, 'Joan the Maid') at the propaganda valuation of Shakespeare's sources: sexually pro-miscuous and a witch. To everyone else she is precisely what she claims to be: a loyal soldier of France and of God, brave, heroic and patriotically concerned for the common people of her country who are suffering at English hands. Her gender is quite irrelevant.

In Act Five, Shakespeare tilts his portrayal towards his (anti-French, anti-Catholic) sources, showing us La Pucelle conjuring up devils and later, when she is arrested, claiming immunity from execution on the false grounds that she is of royal blood and is pregnant, then shouting insults and spitting hate when the attempt fails and she is dragged to death. There has been no hint of this kind of character in her earlier scenes, where she has behaved throughout quite differently from the way her enemies describe her. Two explanations are suggested. In one, what we see in Act Five is the real Joan, and her behaviour elsewhere is cynical and ironical. In the other, her terror and hysteria when things go wrong are extreme but perfectly natural reactions, surprising in the woman of action we have seen in the rest of the play but also moving, injecting humanity into the character and show-ing us the Joan of the sources in an utterly new light – a typical Shakespearean surprise.

TALBOT (*Part I*) Talbot is Joan of Arc's chief rival, both physically (in that they are fighting for the same towns) and spir-itually (in that they are both brave, noble and heroic). He is not a politician but a warrior, and his marked difference from the other English grandees, bickering and plotting, putting their own interests before their country, is symbolized by his staying in France throughout the action. He is the first example of one of Shakespeare's favourite characters, the decent, patriotic soldier. Henry V is the pinnacle of the type, but Bolingbroke in *Richard II*, Antony in *Julius Caesar*, Cassio in *Othello* and Enobarbus in *Antony and Cleopatra* all draw on it.

JACK CADE (*Part II*) The real-life Jack Cade was a minor land-owner in Kent who organized a kind of middle-class revolt against the government. He and his followers published a pamphlet com-plaining of high taxes, extravagance in high places and the over-prominence of Suffolk in public life. They marched on London, and the government first panicked (imprisoning and then execut-ing Lord Say, who in real life was not the saintly figure of the play but an extortionate Kent landlord), and then stirred up the citizens against them and sent them home in disorder. Cade was killed by Iden, as in the play – but Iden was no ordinary house-holder but another Kentish placeman.

Shakespeare ignored all this completely. He turned Cade and his supporters into a kind of macabre comic turn, perhaps specifically intended for the acting company's group of comedians. Historical truth is jettisoned as Cade sets up a kind of parody court in Kent, for all the world like a mafia boss or a banana-republic dictator distributing rewards to his followers and arbitrary punishment to anyone he dislikes. The scenes are fast, funny and fascist – but the ironical point is also quite explicit. The behaviour of Cade and his 'rabblement' almost exactly parallels to that of the lords and courtiers at the heart of the main political action. There is nothing but rank to choose between them.

DUCHESS OF GLOUCESTER (*Part II*) A remarkably stupid person who happens to be married to one of the most powerful people in the kingdom (the Lord Protector, regent and heir apparent to the young King), the Duchess is determined that Gloucester will take the throne for himself. When he refuses, she turns to a group of witches led by John Hume, hoping to bring about a change of heart by magic. Hume is in fact a spy, sent by Suffolk to entrap Gloucester, and the Duchess's involvement with him leads to her own public humiliation and her husband's death.

SAUNDER SIMPCOX (*Part II*) While King Henry and Gloucester are hawking near St Albans, the townsfolk bring them one Saunder Simpcox, who claims that he was blinded and paralysed years before when he fell out of a plum tree, but now thanks to a miracle has been completely cured. The young, gullible Henry is fooled by this, but Gloucester questions Simpcox more closely and shows that he is a conman

SON THAT HAS KILLED HIS FATHER AND FATHER THAT HAS KILLED HIS SON (*Part III*) At the battle of Towton, Henry has no stomach for the fight, and moves to one side, wishing that he were an ordinary person rather than a king. At this point, the Son comes in with a corpse to loot, and finds to his horror that it is his father's, and a Father arrives with another corpse, only to find that it is his son's. Henry watches them, unseen, and when they have gone reflects sadly on what civil war has done to England.

🐾 *About the plays*

It used to be thought that Shakespeare was only one of several authors involved in the four-play cycle formed by *Henry VI* and *Richard III*. Many dramatists were said to have contributed scenes and ideas to a company-created spectacle, and Shakespeare's role was less that of original author than editor and reviser, putting order into a pile of chaotic manuscript.

This view fits the plays into a type of drama already old-fashioned by Shakespeare's time: the historical pageant. Fifty years before, Henry VIII had favoured these, and Elizabeth I, as a young woman, had taken part in them herself each year on the anniversary of her accession. Jousting, feasting, song, dance, tumbling and animal-baiting all played their part – and actors performed scenes from English history, patriotic snippets strung together like the Biblical scenes of medieval Mystery Plays. As a boy of eleven, Shakespeare may have seen one of the most spectacular of all these pageants, at Kenilworth in 1575. (He later described it in *A Midsummer Night's Dream*.)

Probably, when Shakespeare's acting-company settled in London, it had a trunkful of scripts used in pageants in earlier, touring days: scenes dealing with events from the Wars of the Roses, England's wars in France and the murderous career attributed to Richard III. Ideas and episodes from these scenes – the death of Joan of Arc, Cade's rebellion, Queen Margaret and the paper crown – may have found their way into Shakespeare's mind, if not verbatim into his script. But the concept behind the four plays (a Wars of the Roses trilogy followed by close-focus attention on Richard III) has the audacity of a single creative mind, not a committee, and its execution, despite occasional woodenness, dazzlingly foreshadows many preoccupations and stylistic strategies in Shakespeare's later work. Clinchingly, each play is better written than the one before: the mark of a young author learning by experience.

For dramatic purposes, Shakespeare collapses historical time, reducing fifty years to a few emblematic moments, and reshaping or omitting details which fail to fit his over-arching dramatic scheme. In history, Burgundy defected from the English side to the French several years after Joan's execution; in *Part I*, Joan persuades him to do so, by a moving description of France's suffering at English hands. York, in history, had no connection with Jack Cade; in *Part II* Shakespeare makes them political allies. Queen Margaret uses Gloucester's wife's supposed interest in witchcraft to engineer his downfall in *Part II*; in real history, the Duchess of Gloucester was exiled before Margaret ever came to England. The squabbling between Lancastrians and Yorkists is condensed from decades to a kind of continuous ferment which focuses the entire dramatic action.

Shakespeare's inexperience is shown, perhaps, in the plethora of indistinguishable lords, some appearing for a single speech or line, others bewilderingly changing names and ranks as the plays proceed. (In later plays, he solved this problem by reducing the numbers and sharply characterizing each important individual.) The verse, similarly, is often undifferentiated: lines could be swapped between characters without affecting character or meaning. But time and again this continuum is interrupted by flashes of true Shakespearean genius. The non-noble characters – Cade and his followers, Whitmore the pirate, Simpcox, Joan's father – are drawn from that teeming pool of humanity so characteristic of his work. Joan is an unexpected and volatile blend of virginal innocence and crop-headed bravado: a wonderful part for an adolescent actor. Among the aristocratic characters, Talbot's character and lines are worthy of *Henry V*; Gloucester exemplifies the tragic clash, so common in later Shakespeare, between public statesmanship and private anguish; Margaret's devious, vehement character superbly develops from play to play (and is beautifully matched by the sliminess of her co-conspirator Suffolk); above all, Richard Plantagenet is so powerfully characterized that he overwhelms the second half of *Part III* and demands an entire play of his own: *Richard III*, a clear case of dramatic potential overwhelming actual history.

☞ *In performance*

The trilogy was popular in Shakespeare's lifetime, *Part I* especially being a box-office winner. Later generations, concentrating on Shakespeare's later plays, neglected it almost completely. *Part I* was revived once (almost completely rewritten) in 1738, *Part II* for German celebrations of the Shakespeare tricentennial in 1864 and *Part III* not at all. In 1906 Frank Benson revived the whole trilogy for the first time, and it has had sporadic performances since: in the US in 1935, at Birmingham in 1951–3, at the RSC in 1977 and 1988. It has also become known in adaptation: as part of *An Age of Kings* (1960) and *The Wars of the Roses* (1963–4). Apart from that, the rest is – largely unjustified – silence.

TALBOT

    O thou whose wounds become hard-favoured death
    Speak to thy father ere thou yield thy breath.
    Brave Death by speaking, whether he will or no;
    Imagine him a Frenchman and thy foe.
    Poor boy, he smiles, methinks as who should say
    Had death been French, then death had died today.
    Come, come and lay him in his father's arms.
    My spirit can no longer bear these harms.
    Soldiers, adieu. I have what I would have
    Now my old arms are young John Talbot's grave. (*dies*)
                        [Part I, IV, vii]

MARGARET

    A crown for York. And lords bow low to him.
    Hold you his hands whilst I do set it on.
          (*putting a paper crown on his head*)
    Ay, marry sir, now looks he like a king.
    Ay, this is he that took King Henry's chair,
    And this is he was his adopted heir. [Part III, I, iv]

Henry VIII

☞ Sources

Raphael Holinshed, *Chronicles*; Edward Hall, *The Union of the Two Noble and Illustrious Families of Lancaster and York*. Cranmer's trial in Act Five is based on a verbatim account in John Foxe, *Book of Martyrs*.

☞ Story of the play

The surface glitter and pomp of Henry's court mask a plot, led by Lord Abergavenny and the Duke of Buckingham, to discredit Cardinal Wolsey, the king's adviser. Their real objection is that he symbolizes the power and influence of the Catholic Church; their specific charges are that his personal ambition is leading him to bypass the king in making decisions of state. Wolsey is aware of the plot, and before it can come to fruition Buckingham is arrested and condemned for treason.

Henry has separated from Queen Katharine because she has borne him no heir. At a masque in Wolsey's house, he dances with Anne Bullen. Wolsey discovers a legal technicality about the King's marriage to Katharine which should enable it to be annulled, and advises Katharine to throw herself on the King's mercy. Instead she retreats to the country and petitions the Pope for help. Henry discovers that Wolsey has been plundering state funds, and that he has asked the Pope to delay the annulment until he (Wolsey) can eliminate the Protestant Anne Bullen. He dismisses Wolsey, appoints Thomas Cranmer Archbishop of Canterbury and marries Anne Bullen in a dazzling ceremony.

Wolsey and Katharine both die. The nobles continue plotting, this time accusing Cranmer, before the Council, of heresy. Henry, on his way to visit Anne Bullen (who has just had a child, Elizabeth), guarantees him royal immunity, and when the Council condemns him to the Tower, cancels the order. He asks Cranmer to be

Elizabeth's godfather, and at the christening ceremony Cranmer speaks a paean of praise to the new princess and the glories she will one day bring the British people.

The play's spectacle is remarkable: the Act One masque, Council scenes in Acts Two and Five, Anne Bullen's coronation in Act Four, a ballet of 'spirits of peace' dreamed by the delirious Katharine in Act Four, and the christening of Princess Elizabeth that ends the action. Stage directions give details of costumes, music and effects. These included fireworks and cannonfire – the cause, on 29 June 1613, of a fire which destroyed the Globe Theatre.

☞ Characters

King Henry VIII	Lord Sands
Queen Katharine	Denny, Guildford, Lovell, Vaux,
Anne Bullen, *her maid of honour*	*knights*
Cardinal Wolsey	Cromwell, Griffith, Old Lady,
Cardinal Campeius	Patience, *servants*
Capucius, *French ambassador*	Attendants, Bishops, Crier,
Cranmer, Archbishop of	Doctor, Door-Keeper, Garter
Canterbury	King-at-Arms, Guards,
Dukes of Buckingham, Norfolk,	Ladies, Lords, Officers, Page,
Suffolk, Surrey	Porter, Porter's Man, Scribes,
Lord Chamberlain	Surveyor, Women-in-Waiting
Lord Chancellor	
Bishops of Winchester,	
Lincoln	

HENRY Henry is never seen in domestic, intimate scenes. He is presented throughout as a kind of gorgeous figurehead, like a king on a playing-card or the famous Holbein portrait come to life. He presides at meetings and ceremonies, meets ambassadors and plays his role in masques and dances. It is only at the end, when he attacks the Council for condemning Cranmer, that we see any real glimpse of the human being behind the royal mask.

CARDINAL WOLSEY Henry's nobles, led by Buckingham, Norfolk, Surrey and Suffolk, hate Wolsey because he is a Catholic prelate (and therefore brings the undue influence of Rome into

English affairs) and because his power far eclipses their own. For his part, Wolsey is a silky, urbane politician. When Henry demands to know why he has used the King's name to raise illegal taxes, he first claims injured innocence – 'If I am traduc'd by ignorant tongues . . . let me say / 'Tis but the fate of place, and the rough brake / That virtue must go through' – then has the taxes cancelled and spreads the word that the King has done this thanks to his (Wolsey's) influence. He wheedles Katharine to agree to the annulment of her marriage and then, behind her back, writes to the Pope to ask him to delay it. He is so self-assured that he even gives Henry orders in his own court: 'Most gracious sire / In humblest manner I require your highness / . . . to declare, in hearing / Of all these ears . . . whether ever I / Did broach this business to your highness . . .' Norfolk says that 'like the eldest son of Fortune', he 'turns what he list' – and Norfolk is right.

So far, Wolsey is two-dimensional. He claims in a soliloquy that his plotting is for religious reasons (to prevent the 'spleeny Lutheran' Anne Bullen becoming queen), but in effect he is exactly the self-delighted, audience-wooing 'machiavel' (ironical Italian schemer) so popular in Elizabethan and Jacobean drama. However, when Henry is given uncontrovertible evidence about his greed and deviousness and he is finally brought down, Wolsey bids 'a long farewell to all his greatness', reflects that 'Had I but served my God with half the zeal / I served my king, he would not in mine age / Have left me naked to mine enemies', retreats to a monastery and dies 'in repentance / Continual meditations, tears and sorrows'. Though there is arrogance in this – he is as self-obsessed in repentance as he was in power – there is also humanity. His character acquires dignity before our eyes, and the change materially affects our view of everything we have seen or heard him do till now.

QUEEN KATHARINE Katharine of Aragon was briefly married to Henry's elder brother Arthur, but Arthur died a few months later and Henry married her in 1509, having been granted a dispensation from the Pope to do so despite the law that no man should marry his brother's widow. (The technical reason was that the first marriage had never been consummated.) Katharine and Henry were married for twenty years before the king's roving eye led him to the Bullen family. (Anne's elder sister was his mistress for six years, and as soon as Anne was old enough – and returned from France, where she spent her adolescence – he transferred his affection to her.)

Henry VIII plays down any intimacy between Henry and Katharine. The Queen is presented as a woman of radiant middle age, secure and innocent, whose life is suddenly destroyed when Wolsey tells her that her twenty-year marriage has been illegal and that unless she agrees to an annulment she will be dragged through the courts. Katharine responds at first with fury ('Would I had never trod this English earth / Or felt the flatteries that grow upon it'), but then gathers her dignity and submits with a kind of bitter grace ('Come, reverend fathers / Bestow your counsels on me. She now begs / That little thought, when she set footing here / She should have bought her dignities so dear'). We next see her in one of the play's most moving scenes, on her deathbed, talking to her loyal servants, hearing news of Anne Bullen's coronation, and sending Henry a letter in which she begs him to look after their daughter Mary. Her last words are a message of love for the King ('Tell him, in death I blessed him') and a request that her dignity, and innocence, be maintained to the last: 'Let me be used with honour. Strew me over / With maiden flowers, that all the world may know / I was a chaste wife to my grave. Embalm me / Then lay me forth: although unqueened, yet like / A queen, and daughter to a king, inter me. / I can no more'. Here and throughout the play, the quality she shows and the poetry she speaks stand in ironical, marked contrast to the politicking of almost everyone else involved. In a world corrupted by lusts and wants of every kind (for power, gold, position, sex, children), she is a beacon of purity, and her presence as a character (matched only by Wolsey's) is the glory of the play.

ANNE BULLEN Wolsey calls Anne a 'spleeny Lutheran', but this is more his excuse for trying to stop her marriage to Henry than a true description, and there is no sign of it in anything she does or says. She is a charming young woman, good at small talk (when she exchanges witty remarks with Sands at a dinner-party), good at dancing, and kind to Queen Katharine (she feels sorry for her and is reluctant to replace her). But for all that, she accepts her bawdy old servant's advice to make the most of the King's infatuation, and is happy to share his bed and become pregnant with his child.

THOMAS CRANMER, ARCHBISHOP OF CANTERBURY

In history Cranmer was a scholar and ascetic, one of the founders of the Church of England and the chief author of its articles of faith and its liturgy. He was burned for heresy by the Catholic queen Mary. Writing sixty years later, in the reign of James I, Shakespeare and his co-author(s) somewhat daringly present Cranmer in this play as a kind of walking Protestant saint, a man so holy and so apparently guileless that Henry has to ask him 'Know you not / How your state stands i' the world . . . ? / Your enemies are many, and not small . . .' Cranmer certainly *does* know, but proclaims both his guiltlessness and his assurance of royal favour ('God and your majesty / Protect mine innocence . . .') – and Henry rewards his trust by rounding on the Council which is trying him for heresy, and then by making him godfather to the infant Princess Elizabeth.

About the play

Scholars used to dispute the authorship of *Henry VIII*, attributing it in part or in whole to John Fletcher and/or Philip Massinger. Some say that Shakespeare wrote only a handful of scenes, those centring on Katharine, Anne and the Wolsey of the 'long farewell to all my greatness'. Latest opinion, however, claims the whole play for Shakespeare, and sees him as revisiting, at the very end of his career, the kind of historical pageants which were popular in his boyhood and which inspired his earliest pieces of playmaking, the *Henry VI* trilogy. As in those pageants, the scenes are not dovetailed into a homogeneous intellectual structure, but strung together so that each makes its own effect; the characters (particularly the King's) are grandly but shallowly drawn, and effect tends to predominate over philosophical or dramatic substance.

By the 1610s, this kind of looser structure was the prevailing theatrical mode, influenced partly by the transcendental fairy-tale style of Shakespeare's own late romances, and partly by such up-and-coming writers as Beaumont and Fletcher and the writers of masques for Court and the Blackfriars Theatre (which Shakespeare's company used for their winter seasons from 1609). *Henry VIII* is a hybrid piece. At one level it is all pomp and spectacle, with a cumulative magnificence expressed in verse which is, like that of its near contemporary *Cymbeline*, compact, gestural and natural. These ceremonial passages (the ones formerly attributed to Shakespeare's collaborator) are interspersed with scenes of intimate political and psychological realism, social idiosyncrasy and human particularity, focused on such magnificently layered creations as Wolsey or Katharine, who are among Shakespeare's finest characters and whose moral dilemmas, intrigues and sufferings illuminate the action.

Of all Shakespeare's dramatizations of history *Henry VIII* is closest in time to contemporary events (written only three generations after what it describes), and is a delicate piece of historical balancing. Henry's break with Rome and the massive cultural, religious and political changes brought about by the Reformation were still recent history whose impact was felt on people's everyday lives. What Shakespeare mythologizes – in a way whose consolatory power is, as it were, a political version of the late romances – is that out of desperate struggle (the birth of modern England, the theme which underlies all Shakespeare's historical writing) emerges a new unity, embodied first in Elizabeth and then in her successor James, who is mystically referred to in the final, prophetic speech of Cranmer quoted below.

To be sure, the first part of the play does contain the anti-Catholicism standard at the period, and Wolsey is shown as the insinuating and dangerous influence of the Papacy. But *Henry VIII* was written for a Stuart, not Tudor, audience, and Shakespeare goes out of his way in the later scenes to let us sympathize with both Wolsey and Henry's estranged Catholic wife Katharine. It is as if in writing the play (significantly subtitled *All Is True*) he wanted it to serve two purposes: to remind his traditional audience of the legitimizing myth of Elizabeth I, and to provide his patron James I (who was much more generously disposed to Catholicism) with his own mythic resolution of the national agony. At the end, characteristically, Shakespeare seems to project beyond the religious and cultural divisions of the sixteenth-century, still not resolved in James' time, into a romanticized notion of a better land: 'Peace, plenty, love, truth, terror / That were the servants to this chosen infant / Shall then be his and like a vine grow to him. / Wherever the bright sun of Heaven shall shine / His honour and the greatness of his name / Shall be and make new nations. He shall flourish / And like a mountain cedar reach his branches / To all the plains about him. Our children's children / Shall see this and bless Heaven.' Such a prophecy must have provoked wry smiles in not a few of his spectators.

☞ *In performance*

The notorious 1613 performance of *Henry VIII* (when the Globe Theatre burned down) does not seem to have deterred later managements: the play was popular for its spectacular effects and was regularly staged with casts of several hundred, pyrotechnic effects, real horses, coaches and soldiers, and costumes modelled on the most lavish court paintings of the Elizabethan period. Well-known actors who triumphed in the play include David Garrick and Charles Laughton as Henry (Laughton drawing on his recent success in the 1933 film *The Private Life of Henry VIII*, no connection with Shakespeare, Fletcher or Massinger), John Philip Kemble (Cranmer), Herbert Beerbohm Tree, Henry Irving and John Gielgud (Wolsey) and Sarah Siddons, Ellen Terry, Sybil Thorndike, Edith Evans and Flora Robson (Katharine).

Julius Caesar

📖 Sources

Plutarch, *Lives*. Plays about Caesar had been popular in the 1580s, and as a young man Shakespeare may have seen and/or performed in them; in *Hamlet* Polonius refers to one of them.

📖 Story of the play

At the end of a war between two rival military factions, Caesar has defeated Pompey and is idolized by the Roman crowd. However, the Senators suspect that he has ambitions to abolish the Republic and become sole ruler – suspicions confirmed when they hear that the people are clamouring for him to be crowned king. A conspiracy is formed to assassinate Caesar, and Cassius tries to recruit his friend Brutus into it. (Brutus's ancestor toppled an earlier tyrant king, Tarquin the Proud.)

Despite fearful omens, the nightmares of his wife Calphurnia and the warnings of a Soothsayer, Caesar insists on going to the Senate house on the Ides (15th) of March. The conspirators surround him and stab him dead. Civil war is imminent between the senatorial party (led by Cassius and the more reluctant Brutus) and the Caesarians (led by Caesar's lieutenant Mark Antony and the young Octavius, Caesar's nephew). In a set-piece scene, as Caesar's body lies in state before the people, Brutus and Antony make speeches about his assassination. Brutus says that the murder was essential to save Rome from tyranny; Antony says that Caesar loved the people and has left them his estates in his will. The people riot and Brutus and Cassius escape with their lives.

The battle-lines are set: on one side are Antony and Octavius, and on the other are Cassius, Brutus and their army. Brutus and Cassius have a prickly argument about trust and honour, and make an uneasy truce. Brutus sleeps, but is visited by Caesar's ghost saying he will 'meet him at Philippi'. At Philippi, Brutus and Cassius each command a different wing of their army, Cassius against Antony, Brutus against Octavius. Each says he will commit suicide rather than be captured – and when they lose in the battle which follows, they do so. The play ends with Antony and Octavius triumphant, ordering an honourable burial for Brutus on the grounds that he was 'the noblest Roman of them all'.

☞ *Characters*

Julius Caesar
Calpurnia, *his wife*
Marcus Antonius, *his lieutenant*
Octavius, *his nephew*
Lepidus, *triumvir with Antony and Octavius*
Marcus Brutus, Caius Cassius, Casca, Cinna, Decius Brutus, Ligarius, Metellus Cimber, Trebonius, *conspirators*
Portia, *Brutus' wife*
Cicero, Popilius Lena, Publius, *senators*

Flavius, Marullus, *tribunes*
Cinna *the poet*
Young Cato, Lucilius, Messala, Titinius, Volumnius, *friends and supporters of Brutus and Cassius*
Claudius, Clitus, Dardanius, Lucius, Strato, Varro, *Brutus' servants*
Pindarus, *Cassius' servant*
Attendants, Citizens, Guards, Poet, Senators, Soldiers, Soothsayer

CAESAR Historians endlessly ask why the real-life Caesar was assassinated, and their answers range from the politics of an entire century (the evolution of Rome from republican to imperial rule) to some kind of debilitating illness. Dramatic licence allows Shakespeare to be both blunter and subtler. His Caesar dies because he is the brightest star in the Roman firmament, the 'colossus', in Cassius' words, who bestrides the whole world while lesser mortals 'Walk under his huge legs and peep about / To find dishonourable graves.'

Caesar is a charismatic tyrant, favouring his acolytes and patronizing, ignoring or neutralizing his opponents. He is so powerful, and so much part of the scenery of power, that he can be toppled only by a conspiracy of all kinds and conditions of people, including those who love him. Caesar's nobility – enhanced too often in performances by elderly, well-known actors – and his personal charm belie the fact that he is also arrogant, self-absorbed and convinced of his own invulnerability. Even after death he haunts the play: just as the first half was about removing him, so the second half is about coping with his absence.

BRUTUS There is something of Hamlet in Brutus. His instincts are for thought, not action: he is a scholar and ascetic, preferring quiet hours with his books to the hurly-burly of the forum or senate-house. He is a kind husband, considerate master and gentle friend, easy meat for the ambitious, more pragmatic Cassius – and even when he is convinced and drawn into the conspiracy he moves like a man in a nightmare, constantly forced to take actions (plotting, murder, commanding soldiers) which are outside his normal nature. He finds ways to cope with this, does what he convinces himself he has to do, and it is only when things happen which are against all rationality (Portia's suicide; the appearance of Caesar's ghost before Philippi) that he loses his way and his world falls in around him.

The real-life Brutus was a follower of the Stoic philosophy, whose adherents believed that they should live a life of self-denial and service. Shakespeare shows the attractive side of this, but also makes clear that it is out of date in the dangerous politics which suddenly engulf the Roman ruling class. In this world, Brutus is just as much of an anachronism as Caesar. Caesar falls because he refuses to compromise with the 'tide in the affairs of men' when it clearly turns against him. Brutus tries to swim with the current, but fails and is forced to one last act of violence: his suicide. If the revolution needs intellectuals, Brutus is one, but so also does he show the limitations of that group.

CASSIUS In contrast to the Stoic Brutus, with his ideals of self-denial and service to others, Cassius is an Epicurean. He believes that each moment should be taken as it comes, that chance rules all and that life is not for questioning, but for living. He knows what his goals are, but he is a political opportunist, seizing what comes his way and adapting his plans and his approach to fit each new circumstance. He is physically fearless – and scorns Caesar for weakness – but is wary of events and prone to panic when things seem to be moving out of his control. (He draws back at the last moment before the assassination, and Brutus has to reassure him. Before Philippi, he loses his nerve entirely, and after the battle he is so unmanned by news of defeat that he stabs himself dead.)

The pull in Cassius' character between ambition and impetuosity makes him as unsuited as Brutus to the multifarious world of Roman politics. Unlike Brutus he is a man of action, but in the end both suffer from the same flaw: dissatisfied with the way things are, they are unable to reshape their own natures enough to bring about the change they long for.

PORTIA Brutus's beloved wife ('As dear to me as are the ruddy drops / That visit my sad heart') has a few short speeches only, full of concern for her husband and panic when she hears no news of him. In the scene before Philippi, when Brutus is 'sick of many griefs' and quarrels distractedly with Cassius, he suddenly reveals that Portia has been so grieved by his long absence and the growing power of Octavius and Antony that she has committed suicide. Although he tries to put it from him ('Speak no more of her. Give me a bowl of wine . . .'), this is the hammer-blow which marks the beginning of his decline.

ANTONY Antony's irruption into the play at the beginning of Act Three is a major dramatic surprise. Until then, the action has been concerned with Caesar's tyrannical silkiness and the growing momentum of the conspiracy. Antony has hardly appeared: half a dozen lines, some three dozen words. The cathartic brutality of the assassination crowns this movement of the play, leaving the conspirators in a kind of daze. They argue about what to do next, Brutus says he will appease the mob – and it is at this point that Antony swings into the action. He is the first person to weep openly at Caesar's death, and the moral authority this gives him not only throws a searing light on the politics which have led to the murder, but also sets up his blunt, soldierly sarcasm in the funeral oration (' . . . and Brutus is an honourable man').

However, Antony has already shown us the other side of his character. On an empty stage, he has promised civil war to Caesar's body: 'All pity choked with custom of fell deeds', he will

'Cry havoc, and let slip the dogs of war / That this foul deed shall smell above the earth . . .' Almost immediately after the funeral oration we see him with Octavius and Lepidus, making lists of people to be eliminated ('These many, then, shall die; their names are pricked'), and he includes his own nephew. Face to face with Brutus and Cassius before Philippi, he begins mildly ('In your bad strokes, Brutus, you give good words: / Witness the hole you made in Caesar's heart / Crying "Long live! Hail Caesar!"'), but soon turns to savagery ('You showed your teeth like apes, and fawned like hounds / And bowed like bondsmen, kissing Caesar's feet . . .'). He is like a raging animal, and his one remaining speech in the play, his ringing epitaph for Brutus ('This was the noblest Roman of them all') does nothing to change the impression that he is one of the most intemperate and dangerous men in Rome.

☞ About the play

The play's historical framework could hardly be simpler. Caesar's constitutional ambitions anger a group of Roman aristocrats who mount a conspiracy to assassinate him. Far from resolving the situation, his murder leads to division among the conspirators and to civil war. The conspirators are defeated at the battle of Philippi. On this scaffolding Shakespeare builds a complex study of political interaction, showing the way people of widely differing characters and ideals subordinate their own natures for a common end (or fail to do so), how groups are formed and the tensions which split them apart. The contest is not merely between rivals or uneasy allies, but between the ideals and ambitions people have and the qualities of character needed to fulfil them. Behind all the machinations and compromises are two large, contrasted groups caught up in the power play: the trembling, ineffective Senate, and the common citizens who once supported Caesar and whom Antony wins over against the conspirators ('Friends, Romans, countrymen . . .') even while planning to engulf them in a civil war which will glut the earth with 'carrion men, groaning for burial'.

The play has striking relevance to contemporary Elizabethan politics. Like 1590s London, Shakespeare's Rome is a busy city, anonymous and frightening, bloodthirsty and cruel, with a volatile plebeian mob and a divided ruling class. But it boasts a group of aristocrats with intellectual application who are prepared to risk all in the cause of freedom, and the play shows their reaction when the state's most powerful individual steps beyond a position validated by right or merit. The resonances are clear both for the Earl of Essex (who led an unsuccessful rebellion against Queen Elizabeth shortly after *Julius Caesar* was written) and for his friend and sympathizer the Earl of Southampton (Shakespeare's patron).

In contrast to his largely unsympathetic portrayal of Caesar, Octavius and Antony, Shakespeare made Brutus and Cassius figures of tremendous sophistication and humanity. Because Brutus is led by his conscience and is determined always to act according to the highest principles, he is politically less effective. His decision to assassinate Caesar is motivated by love of country and freedom rather than by malice or personal ambition. Cassius's impulse is more genuinely revolutionary, but he is also an individualist who finds Caesar's arrogance an affront to his own sense of dignity and worth. Shakespeare's political point is that it is only through the alliance of men of such diverse personalities and principles that the danger which Caesar represents can be averted.

Because of Brutus's personal revulsion from the cruelty required actually to murder Caesar, the assassination acquires the aura of a religious act, a kind of sacrifice. His exhortation to the conspirators – 'Stoop Romans stoop / And let us bathe our hands in Caesar's blood / Up to the elbows and besmear our swords / Then walk we forth even to the market place / And waving our red weapons o'er our heads / Let's all cry peace, freedom and liberty' – raises questions, relevant to any rebellion against tyranny, about the rightness of doing wrong (in this case shedding blood) to prevent greater wrong, and whether the new rulers will prove as tyrannical as the old. Such questions, arising here in an objective way about a historically distant event, are typical of *Julius Caesar*'s anticipation of the complexities and contradictions in the debate between monarchy and republicanism which was to lead to revolution in England forty years after the play was written, and far more convulsively elsewhere in the centuries that followed. In such a context, Cassius's question in Act Three – 'How many ages hence / Shall this our lofty scene be acted over / In states unborn and accents yet unknown . . . ?' – takes on more than a merely theatrical meaning.

In performance

From its first known performance, on 21 September 1599, *Julius Caesar* has been one of Shakespeare's most popular plays. A main attraction seems to have been its success as a 'company' play, interest resting not on a star performer but on the interaction between individuals. This can be seen in the crowd scenes, and also in the way that the leading characters embody the interlocking of different kinds of political and philosophical temperament in a particularly lively and 'human' way. In performance, two especially notable versions were the 1864 American production, in which Brutus, Cassius and Antony were played by the three Booth brothers (respectively, Edwin, Junius Brutus and John Wilkes), and the 1953 film starring Marlon Brando (Antony), John Gielgud (Cassius), James Mason (Brutus), and Louis Calhern (Caesar).

CASSIUS
> Why man, he doth bestride the narrow world
> Like a Colossus, and we petty men
> Walk under his huge legs, and peep about
> To find ourselves dishonourable graves. [I, ii]

BRUTUS
> O Antony, beg not your death of us
> Though now we must appear bloody and cruel
> As by our hands and this our present act
> You see we do. Yet see you but our hands
> And the bleeding business they have done.
> Our hearts you see not. They are pitiful. [III, i]

King John

☞ Sources

Raphael Holinshed, *Chronicles*. The play is related to an anonymous piece, *The Troublesome Reign of King John*, owned by Shakespeare's company and published in 1591, but scholars do not agree on which play came first.

☞ Story of the play

King John is unpopular. His courtiers are at his throat, and Philip, king of France, is demanding that he abdicate in favour of his nephew, the saintly child Arthur. At this point John is asked to legislate in a dispute between Robert Faulconbridge and his bastard brother Philip, who claims the inheritance. Philip's mother reveals that his father was John's brother, Richard the Lionheart, and John immediately knights him and makes him his favourite. The Bastard proceeds to swagger about the court, insulting the rebellious lords and mocking emissaries from France and Austria.

John's quarrel with France escalates to war. At the siege of Angiers, peace is made on condition that John's niece Blanche, princess of Spain, marries the French dauphin Lewis. John elevates Arthur to the Duke of Bretagne, hoping that this will end his claims to the English throne. Next, he quarrels with the Pope (refusing to accept Rome's nominee as Archbishop of Canterbury), and is excommunicated. While the Bastard leads triumphant armies against the Austrians, John imprisons Arthur and orders his henchman Hubert de Burgh to blind and murder him. Constance, Arthur's mother, suggests to the French dauphin that he invade England and seize the throne.

Hubert is so struck by Arthur's saintliness that he can't bring himself to kill him. The French, egged on by the Pope, invade England, and the Bastard hurries home to defend his country.

Arthur tries to escape from prison by jumping from the battle-ments, and is killed. John tries to avoid war by accepting the Pope's demands, but the Bastard insists that the English stand and fight. John is defeated in battle, but when his rebellious lords hear the French plan to assassinate them, they rally to the English cause and the French retreat. News of this reaches John on his deathbed: he has been mysteriously poisoned. John's son Henry is proclaimed king, and the Bastard claims, in a ringing speech, that Britain will never be conquered so long as it 'to itself do rest but true'.

🖙 Characters

King John
Henry, *his son*
Queen Elinor, *his mother*
Arthur, *his nephew*
Constance, *Arthur's mother*
The Bastard (*Philip Faulconbridge, son of Richard the Lionheart*)
Lady Faulconbridge, *his mother*
Robert Faulconbridge, *his half-brother*
Hubert de Burgh
Earls of Essex, Pembroke, Salisbury
Lord Bigot
Philip II, *King of France*

Lewis, *his son*
Archduke of Austria
Cardinal Pandulph
Chatillon, *French ambassador*
Peter of Pomfret, *mad Yorkshire prophet*
Gurney, *servant of Lady Faulconbridge*
Melun, *a French lord*
Blanch, *John's niece, princess of Castille*
Attendants, Citizens of Angiers, Executioners, Heralds, Lords, Messengers, Officers, Sheriff, Soldiers

JOHN John is an incompetent and dangerous buffoon, thrust by circumstances (the death of his charismatic brother Richard the Lionheart and the youth of Richard's son and heir Arthur) on to a throne he is incapable of filling. His nobles resent him, his formid-able Plantagenet grandmother Elinor scorns him, his European neighbours (led by France and Austria) are out to topple him. Everything he does to try and improve the situation makes matters worse. His only allies are the Bastard (whom he plucked from obscurity and made favourite, hardly improving the temper of his courtiers) and Hubert de Burgh (a politician from Angiers whom he makes Lord Chamberlain, again to the annoyance of his nobles). John arranges for Hubert to murder Arthur, so legitimizing his own position on the throne – and Hubert bungles it. To protect the territory he wins in France, he signs a humiliating treaty which gives away far more than he ever gained. When the French army invades England he tries to get them to withdraw by giving up his opposition to Papal power in the country – and the army stays anyway. To finance his wars, he lets the Bastard plunder abbeys in the North of England – and later, when the King hides from pursuit, he rashly chooses one of those abbeys and is poisoned by a resentful monk.

John is unhappy even with the language of royalty. Facing his terrifying enemies, the kings of France and Austria, he nerves himself to quarrel but then dissipates his anger by the inept words he chooses: 'Peace be to France, if France in peace permit/Our just and lineal entrance to our own! / If not, bleed France, and peace ascend to Heaven!' Trying to show relaxed firmness to his lords, he ties his tongue in knots to the point where the words reveal nothing except his own fatuity: 'Some reasons of this double coronation / I have possess'd you with, and think them strong; / And more, more strong than lesser is my fear / I shall indue you with; meantime but ask / What you would have reform'd that is not well / And well you shall perceive how willingly / I will both hear and grant you your requests?' At the end, when he is alone and dying of poison, Shakespeare does give him true poetry, true pathos and true humanity – 'Poisoned, ill fare, dead, forsook, cast off / And none of you will bid the winter come / To thrust his icy fingers in my maw; / Nor let my kingdom's rivers take their course / Through my burnt bosom . . .' – only to remind us at the very last moment that John is really a buffoon, by letting him die, unnoticed, while the Bastard is still talking to him.

BASTARD   In many ways, the Bastard is a companion part to Richard in *Henry VI*, *Part III* and *Richard III*, written a couple of years before. He talks regularly to the audience, taking us into his confidence, offering a mocking commentary on everyone else in the action and revealing his own thoughts and intentions with self-delighted relish. He takes sardonic delight in the anarchy he sees all round him ('Mad world! Mad kings! Mad composition!'), and announces that since everyone else is scrambling for position and wealth, he will do the same ('Gain be my lord, for I will worship thee!') – exactly what one might expect from someone who started a quarrel with his legitimate half-brother for land and was then unexpectedly revealed to be the son of one king (Richard the Lionheart) and made the favourite of another (John).

As a newcomer at court, the Bastard has no time for ceremony or pomposity. He is especially sharp with the silkily menacing Archduke of Austria, capping his every utterance with the nonsense-phrase 'And hang a calf-skin on these recreant limbs' and refusing to be shamed or threatened into silence. He represents the Plantagenet boldness which King John so conspicuously lacks, and it is no surprise, later in the action, when he removes himself entirely from the plotting at court, raises an army and takes the field against England's enemies.

The Bastard's metamorphosis from lordly jester to national hero is one of the two main dramatic movements of the play. The action shows him growing in moral stature and nobility in an exact reversal of John's decline into futility and impotence. His language is gradually purged of its mocking tone and acquires instead a patriotic, unironic grandeur which prefigures the great battle-speeches of *Henry V*: 'O inglorious league! / Shall we, upon the footing of our land / Send fair-play orders and make compromise / Insinuation, parley and base truce / To arms invasive? Shall a beardless boy / A cocker'd silken wanton, brave our fields / And flash his spirit in a warlike soil / Mocking the air with colours idly spread, / And find no check . . . ?' None the less, this development is a conjuring trick. For all his bravery, the Bastard is just as false a representative of royal glory on the battlefield as John is of royal political diplomacy. He may flourish – and he does so magnificently – but the world he succeeds in is a dunghill of lies and moral compromise, and even his most heartfelt-seeming utterances (for example his moving epitaph for John, 'Art thou gone? I do but stay behind / To do the office for thee of revenge . . .') are tainted by his surroundings. He appears from nowhere like a shooting star, burns brightly and is quickly gone, one of young Shakespeare's most cynical creations in this most irony-soaked of plays.

HUBERT DE BURGH Hubert is a local politician from Angiers. When his city is under threat from both the French and the English, and siding with either will involve extermination by the other, he cannily suggests that the two sides unite and make a dynastic marriage between Blanch and Lewis: this 'shall do more than battery can / To our fast-closed gates: for, at this match / The mouth of passage shall we fling wide open / And give you entrance'. John, impressed with this, makes Hubert his chamberlain, and gives the boy Arthur into his 'safekeeping', making it very clear that this means oblivion for Arthur. Hubert goes to the boy in prison, determined to blind him and kill him – but is so moved by Arthur's bravery and nobility that he lets him live, hides him and tells John that he is dead. (The ruse fails, as Arthur, trying to escape, falls from the battlements and breaks his neck.) Throughout, Hubert is presented either as an honest man, making the best of terrible situations and bewildered by the villainy all round him, or as one of the most devious, self-seeking and morally vacuous people in the play.

☞ About the play

King John has always been something of the runt in the litter of Shakespeare's plays on English history: not as magnificent as the 'major' tetralogy (*Richard II*, *Henry IV Parts I and II*, *Henry V*), not as enthralling or varied as the 'minor' tetralogy (*Henry VI*, *Parts I–III*, *Richard III*), not as mysterious as *Cymbeline* or as spectacular as *Henry VIII*. Some scholars place it early, claiming it as a revision of one of the old chronicle-histories owned by Shakespeare's company. Others give it a later date and explain what they see as inconsistencies of style and level by saying that what we have is unfinished, possibly laid aside because *Richard II*, *Romeo and Juliet* and *A Midsummer Night's Dream* were clamouring in Shakespeare's mind.

All such judgements assume that *King John* is serious – and certainly, when it is read and not seen, bumpiness and occasional perfunctoriness leap from the page. In performance, however, an entirely different play emerges: fast-moving black comedy, asking the question 'What happens in a state if its king is a dangerous buffoon?' and answering it with a blend of saturnine irony and the macabre shenanigans of *Titus Andronicus*. *Richard II* treats a similar question in a serious way and is history made tragedy; *King John* puts red noses on politics and ethics, and makes them farce.

The play ruthlessly reshapes the historical narrative. In 'real' history, Arthur's death was a passing moment in John's reign, far less significant than the King's quarrel with the Pope (which Shakespeare reduces to merely rhetorical posturing). The signing of Magna Carta, of such symbolic importance in later English history, is not even mentioned in the play. Characters of enormous historical weight – Cardinal Pandulph, the Dauphin, Queen Eleanor – have their humanity compressed until they exhibit single emotions or obsessions and are allowed no development. By contrast, Shakespeare takes John and Hubert, two people who are colourless in the historical record, and develops their characters at length: their growth in the action, together with that of the Bastard (an invented character), is the play's main psychological focus.

It was a favourite technique in drama of Shakespeare's time (perhaps imitated from the morality-plays of three generations earlier) to take the qualities thought to make up a 'whole' individual – nobility, compassion, honour, anger and so on – and parcel them out among the characters. In *King John*, Shakespeare divides his chosen character-qualities among the three principals and then, so to speak, leaves them to fight it out between them. Hubert combines political cunning and cowardice. Having wavered between two powerful adversaries (France and England), he supports John so sycophantically that he agrees to murder Arthur to please him, and then, faced down by the boy himself and by his own conscience, collapses into a self-lacerating penitence which would be admirable if he had shown any previous grace or nobility of character. John and the Bastard are mirror-images, and their character-journeys, like those of Richard and Bolingbroke in *Richard II*, move in opposite directions. John's initial nobility and heroism are subverted by his panic about legitimizing his place on his brother's throne; as the play proceeds he becomes ever more baffled, malign and ineffectual, until he dies one of the most absurd and pointless deaths in Shakespeare. The Bastard's initial sharp-tongued detachment from courtly manners gradually gives way to patriotism, heroism and true nobility.

In terms of the play's underlying theme (moral and political legitimacy), the point of all this is plain. But the tone is satirical and subversive, far removed from the poetic and reflective treatment of a similar philosophical journey in *Richard II* or the certainties of *Henry V*. *King John* turns the Establishment into a joke, treats grandees as buffoons or knaves, and offers no palliatives (save for the Bastard's speech, 'Come the three corners of the world in arms') to the prevailing political myth of its time, the glory that was Elizabethan England. It is a wry, uncomfortable play, and its unsettling nature is increased, not diminished, by the speed of its action and the baleful glitter of its dialogue.

☞ In performance

King John had two periods of popularity: in Shakespeare's own day and at the time of the French Revolution (when its anti-French sentiments guaranteed success). In Charles Kemble's 1823 production it inaugurated the nineteenth-century fashion for performing Shakespeare in 'costumes authentic to its period': a kind of theatrical pre-Raphaelitism. In 1899 scenes from it were the first Shakespeare ever filmed. The most respected twentieth-century productions were Peter Brook's in 1945, starring Paul Scofield (the Bastard), and the 1984 TV version starring Leonard Rossiter (King John).

King Lear

👉 Sources

Main plot: *King Leir*, an old play owned by Shakespeare's company. Gloucester plot: Philip Sidney, *Arcadia*.

👉 Story of the play

Lear has decided to divide his kingdom into three and to give the largest part to whichever of his daughters loves him most. Goneril and Regan falsely profess love, and he divides the kingdom between them. Their sister Cordelia refuses to flatter, and he exiles her to France, whose king she is to marry. The loyal Earl of Kent tries to argue with Lear and is also banished, but returns in disguise to look out for his master. In a second plot, Edmund, the illegitimate son of the Earl of Gloucester, sets in motion a plan to dispossess his legitimate brother Edgar by persuading Gloucester that Edgar intends to murder him.

Goneril and Regan insult Lear by refusing to accommodate his large entourage. Lear rushes outside in a storm, with no companions but his Fool and the disguised Kent. Sheltering in a hut, they meet Edgar (now banished by his father and disguised as Poor Tom, a lunatic). Gloucester takes Lear into his castle, where the old man, driven mad by suffering, 'tries' Goneril and Regan in his mind for treason and lack of love. Gloucester, knowing that they are plotting to kill Lear, sends him to safety in Dover, where Cordelia has just landed with a French besieging force. Edmund tells Regan and her husband Cornwall of this 'treason', and they blind Gloucester and send him into the wilderness to die. Edgar, still disguised as Poor Tom, meets his father and promises to take him to Dover. On Dover cliff he cures him of his suicidal intent, and they meet the mad King.

Goneril and Regan are both in love with Edmund, and Edgar intercepts a love-letter from Goneril and reveals it to her husband

Albany. For the moment, Albany can do nothing: he is one of the leaders of the English army which defeats the French. But then he forces Edmund to defend himself by combat against all challengers, and the 'yokel' Edgar fights and fatally wounds him. News comes that Goneril has poisoned Regan and committed suicide. With his dying breath, Edmund reveals that he has ordered the deaths of Lear and Cordelia. Albany sends a reprieve – but too late. Lear finds Cordelia dead in prison, mourns for her and dies.

☞ *Characters*

King Lear	**Fool**
Cordelia, Goneril, Regan, *his*	**Oswald,** *Goneril's steward*
daughters	**Attendants, Courtiers, Curan,**
Cornwall, *Regan's husband*	**Gentleman, Heralds, King of**
Albany, *Goneril's husband*	**France, Burgundy,**
Earls of Gloucester, Kent	**Messengers, Old Man,**
Edgar, Edmund, *Gloucester's sons*	**Soldiers**

LEAR At the start of the play, Lear is imperious and arrogant, with a powerful sense of his own royal position and dignity – qualities aggravated rather than tempered by extreme old age. He calls himself impotent, but woe betide anyone who acts on the description.

The contrast between this self-image and Lear's real position (he *is* a 'foolish, fond old man' and has given away all his true authority) drives him to madness – and with it, paradoxically, to the discovery of the true nature of compassion and self-knowledge. His sufferings pour humanity into him. Tragically for him, the knowledge comes at the very moment when he loses the most valuable possession he ever had (his beloved Cordelia) – but because of his moral journey, his despair ('Look on her, look, her lips / Look there . . .') and death are moving, not sentimental, and provide true Aristotelian catharsis.

GONERIL AND REGAN Lear's elder daughters are fire and ice. Goneril is intemperateness personified. No sooner does she have her share of Lear's estate than she pours humiliation on him. Married to a weak husband (Albany), she forms a sexual bond with Edmund, and plots to murder Albany. When Regan, her rival for Edmund's bed, threatens to reveal this to Albany, Goneril poisons her and stabs herself dead – and her rage is so volcanic that the very knife is 'hot, it smokes'. She is the embodiment of all her father's rash forcefulness and rage.

Regan, by contrast, is imperious and wastes no words. Instead of shouting, as Goneril does, she plots in the shadows, leaving Goneril, for example, to utter the words which humiliate their father. Her high point of evil is when she urges her husband Cornwall to put out Gloucester's eyes. Her low point is when she transfers her affection to Edmund – and she dies for that, not stabbed cleanly and openly but poisoned in the dark where she belongs.

EDGAR Gloucester's elder son at first seems like the mirror-image of his brother Edmund: legitimate, light, good, honest. But events shock him and change him, until he begins to use a benign form of Edmund's cunning. He reinvents himself and his life, and his succession of disguises, his alternative reality, fools everyone, right up to the moment when, after killing Edmund in single combat – light symbolically conquering dark – he is revealed as his bloodstained country's only hope of salvation.

EDMUND Edmund is that favourite kind of Shakespearean villain: intellectually able, rational and morally null – and he shares his thoughts with us in saturnine, ironical soliloquies. If, as some say, he and Edgar are like dark and light halves of the same divided personality, it is because Edmund never comes to terms with the light which is the other part of himself, as Edgar does with the dark, that he is bound in the end to lose.

CORDELIA Lear thinks of his daughter less as a human being than as a kind of plaything, to be cherished or thrown down at whim. In fact, just as Regan and Goneril are refractions of Lear's choler and imperiousness, so Cordelia has inherited his dignity, honour and integrity. The play shows him working out his path to the understanding of these qualities, and therefore to Cordelia. The part is small, but crucial to both action and meaning.

FOOL The Fool spars verbally with Kent and with Edgar (disguised as 'Poor Tom'), and has one-liners in plenty for his master. In essence he is a political and psychological satirist. Real laughter has long drained out of him, and he is one of Shakespeare's most haunted, derelict creations.

GLOUCESTER Like Lear, Gloucester is an old man who mistakes the true natures of his children and suffers for it. In absolute terms, he committed a real sin (when he fathered a bastard son in a moment of 'blind' lechery), and his punishments are, first, metaphorical blindness (when he fails to recognize Edgar) and then literal blinding by Cornwall. He is, like Lear, allowed a vision of truth, but because he is a figure with little tragic dignity, that recognition is stoical rather than truly cathartic, and is described more than felt. In the balance between the play's two plots, he is Lear's shadow, and the moral contrast between them is one of his most important functions.

☞ *About the play*

The title of one of Goya's most terrifying etchings could be used as an epigraph to *King Lear*: 'The sleep of reason produces monsters'. Consistent themes in the play are the nature of human reason, what happens when what we take to be reason is mistaken or perverted, and the way pursuit of a rational approach to experience comes up against the soft fleshiness of human beings.

The play begins with Lear's own disastrous flight from reason. Foolishly, he thinks that a divided kingdom will survive and that his daughters' love is a commodity which can be quantified and rewarded. The disasters which flow from this are personal, political and cosmic: the King's own self, the selves of everyone around him, the state of Albion and the universe itself do battle with each other and themselves. In the 'absurd' world which results, rationality is folly, disguise is true nature and insanity is sane. The objections of Goneril and Regan to their father's extravagance are part of a perverted and deadly view of what human life is for. Kent can sustain his 'irrational' loyalty to the mad king only by assuming the disguise of an uneducated peasant. The only way for Edgar to maintain his true nature is to pretend to be mad. The Fool, apparently well beyond reason, consistently speaks wisdom and gives sane advice. And crucially, in a world where (what is taken for) reason has become the mask of savagery and decency must disguise itself as poverty or madness, the 'irrational' needs of real humanity are consistently forgotten. As Lear says bleakly in Act Three, 'Allow not nature more than nature needs / Man's life is cheap as beast's.'

It is at this point, at the height of the physical and psychological storm engendered by the sleep of reason, that Shakespeare shows us grounds for optimism and hope. In a world of apparently total despair, in which his characters have been stripped of shelter, warmth, food and clothing – every protection for their physical frailness – they still find inside themselves those qualities which make them human: need and ability to communicate, altruism, kindness, wit, energy and dreams. Shakespeare's vision is not merely that our world is awry and that we have made it so, but that even in the teeth of the Apocalypse we can change it for the better. The outcasts of Act Three can be identified with the preachers who helped bring about social revolution in England a generation after the play was written. Like Edgar, these prophets – Ranters, Levellers and others – dressed social and religious criticism in the Old Testament and the apparently insane language of inspiration.

One of the components of Lear's own tragedy is that he sees none of this possibility until it is too late. It is only in the midst of the storm that he finds concern for the victims of the society over which he has ruled: 'Poor naked wretches wheresoever you are / That bide the pelting of this pitiless storm / How shall your houseless heads and unfed sides / Your looped and windowed raggedness defend you / From seasons such as these?' Shakespeare plunges us fully into this despair, makes us follow his suffering characters as they explore the very limits of their agony – not only Lear, with his vision of 'unaccommodated man' stripped naked by a world in which human values have been lost, but Gloucester, whose blinding pitilessly embodies one of the play's darkest themes: the invasion of cold iron into the softest and most sensitive place in the human anatomy.

Shakespeare's use of the ironic distance between what happens to the characters in a work of art (who live only in their own dimension) and the meaning of those events places *King Lear* in the company of such works as the Book of Job or Michelangelo's *Last Judgement*. As soon as the storm is over, as soon as we have followed his characters into the pit of suffering, he characteristically begins to build up the alternative picture, of change, of self-redemption. The disguised Edgar, finding his father Gloucester so wasted by suffering that he can think of no solution but suicide, tricks him into realizing the futility of this desire for extinction, and brings him face to face with the indissoluble nature of humanity. Lear's attacks on the wickedness of the world ('Plate sins with gold / And the strong lance of justice hurtless breaks. / Arm it in rags, a pigmy's straw does pierce it') and his raging against his sons-in-law ('Kill, kill, kill, kill, kill, kill') give way, with the arrival of Cordelia's French army, to a kind of exhausted, unsentimental acceptance of his own condition: 'I am a very foolish fond old man . . . / And to deal plainly / I fear I am not in my perfect mind.'

Even if the characters have, by the start of Act Five, reached the harbours of sanity and self-knowledge, there is still the final struggle for the soul of the kingdom, the metaphysical battle between the *realpolitik* of Lear's enemies and the humane society we have so far seen only as dream or prophecy. This is enacted in a ritualized, almost fairy-tale way, with heralds, trumpets and single combat. At the play's climax, Shakespeare plays a trump card. In his source, everything ended happily: Cordelia and Lear alive, a bright future forged in the crucible of pain. In the 1681 revision of the play, Cordelia even married Edgar. But art on the level of *King Lear* makes no such compromises. Shakespeare leaves the sorting-out of society, the awakening of reason from its tormented sleep, to happen in the wings, and narrows the focus onto his central character and the tragic truth that realization and awakening have come too late to help that character. Lear's Britain may be redeemed by what Lear has suffered, but what is that to him, with his daughter's body in his arms? The significance of everything shrinks to nothing next to the death of a child, and death, however it comes, is harsh and cruel: 'Thou'lt come no more / Never, never, never, never, never.' In the face of that insurmountable fact, all castles of reason – ethics, morality, politics and metaphysics – collapse round the speaker's feet. We, the audience, see that the world should and can be better ordered, but that cathartic knowledge is denied to the individual victims of disorder. The point is bleak (and strikingly unChristian, sidestepping ideas of external absolution and redemption) but clear. Human society is a construct of reason, and will survive so long as it takes account of the peculiarities of each irreplacable individual.

☞ *In performance*

Nahum Tate's happy-ending version of *Lear* (1681) held the stage for 150 years; William Macready (1838) has the distinction of returning the original text to the repertory. From then on, the play has attracted actors of the first rank (Edwin Booth, Henry Irving, John Gielgud, Paul Scofield and Robert Stephens have been particularly admired). Scofield's performance, directed by Peter Brook, was filmed in 1970. Other films include Kurosawa's *Ran* (1985) and Kosintzev's *King Lear*, one of the finest realizations of the play in any other medium.

LEAR

Nothing will come of nothing. Speak again. [I, i]

GLOUCESTER

As flies to wanton boys, are we to the gods
They kill us for their sport. [IV, i]

LEAR

When we are born we cry that we are come
To this great stage of fools. [IV, v]

Love's Labour's Lost

☞ Sources

Original. Shakespeare may have been sending up a debate, current at the time, about whether the best way to cope with life was to immerse oneself in it or to withdraw to an existence of studious contemplation. The Russian masquerade may have been added after a similar event at the 1594 Gray's Inn Christmas Revels, during which Shakespeare acted in *The Comedy of Errors*.

☞ Story of the play

King Ferdinand of Navarre and his courtiers Berowne, Dumain and Longaville vow to devote themselves for three years to study and self-denial (especially from female company). The first person to fall foul of the vow is Costard the clown, arrested for talking to the country wench Jaquenetta. He is put in the charge of a visiting Spanish grandee, Don Armado – who also loves Jaquenetta.

The Princess of France, with her ladies Rosaline, Katharine and Maria, comes to court on a diplomatic errand. Ferdinand and his lords are reluctant to talk to them, but it is soon clear that love is in the air.

Now the cross-purposes begin. Armado gives Costard a letter for Jaquenetta, and Berowne sends him with a poem to Rosaline. Costard misdelivers them. Berowne mocks the other lords' love-sickness – each has heard the others trying to write poems to send to the women they love – and is then discomfited when the schoolmaster Holofernes arrives with *his* (Berowne's) sonnet. The young men agree that love itself is a subject worth studying, and decide to test their ladies' devotion by disguising themselves as visiting Russians and courting them.

Holofernes, meanwhile, has been rehearsing a pageant to entertain the court; his cast is Armado, Moth, Costard, Sir Nathaniel the curate and Dull the constable. The courtiers gather, the lords disguised as Russians and the ladies (who knew in advance what was happening) masked and wearing each other's jewellery. Chaos ensues, and the pageant is abandoned. Costard is about to fight Armado for Jaquenetta, when news arrives that the King of France, the Princess's father, has died. The ladies prepare to leave, telling the crestfallen lords to live one year in seclusion and then, if their love stays firm, to come courting a second time. The play ends with music: 'When daisies pied' (a song of spring) and 'When icicles hang by the wall' (a song of winter).

Characters

Ferdinand, *King of Navarre*	Holofernes, *schoolmaster*
Berowne, Dumain, Longaville, *his lords*	Sir Nathaniel, *curate*
	Dull, *constable*
Princess of France	Costard, Jaquenetta, *rustics*
Katharine, Maria, Rosaline, *her ladies*	Attendants, Forester, Lords Boyet, Marcade, Other Lords, Villagers
Don Adriano de Armado	
Moth, *his page*	

BEROWNE From the start, Berowne is sceptical about the young King's plan. He agrees to take part out of curiosity (to see if it is possible) – and then, almost as soon as he sees Rosaline and begins points-scoring conversation with her (*Berowne*: 'Did I not dance with you in Brabant once?' *Rosaline*: 'Did I not dance with you in Brabant once?' *Berowne*: 'I know you did.' *Rosaline*: 'How needless was it, then to ask the question'), his worst fears are realized and he falls in love. He mocks himself for weak-mindedness ('This wimpled, whining, purblind, wayward boy / This senior-junior, giant-dwarf Dan Cupid / ... O my little heart! / And I to be a corporal in his field / And wear his colours like a tumbler's hoop ...'), but there is more than a hint of enjoyment in his ruefulness. At first he encourages the younger lords' flirting-games and their masquerade as Russians, but the deeper in love he falls, the less time he has for such extravagance, and he finally rejects altogether its 'Taffeta phrases, silken terms precise / Three-piled hyperboles, spruce affection / Figures pedantical ...'

in favour of 'honest wooing'. Unfortunately, the initiative in his relationship with Rosaline has by now passed to her, and when she goes back to France with the Princess she leaves him not merely to reflect on the true meaning of love, but to spend the time charitably visiting the sick in hospital.

Love's Labour's Lost is a charade, and it would be foolish to over-solemnize it. But Berowne's depth of character makes him guardian of the human truth behind the games, and our guarantee that however much young people may be giddy and inconstant, 'affection's men at arms', they will all grow up one day.

ROSALINE Rosaline is self-possessed, witty and brighter than anyone in the play except Berowne. Some see her as a dramatic version of the Dark Lady of the Sonnets, others as a prototype of Beatrice in *Much Ado About Nothing* or Rosalind in *As You Like It*. When the French ladies first come to court, she and Berowne are immediately drawn to one another. They begin by fencing with words, then Berowne falls head over heels in love with her, and she with him. But he is unaware of this, and she decides, mischievously, to have as much fun from the situation as possible, to bring it about: 'That he should be my fool, and I his fate . . .'

THE YOUNG LOVERS The principal lovers, in terms of rank, are Ferdinand and the Princess of France. Ferdinand is charming, well-mannered and puppyish, and easily persuades the others to go along with his foolish idea, just for the fun of it. The Princess is older, and at first tends to keep her distance – then, hearing that the gentlemen plan to disguise themselves as Russians, enters into the spirit of things and proposes that the women exchange identities, wear masks and seize the initiative in the game of love.

Of the attendant lords and ladies, Dumain is the most thoroughly characterized, after Berowne. He is just as young and self-conscious as the others, but blunter and far more ironical. His love poem, for example, is a piece of doggerel which hardly bothers to go through the poetic motions – 'On a day – alack the day! – / Love, whose month is ever May / Spied a blossom passing fair / Playing on the wanton air . . .' – and his mockery of Holofernes during the pageant is mercilessly unsentimental. He is matched with Katharine, the oldest and wittiest of the French ladies, after Rosaline. The fourth lord, Longaville, is tall, gawky, languishing, and beautifully mismatched with the cheerful, bustling Maria.

ARMADO Armado is one of the first tourists in European literature, a 'refined traveller of Spain' who is 'haunting' the court of Navarre. He has fallen in love with a country girl, Jaquenetta, and when his rival, the clown Costard, is found illicitly talking to her, the King condemns him to 'a week with bran and water' and mischievously puts Armado in charge of seeing that this sentence is carried out.

As well as providing the motor of this second plot, Armado fills the play with superbly fantastical language. He is a linguistic fop – 'A man in all the world's new fashion planted / That hath a mint of phrases in his brain / One whom the music of his own vain tongue / Doth ravish like enchanting harmony' – and his preening and gobbling make him an excellent foil to those other verbal pyrotechnicians in the play, Berowne, Holofernes and Moth.

MOTH Moth (in Shakespeare's day, this was pronounced like the French word *mot*, 'word') is a small child, Armado's cheeky page-boy. He spends his time catching his Spanish master in silky verbal traps, making phrases which quite belie his years, with a gusto to equal Berowne himself – for example when he tells Armado that the best way to court Jaquenetta is 'to jig off a tune at the tongue's end, canary to it with your feet, hammer it with turning up your eyelids, sigh a note and sing a note . . . with your hat penthouse-like o'er the shop of your eyes'.

JAQUENETTA Armado's beloved is a pert village girl, and their verbal sparring is a kind of farce-equivalent to the high-comedy repartee of Berowne, Rosaline and the other courtiers: *Armado*: 'Maid –' *Jaquenetta*: 'Man.' *Armado*: 'I will visit thee at the lodge.' *Jaquenetta*: 'That's hereby.' *Armado*: 'I know where it is situate.' *Jaquenetta*: 'Lord, how wise you are!'

HOLOFERNES The schoolmaster who contrives the pageant of the Nine Worthies (and plays at least three of them himself) is a linguistic pedant. He spends much of his time swapping grammar with his friend, the dim-witted curate Sir Nathaniel – as Moth says, 'they have been at feast of languages, and stolen the scraps'. But this amiable wrangling, like the rehearsals for Holofernes' ludicrous pageant, is warm and charming, a splendid foil for the emotionless point-scoring of the courtiers who make such merciless fun when they perform their show.

COSTARD Costard is a 'clown' (that is, countryman), not the melancholy jester of other Shakespeare plays but a young village lad, in love with Jaquenetta and happy to stand up for himself (and her) even to Armado, even in front of the court. He is a similar character to Speed or Launce in *The Two Gentlemen of Verona*, or to the Dromios in *The Comedy of Errors*, and may have been played by one of the same actors.

SIR NATHANIEL Sir Nathaniel is a doddery old curate, Holofernes' friend and straight man. At the performance of the pageant (where he is cast as Alexander the Great) he is completely overcome when Berowne interrupts him with witty repartee, and Costard stands up for him: 'O, sir, you have overthrown Alisander the Conqueror . . . a foolish mild man, an honest man, look you . . . a marvellous good neighbour, faith and a very good bowler, but, for Alisander, alas you see how 'tis, a little overparted . . .'

About the play

Love's Labour's Lost is one of those plays which seem difficult on the page (all dense wordplay, leaping from one literary level to another) but work marvellously on stage. It is a sendup of medieval romance, pedantry, pretension, and particularly of a group of aristocratic intellectuals of Shakespeare's day, led by Sir Walter Ralegh, who eschewed the pleasures of the flesh and devoted their lives to the study of arts and sciences with a view to discovering the secrets of the universe, no less. It is a young man's romp, and the youth and greenness of its central characters are crucial to its success. Four solemn young men propose to set up a woman-free 'academy' for three years, forswearing emotion for intellectual discipline – and immediately fall headlong in love with the first young women they set eyes on. Owlishly, they debate what to do and decide to experiment with love. The women are at first breathless with indignation, but before they can work out a suitable response, they too are in love.

This basic situation is gloriously silly and dramatically as reliable as steel – and Shakespeare enriches it with every means at his disposal. The language is engorged with rhymes, puns, tortuous syntax, invented words, sonnets, rhetoric and parody, almost a deconstruction of itself. The supporting cast includes a funny foreigner, a cheeky pageboy, a brainless policeman, a pedant, a yokel and a doddering clergyman. The plot uses not only every farce convention ever invented – impersonation, mistaken identity, wrongly-delivered letters, daft wordplay, drunk scenes, falls and fights – but also a fancy-dress masquerade and one of those 'rude-mechanical' plays-within-a-play which Shakespeare's audiences and actors so relished.

Love's Labour's Lost, like *A Midsummer Night's Dream* and the Montague-Capulet squabbles in *Romeo and Juliet* (both plays written at much the same time) is a company piece, following the fate not of individuals but of groups (the lords, the ladies, the low-life characters), developing character against character within each group and contrasting group with group. It is only in Act Five that all three groups come together, in a flurry of charades and cross-purposes – and at this point Shakespeare pulls off a breathtaking dramatic risk. At the height of the shenenigans he brings on a messenger (Marcade) with news that the old King, the Princess's father, has died, and at once 'reality' impinges on the fantasy, the mood darkens and the young couples are forced to take themselves and their futures seriously for a moment. (As Berowne says, 'Mirth cannot move a soul in agony.') Then, after a moment or two of grown-up solemnity, the pleasure starts up again – no longer with unadulterated silliness, but with a sense that the sky can hold clouds as well as sunshine, and that neither our joys nor our sorrows can be fully appreciated without the other. The songs of spring and winter, performed by the whole company to end the play, round off a finale as poignant and as theatrical as the ensemble which ends a Mozart opera.

In later plays, for example *As You Like It* and *Twelfth Night*, Shakespeare perhaps blended his ingredients more deftly, showing the joy within the sorrow and the tears within the smiles in the same characters and at the same moments. *Love's Labour's Lost* was one of his first attempts to blend romantic comedy with farce, and to import the style of each into the other. The play is a young writer's assault on style, headlong and innocent, and has no time for subtlety. Its strength lies partly in this very brashness, but also in the way Shakespeare uses the formality and rigidity of his chosen conventions not only for their own sake but to articulate one of his favourite themes: what happens when young aristocrats, brought up in the formality and intellectual rigidity of court usage, are confronted by the pangs of uncontrollable emotion (love) as well as by the genial anarchy of the countryside and the full-hearted comedy of ordinary people.

☞ *In performance*

Shakespeare tinkered with *Love's Labour's Lost* for some years, culminating in a court performance at Christmas 1597. But the piece was not popular, and dropped out of the repertoire entirely until 1837. It was not until the twentieth century that audiences caught up with its interplay of styles and moods, and it became a particular favourite at Stratford (where it was produced half a dozen times). None the less, perhaps because of its fearsome scholarly reputation (every sentence seeming to bristle with footnotes), not to mention the ensemble style of playing it demands, it is still, quite unjustly, more neglected onstage than any other Shakespeare comedy.

BEROWNE

 From women's eyes this doctrine I derive.
 They sparkle still the right Promethean fire.
 They are the books, the arts, the academes
 That show, contain, and nourish all the world. [IV, iii]

Macbeth

 Source

Raphael Holinshed, *Chronicles*.

 Story of the play

Three witches meet Macbeth and his fellow-general Banquo as they are returning to Scotland after defeating a rebellion against King Duncan. The witches promise Macbeth that he will be 'thane of Cawdor and king hereafter' and tell Banquo that his sons will one day rule. Soon afterwards, Macbeth hears that he has been appointed Thane of Cawdor. Duncan comes to stay in his castle. Macbeth tells his wife the prophecy, and of his misgivings at murdering the King, and she encourages him and mocks him until he does it. The King's sons Malcolm and Donalbain escape and are blamed for the murder.

Macbeth is crowned King. But now, afraid of the prophecy made about Banquo and his sons, he sends assassins to murder them. Banquo is killed, but the boy Fleance – the future ancestor of King James I – escapes. That night at dinner, Macbeth sees Banquo's ghost and reacts with horror. The witches tell him that he is safe till 'Birnam Wood comes to Dunsinane' and that 'no man born of woman' will ever kill him. Hearing that Macduff, Thane of Fife, has fled to England, he orders the murder of Lady Macduff and her children – and this leads Macduff and Malcolm to raise a revolt against him.

Lady Macbeth, tormented by guilt, sleepwalks and confesses about the murders to her doctor. Malcolm and Macduff gather their army in Birnam Wood, and tell the soldiers to camouflage themselves with branches and advance on Dunsinane. Macbeth meets Macduff in single combat, and, horrified to hear that Macduff was born by Caesarean section, 'from his mother's womb untimely ripped', surrenders to his death. He is beheaded and Malcolm becomes King of Scotland.

👉 'The Scottish play'

Actors used to think *Macbeth* unlucky. They renamed it 'the Scottish play' and relished tales of disasters during this or that production. Superstition apart, the piece tends to resist theatrical success. In particular, the writing is so poetically rich that it seems to wriggle free of convincing realization: the *Macbeth* in our minds seems more satisfying than the *Macbeth* before our eyes. Tackling *this* problem is perhaps more likely to lay the ghosts than (say) reciting the 90th Psalm before each show (as was done during one 1926 production).

👉 Characters

Duncan, *King of Scotland*
Malcolm *and* Donalbain, *his sons*
Macbeth
Lady Macbeth
Banquo, Macduff, Lennox, Ross, Menteith, Angus, Caithness, *noblemen of Scotland*
Lady Macduff
Her Son

Siward, *Earl of Northumberland*
Young Siward, *his son*
Fleance, *Banquo's son*
Seyton
Witches
Captain, Doctors, Gentlewoman, Hecate, Murderers, Old Man, Porter, Sergeant

MACBETH   For all Macbeth's brilliant bravery and imagination, he stands no chance against the malignity of Fate. Right at the start of the play, the witches announce that he is the object of their meeting and their spells. He and Banquo have no time to think about the prophecy before the first part is fulfilled: the witches have been off the stage for only twenty lines when news comes that Macbeth is Thane of Cawdor. Almost at once he begins to subordinate his 'good' soldierly qualities – pragmatism, nobility, valour – to ambition and superstition, and his downfall is assured. A couple of scenes later, Lady Macbeth has no problem working on his ambition to make him kill Duncan.

Once the deed is done, accumulating horror saps any remaining capacity in Macbeth for moral choice. He moves from one crime to another – killing the grooms, ordering the deaths of Banquo and his son and Lady Macduff and her innocent family. He still trusts the prophecy that 'no man born of woman' will ever kill him – and when he realizes the irony in that prophecy, he abandons hope and assents gruffly, grimly, to his own death. His tragedy throughout is that although he knows precisely the moral self he is sacrificing (his 'eternal jewel / Given to the common enemy of man'), he can neither wish the knowledge away, nor stop himself.

LADY MACBETH Some say that this part was imitated from Seneca's *Medea*, well-known in Shakespeare's day (and offering similar acting challenges). Lady Macbeth has every one of her husband's qualities in excess: ambition, pride, ruthlessness, superstition. After she calls on the spirits to 'unsex' her and she is freed from the complexities of human relations – among other things, she seems to have no living children – her style becomes practical, intelligent, thorough and driven, but lacking in sympathetic imagination. Then, when she surrenders her psychological power to Macbeth, her repressed nature breaks out in sleep-walking, despair and suicide. She is psychologically far more complex than the 'all-sexuality' or 'the embodiment of evil' often taken as the clue to her character: virtually a textbook study in the redirection of the libido into ambition and control.

MALCOLM Duncan's son is an intellectual prince in a macho world. He personifies qualities which Macbeth so signally throws away. Shakespeare gives him one of the most powerful scenes in the play (Act Four, Scene Three), when he tests Macduff's loyalty by claiming to lack all kingly qualities. When Ross brings news that Macduff's wife and children have been murdered, he urges him to 'make medicines of our great revenge / To cure this deadly grief', and becomes, with Macduff, an unstoppable force.

THE MACDUFF FAMILY The rough strength of Macduff, Thane of Fife, makes him honest and patriotic, a worthy agent of retribution. The root of his character is his love for his family, and his most moving scene is the one where he hears, and accepts, news of their murder: 'All my pretty ones? / Did you say all? O hell kite. All? / What all my pretty chickens and their dam / At one fell swoop?' Shakespeare has already shown us the pathetic Lady Macduff and her eldest son, his father's true heir, concerned even at the moment of his death less for himself than for his mother, his brothers and his country.

BANQUO Macbeth's fellow general matches him in courage but not ambition. Insomnia represents his conscience – and while his conscience still functions, he is safe. One of his best scenes is with his son Fleance (a fly who cannot be swatted, and who, as the witches predict, will one day father a line of kings): a mosaic of tiny details of affection. Soon afterwards, Banquo ends up dead in a ditch. But Fleance survives, as if his father's better self, his innocence, had broken free of the net of ambition, darkness and ethical compromise.

WITCHES The witches, 'weird sisters', were actually 'Wyrd sisters', the Fates in Celtic myth, cool and uninvolved. But Shakespeare, perhaps pandering to his royal master (who wrote an attack on witchcraft) mixes them up with Jacobean demonology, making them a kind of supernatural freak show. The critic Walter Benjamin wrote that every great work of art is also a document in barbarism – and *Macbeth* stands uncomfortably close to the fanatical denunciations of witches common in Europe at the time.

About the play

Holinshed's *Chronicles*, Shakespeare's source, devotes two paragraphs to Macbeth, a legendary Scots warlord who won the throne by murder, was killed in his turn and was succeeded by the son of one of his victims. This son was Fleance, reputed ancestor of King James, before whom Shakespeare's play was first performed.

Holinshed treated the dry bones of this legend as if they were factually true. Shakespeare used them as the foundation for richer work: the political study of a revolutionary coup and its aftermath, and the psychological study of the disintegration of a personality given over to evil without redemption.

The play's political narrative is simple. A leading figure in an emerging country is convinced that supreme power is his by right, and decides, disastrously, to win it by violence. To consolidate his authority, he arranges the deaths not just of rivals and colleagues but also, as things start to spin out of control, of innocent women and children. A state built by violence against the 'enemy without' now turns on the 'enemy within', and degenerates to the point where the leader even commands his minions to 'hang those who speak of fear'. With enormous difficulty, opposition manages to gather itself, and after a terrible battle the country is once again set free.

Events such as these must have had political resonance in the volatile England of 1606, three years after the accession of James I and a few months after the Gunpowder Plot of 1605. But Shakespeare was interested less in specific politics than in the psychology of murder and tyranny, and the way one man's nightmares can rapidly become those of a whole nation. He focuses the discussion not on battles and political accusations or justifications but on the tyrant's own moral and personal disintegration. *Macbeth* is the study of someone who makes a bargain with evil and is thereafter cursed with full self-knowledge and self-disgust, as his attempts to escape draw him ever deeper into moral and existential Hell – a Hell which we, the spectators, have ironically known gaped for him from the moment he stopped to listen to the witches.

At what point in such a descent do a man's crimes jeopardize his humanity? At first sight, in this play, the worst thing Macbeth does, the moment of political and psychological no-return, seems to be Duncan's murder. But Duncan, however saintly, is an old king, and old kings must die if new kings are to rule. Macbeth's acceleration of this process may technically be a crime, but it is also part of a natural evolutionary process. Freud wrote that all sons symbolically kill their fathers to validate their own identities; in society a similar progression is common, as new generations make their way by climbing over old.

Duncan's murder starts Macbeth down a road on which there is no turning back. Each succeeding murder devastates his soul more than the one before. Banquo is presented almost as Macbeth's brother, and his death drives Macbeth to a psychological panic beyond all control. In his desolation of spirit, in the fury for action which he mistakes for resolution, he orders the deaths of Lady Macduff and her children. They are entirely innocent, and their pointless destruction is one of the bleakest moments in the play. After it, and the death of his wife which closely follows it, Macbeth is isolated, at odds even with himself. He says that he has lived long enough, and that existence has lost all meaning, has become 'a tale / Told by an idiot, full of sound and fury / Signifying nothing'.

Shakespeare's predominantly Christian spectators would probably have rejected this view outright, as blasphemy – and a modern, sceptical audience might wonder how far Macbeth's innocent victims would go along with him. But one thing is clear: at this point (the beginning of Act Five), having severed any remaining connection with the rest of humanity and embraced 'absurdity' (in the Ionescan sense of psychological and moral apartness) Macbeth has stepped beyond the pale and must be defeated. In our modern fragmented world, where we are meant to stand by and for ourselves, a moment like this takes on deep resonance.

Macbeth's expression of grim absurdity is not, however, the end of the story, and the play is far more than a study in the psychopathology of ambition and murder. In Act Five Shakespeare sets Macbeth's personal collapse in a new context of political and moral objectivity, in stark contrast to the dark vortex of destruction which has preceded it. If the play can be said to have a positive point, it lies in the way the tyrant is eventually toppled. Opposition to his rule began moments after the discovery of Duncan's body, and slowly gathers force throughout the action. When Macbeth is finally defeated, it is by the forces of life – a point brilliantly made in the symbolic narrative of Shakespeare's play. Unlike Macbeth's own cohorts and supporters, the forces of opposition share each other's pain, give each other strength and are united in sacrifice. They attack the tyrant bearing trees (a symbol of life), and his death comes from a man who embodies the image of a new-born child (Macduff). In contrast to Macbeth's own rise, which begins with sterile and dangerous ambition fuelled by superstition, the spur to opposition is the pure, deep warmth of family emotion. When Macduff hears that his wife and children have been murdered, the depth of his loss is expressed in a register which is irreducibly human. A father's love triggers the life force which hunts and destroys an enemy of life.

☞ In performance

Macbeth may have been written for performance at court during a state visit by the Danish King Christian IV on 7 August, 1606. (Burbage would have played Macbeth.) The play was rewritten by William Davenant in 1663 (the witches given songs and ballets, and the dialogue trimmed to accommodate the new supernatural shenanigans); this version held the stage until Garrick's time (1740s onwards). His success in the role was paralleled half a century later by that of Sarah Siddons as Lady Macbeth.

In the nineteenth century, actors often played Macbeth not as evil but as a suffering colossus, heaping all the play's wickedness on Lady Macbeth. In the twentieth century the psychopathology of both leading characters was more diligently explored, despite some extraordinary aberrations (for example Orson Welles' 'voodoo' staging of 1936, or William Gaskill's existentialist-Hell version of 1966, starring Alec Guinness and Simone Signoret). One of the few widely admired productions of the century was Trevor Nunn's RSC account (1976) starring Ian McKellen and Judi Dench. The play has been filmed a score of times, beginning with a 1906 silent version directed by D.W. Griffith and ranging from Orson Welles' superb (and non-voodoo) 1948 version to Kurosawa's *Throne of Blood* (1957), resiting the story in medieval Japan and universally acclaimed as one of the most successful Shakespeare adaptations ever made.

Measure for Measure

☞ *Sources*

Shakespeare took the Isabella-Angelo-Claudio plot from a story by Giraldus Cinthio, and the germ of his comic sub-plot from George Whetstone's play *Promos and Cassandra*. The play's politics owe debts to a 1598 treatise *The Counsellor*, on the ethics of public office.

☞ *Story of the play*

The Duke of Vienna, thinking that obedience to the laws has become lax, announces that he is leaving the city in charge of his puritanical deputy Angelo. Ostensibly going on pilgrimage, he in fact disguises himself as a friar and returns to see what happens. Angelo rigorously begins to enforce the laws against immorality. He orders the destruction of brothels (including that run by Mistress Overdone and her tapster Pompey), and has the young nobleman Claudio arrested for making his fiancée Juliet pregnant.

   The statutory punishment for Claudio is death. He begs his sister Isabella (a novice nun) to intercede for him with Angelo – and when she does so Angelo is smitten with lust and offers to pardon Claudio if she has sex with him. Indignantly, she refuses. In the prison, Claudio is comforted by a friar (the disguised Duke), who suggests a stratagem. Angelo was once engaged to Mariana but abandoned her. If Isabella pretends to agree to sex, and she and Mariana change places, the deed will be done and Claudio set free.

   The plot works – except that Angelo treacherously orders Claudio's death anyway, and Abhorson the executioner and Pompey (his new assistant) prepare the block. The Friar suggests substituting Barnardine, a convicted murderer, and dressing him in Claudio's clothes, but Barnardine strenuously objects. A pirate, luckily, has in the meantime died in prison, and his head is sent to Angelo as Claudio's.

The Duke now sheds his disguise and 'returns'. Isabella and Mariana confront Angelo. He denies everything, but the Duke, who has revealed his identity as the 'friar', confirms the story. He orders that Angelo must marry Mariana and then be executed, but when Isabella and Mariana plead for Angelo's life, and Claudio is brought in alive, the Duke pardons Angelo. Claudio is now free to marry Juliet, Angelo must marry Mariana, and the Duke proposes that he himself should marry Isabella.

☞ Characters

Duke Vincentio	Abhorson, *the executioner*
Angelo	Barnardine
Claudio	Provost
Isabella, *his sister*	Escalus
Mariana	Varrius, *servant to the Duke*
Lucio	Friar Thomas
Mistress Overdone	Friar Peter
Pompey	Francisca, *a nun*
Constable Elbow	Attendants, Boy, Citizens,
Froth	Lords, Officers

DUKE If the play is taken as comedy, pure and simple, then the Duke is a kind of prankster, inventing the whole charade for his own amusement with little regard for its effect on other people's lives. If, by contrast, it is a more serious piece about the ethics of power, questions arise about his apparent indifference to the lives he meddles in – as if he were a philosopher conducting an investigation into the nature of morality and free will, or the embodiment of some abstract, objective force such as Fate or even God.

At one point in the play, the Duke talks of the obligations of rule – 'He who the sword of Heav'n will bear / Should be as holy as severe . . .' – and condemns Angelo for not living up to this high standard. And for all their apparent immorality and autocracy, his actions do have profoundly moral results. (His failure, for example, to tell Isabella that Claudio has been spared produces necessary moral growth in her.) The question is one of the balance between ends and means.

ANGELO Angelo's tragedy is that his head cannot rule as much as his heart or his loins. At base, he would like to behave like some unemotional ethical assessor, applying logic to human lives in an attempt to rule the unruly and govern the ungovernable. Human nature (his own or other people's) is not part of the equation until he sees, and lusts after, Isabella.

This lust, partly sexual and partly intellectual – he senses in her a moral authority which he does not himself possess and which he can deal with only by attacking – destroys his sense both of his position and of himself. He becomes a self-hater and projects that hatred into public life, in particular when he breaks his bargain to free Claudio. At the end of the play, when the Duke confronts him with himself, he has nowhere to turn and must be redeemed from outside himself (a striking, and deliberate, Christian point). Both his desire for death and his salvation by Isabella and Mariana are as moving as they are logical; heart is at last in tune with head.

ISABELLA Isabella is a favourite late-Shakespearean character, an intellectual young girl who changes and flowers before our eyes. As the play proceeds, she discovers in herself two of the warmest of all human qualities, a capacity for mercy (when she pleads for Angelo's life in the final scene) and a sexuality which evolves from the repression and denial she feels at first, to tremulous but passionate engagement in human relationships: sympathy for Mariana, willingness to beg mercy for Angelo, stunned joy when Claudio is restored to her alive. (Shakespeare gives her no lines here: a masterstroke.) One of the key journeys in the action is from moral introversion, and the psychological sterility it causes, through terror and heartache to full acceptance and openness – and the fact that it is Isabella who makes this journey, in such fairy-tale circumstances, makes her one of the play's most appealing characters.

CLAUDIO An innocent if headstrong young man, who has committed no crime except sleeping with his fiancée, Claudio is suddenly and arbitrarily condemned to death, and his horror at the thought of the grave ('Nay, but to lie in cold obstruction and to rot') is a deliberate reminder of human frailty in the midst of all the cold-blooded legalistic plotting of the surrounding action. Claudio is the personification of human frailty, and the preservation of his life is the play's moral and emotional touchstone.

POMPEY Pompey, the tapster (barman) in Mistress Overdone's brothel, is entirely and self-delightingly shameless. On trial for his life under the immorality act, he argues ethics with the judge (Escalus). He leaps at the chance of saving his own skin by becoming assistant executioner, and revels in the technicalities of his new trade, and in the presence in gaol of so many of his old customers from the brothel: 'Master Rash, he's in for a commodity of brown paper and old ginger . . . Master Caper, at the suit of Master Threepile the mercer . . . young Dizzy . . . Master Deepvow . . . young Dropheir that killed lusty Pudding . . . and I think, forty more, all great doers in our trade and are now "for the Lord's sake".' In a play where the characters are overburdened with scruples of one kind or another, he is that refreshing change, someone with no moral sense whatever.

About the play

Measure for Measure's subject is human relationships, and it focuses on the nature of justice and mercy, and on the privileges and obligations of those who administer them. The phrase 'measure for measure' derives from Christ's sermon on the Mount: 'Judge not, that ye be not judged. For with what judgement ye judge, ye shall be judged, and with what measure ye mete, it shall be measured to you again.'

The play's main strand, the Angelo-Isabella-Claudio story, conforms to the style of black melodrama popular at the time: *The Revenger's Tragedy*, say, or Webster's *The White Devil*. The humour of such plays is dark and savage, hardly a laughing matter; Shakespeare's genius was to combine this with the warm-hearted, 'common-people' comedy of which he was such a master. His 'low-life' bawds, constables and drunks are mined from the same rich seam as Dogberry, Bardolph, Autolycus and the others.

On the page, the play can seem both untidy and morally elusive. On stage, the elements fuse and the philosophical arguments take second place to a powerful and irresistible story-telling energy. At first, the action is straightforward: the Duke hands over his power, Claudio is sentenced, Lucio persuades Isabella to intercede, Angelo demands that she allows him sex, and Isabella presumes that Claudio will die to save her honour. But as soon as Isabella talks to Claudio in the prison, the dynamic changes. Claudio's reluctance to die for Isabella's chastity and his terror at the thought of death shock us with a humanity which revenge-tragedy writers never achieve. The Duke (who has been watching, disguised as a friar) moves the action firmly and ironically from realism to the realms of make-believe when he comforts the devastated Isabella by proposing the 'bed-trick' (substituting one bedmate for another), a staple of romantic fiction at the time. This suggestion poses a crucial moral question: if a law is unjust, what means are justified to evade its actions?

Shakespeare continues to exploit the discordance between romantic fancy and psychological realism. Isabella, too numb to think about moral implications or consequences, agrees with the suggestion. The disguised Duke has an uncomfortable confrontation with the aggressively 'realistic' pimp Pompey. Lucio, attacking the Duke for (as he thinks) going into exile, raises the uncomfortable thought that if the Duke's judgement is questionable, then the very basis of society is shaking. We know (because he has told us) that the Duke's disguise is not whim but serves a deeper, more personal mission of social and psychological exploration. Nothing is what it seems; morality and ethics are shifting and prismatic; our empathy must be not only emotional, with the characters, but also intellectual, with the philosophical and psychological questions they raise in our minds. The 'bed-trick', for example, a simple enough contrivance, is fraught with symbolic and philosophical meaning. Angelo will have sex with one woman (Mariana) thinking that she is another (Isabella). Mariana will have sex with Angelo in the full knowledge that he spurned her earlier. The disjunction between sex and love could hardly be more graphically enacted.

The remaining prison scenes further explore the relativism of justice in the real world and demonstrate why Angelo's absolutist assault on sexuality is unsustainable. The Provost sympathizes with a nobleman (Claudio) while scorning a commoner (Barnardine). The disguised Duke arrives, confident of the success of his romantic scheme, only to find that Angelo, despite having (as he supposes) had sex with Isabella, has cynically ordered Claudio's execution. Failing to manoeuvre the Provost into executing Barnardine instead and swapping their heads, the Duke is forced to resort to his true authority and reveals the seal of his office.

Act Four, Scene Three begins with one of the play's finest confrontations between ordinary people and the world of philosophical moralizing and upper-class gamesmanship, when the 'common murderer' Barnardine rejects the insistence of the Duke/Friar that it's time for him to die, on the grounds that he isn't ready. Like Angelo's schemes before him, the Duke has run up against stubborn humanity. At this point, again at a moment of philosophical impasse, Shakespeare once more blurs genres, fairy tale and melodrama. The Provost plucks out of the air the notion that a pirate, conveniently dead that morning, can be beheaded and passed off as Claudio. The Duke then confronts us with one of the most dizzying philosophical provocations so far, when he tells Isabella that Claudio is dead. How, we may ask, can this possibly be justified? Is it anything more than cruelty heaped on cruelty, the stuff of Jacobean revenge tragedy?

But this is Shakespeare, and there is another Act to come. The Duke 'returns', Isabella begs for justice and Angelo rejects her case. Mariana arrives and describes the 'bed-trick', the Duke reveals that he was the Friar, and sentence is swift: 'Angelo for Claudio, death for death'. But then, as Mariana and Isabella plead for Angelo's life, as love and forgiveness triumph not only over hypocrisy and cruelty but also over the righteous rigours of the law, philosophical resolution and the heart of the play's meaning are finally achieved – and the Duke symbolizes the transformation by a kind of transcendental conjuring trick, producing Claudio alive for all to see and his sister to embrace.

This ending focuses our attention on Isabella and the changes wrought in her by the play's events. Life triumphs; she moves from sterility (the vocation she was forcing on herself) to the warmth of true affection – a journey which stands for that of everyone in the play, and of society at large. Underpinning all the melodramatic implausibilities of the action and the complex dialectic between justice and mercy is the resolution of another, deeper, set of contradictory energies: the replacement (thanks to the Duke's profound experiment) of cruelty and exploitation with forgiveness, love and the possibility of a new, non-legalistic and genuine contract in human life.

☞ In performance

Measure for Measure has had mixed fortunes. Isabella, one of Shakespeare's most luminous parts for women, has always guaranteed performances, and she has been played by leading actors of distinction from Anne Bracegirdle in the 1690s to Juliet Stevenson in the 1980s; Sarah Siddons and Flora Robson made the part particularly their own. But for two hundred years, the play was known in truncated and adapted versions, omitting the 'low-life' sub-plot and replacing it with songs. The full text was restored in the nineteenth century by John Philip Kemble (who himself regularly played the Duke), but the play found true success only in the twentieth century, when it began to be performed worldwide. Charles Laughton and John Gielgud had notable success as Angelo, the latter in Peter Brook's 1950 ground-breaking Stratford production. There have been two (undistinguished) films and a number of operas, notably *Das Liebesverbot* ('The Ban on Love') by the 21-year-old Wagner.

ANGELO
   What's this? What's this? Is this her fault or mine?
   The tempter or the tempted, who sins most ha? [II, i]

The Merchant of Venice

🔖 Sources

Giovanni Fiorentino's *The Simpleton* contains the story of Portia, Bassanio, Antonio and Shylock. The idea of the three caskets may have come from the anonymous story-collection *Gesta Romanorum*.

🔖 Story of the play

In Belmont, Portia sets would-be husbands a challenge: her picture is in one of three caskets made of gold, silver and lead, and they must choose. The man who picks the right casket will be her husband; those who fail will forfeit all they own. Bassanio, a young Venetian, decides to accept this challenge. To finance it, he borrows money from his friend Antonio, who in turn asks a loan from the moneylender Shylock. Antonio promises to pay Shylock back in three months, when his merchant-ships return from foreign voyages. Shylock demands a pound of his flesh if he fails.

At Belmont, the princes of Morocco and Aragon choose the wrong caskets. In Venice, Shylock's daughter Jessica steals her father's money and leaves his house for ever, joining her beloved Lorenzo in Belmont. Bassanio sails for Belmont, undertakes the trial of the caskets and makes the right choice. Celebrations are interrupted by news that Antonio's merchant-ships are lost and that Shylock insists on the letter of his agreement. Portia decides to disguise herself as a lawyer and plead Antonio's case in court. Nerissa (her maid, engaged to Bassanio's friend Gratiano) disguises herself as a lawyer's clerk.

At the trial, Shylock demands his pound of flesh and is unmoved by Portia's impassioned speech about the nature of mercy. She then invokes the original agreement: he can have his pound of flesh only if he cuts it without drawing a single drop of blood. Defeated, Shylock is forced to hand half his wealth to

Antonio (who passes it to Jessica and Lorenzo), and to become a Christian. Bassanio and Gratiano pay the 'lawyer' and 'clerk' with rings given them earlier by Portia and Nerissa.

Back in Belmont, and no longer disguised, Portia and Nerissa demand their rings, and when Bassanio and Gratiano say they have lost them, magnanimously give them 'new ones' – the originals again. All confusion over, the lovers fall into each other's arms – and Antonio is told the happy news that three of his ships have not, after all, been sunk but are safe in harbour.

☞ *Characters*

Portia, *heiress of Belmont*
Nerissa, *her gentlewoman*
Princes of Morocco,
  Aragon, *her suitors*
Duke of Venice
Antonio, Bassanio, Gratiano,
  Salerio, Solanio, *Venetian*
  merchants
Shylock
Jessica, *his daughter*

Lorenzo, *in love with her*
Launcelot Gobbo, *Shylock's*
  servant
Old Gobbo, *his father*
Tubal, *Shylock's friend*
Balthasar, Leonardo, Stephano,
  servants
Attendants, Gaolers, Magnif-
  icoes, Officers, Servants

PORTIA Portia is rich, bright and bored. She keeps herself amused by playing games: putting her suitors through the ordeal of the three caskets, disguising herself as a lawyer and going to plead a real case in a real court, playing the trick on Bassanio with the keepsake-ring. All these games are gambles with Fate, disastrous if they turn out wrong.

The trial-scene shows Portia discovering, and revealing, true depth of character. The 'quality of mercy' speech is not cold rhetoric, but a heartfelt declaration of human truth – and it is matched by the way her games-playing with the suitors turns into a test of real love with Bassanio. As her character develops, so her language grows poetically ever richer, and she becomes the source of all the play's radiance and warmth.

SHYLOCK For other characters in the play, Shylock is a figure of darkness. His servant Gobbo calls him 'the fiend at mine elbow' and when Jessica (Shylock's daughter) leaves him she says she is escaping from 'a house of hell'. Antonio and Bassanio, borrowing money from him, treat him with contempt, and he responds in kind. During the trial all sympathy is with Antonio (hardly surprising in view of Shylock's gloating language and the way he sharpens a knife to take his pound of flesh), and there is a kind of savage joy when Portia tricks him. (Gratiano howls at him with true anti-semitic savagery.) Shakespeare allows him no redemption: it is made plain that his imminent conversion to Christianity is punishment (or self-mortification) and not the epiphany his Christian hearers might imagine.

All these attitudes, however, reveal as much about the people who hold them as they do about Shylock himself. He is a lonely, joyless man who has built his life obsessively round religion, his daughter and his money. When all three are threatened he collapses into a kind of madness – and that, paradoxically, elevates his stature as a dramatic character. Shakespeare shows us the reverse side of the image everyone has of him, and it is pitiful and moving.

ANTONIO Antonio, the merchant of the play's title, is enigmatic. Some see him as timid, melancholy and absurdly over-generous, an innocent fly caught in Shylock's web. Others find him frigid and unbending, a kind of Christian Shylock. The part is small, he is given few opportunities to show or develop character, and even in the sunny final Act he speaks only a handful of lines and stands aloof from the happiness all round him.

BASSANIO In productions which take a sour view of all the characters in the play, Bassanio is sometimes played as a callous fortune-hunter. But he can also be seen as pure-hearted and honest, one of the most amiable men in Venice. Although he makes preliminary arrangements over Antonio's bond with Shylock (which is to benefit him, since the money is to finance his wooing of Portia), he is so horrified by the conditions that he tries to persuade Antonio to end it. Faced with the trial of the three caskets, he chooses lead rather than gold or silver because he values truth in a world which is 'still deceived by ornament'. He and Portia are well-matched: as the play proceeds she works her way through to the seriousness and integrity he possesses from the start.

JESSICA Jessica is sometimes seen as a pure, innocent girl who is oppressed by her father Shylock, escaping to radiant happiness when she finds true love with Lorenzo. (The soaring ecstasy of their poetry supports this view.) On the other hand, she not only betrays her father and steals his money, she leaves his house, and renounces her religion to join the Christians.

GRATIANO Gratiano is absolutely unable to control his tongue: even his friend Bassanio says that he speaks 'a great deal of nothing' and tells him that he is 'too wild, too rude, and bold . . .' In the trial scene, after Portia tricks Shylock, his outburst of capering joy is particularly offensive: 'O upright judge! Mark, Jew! O learned judge! . . . / O Jew, an upright judge, a learned judge!' He is no match for the bright, mocking Nerissa, and his sullen surprise when she reveals that she, all the time, was the lawyer's clerk who accompanied Portia to court is symptomatic of the way his brains tend to lag behind his tongue.

☞ About the play

Shakespeare's source centres on an heiress, Portia, who tests would-be suitors by ordeal, confiscating their goods and sending them packing if they fail. One suitor, Giannetto of Venice, fails the test twice, but borrows money to make a third attempt – and when the debt is called in Portia disguises herself as a lawyer, pleads his case in court and wins. She marries him and they live happily ever after. In this version, the suitor and moneylender are minor figures, and the characters have no psychological depth. It belongs to the same world of romantic fairy tale as another story drawn on by Shakespeare in this play, about an heiress who invited her suitors to choose among three caskets, gold, silver and lead.

As always, Shakespeare adapted his source-material to suit his own purposes, and transformed it in the process. In particular, he developed the world of the original story's secondary characters,

Portia's Venetian lover (here renamed Bassanio), his friend Antonio who lends him money to court her, and the usurer Shylock who lends the money to Antonio in the first place. This enrichment of the Venetian dimension allowed him to set up two crucial antitheses: between materialism and emotion and between love and hate. The Venetian world is sophisticated but coldly materialist. Commerce – a matter of cargo-lists, banking arrangements, contracts and household accounts – is all-important. When Bassanio falls in love outside Venice and outside this system, Antonio is bewildered – the play begins with him saying, 'In sooth, I know not why I am so sad' – and his apprehension of loss is to do entirely with his friend and not his ducats (which at this point he thinks are safe at sea). When Shylock's daughter Jessica elopes with Lorenzo, Shylock's anguish similarly leads him to blur his love for her and the money she has stolen in lieu of dowry – 'My daughter, my daughter and my ducats!'

In such a world, where people make deals instead of intimate conversation, the irruption of feeling leads to tongue-tied bewilderment, fury and cruelty. By contrast, in Portia's Belmont, wealth is taken for granted, and all the talk is of games, music, laughter and love. When Portia hears that Antonio is in danger of his life because of his loan to Bassanio, her first thought is simply to pay the debt, and her second is to dress as a lawyer and plead for him in court, a masquerade straight out of fairy tale. During the masquerade (in the 'quality of mercy' speech) she at last reveals true feeling and intellectual drive, releasing the play from the realm of fantasy. Emotion and materialism confront each other – a standoff which commerce, in the shape of Shylock's sterile insistence on the letter of a contract, is bound to lose – and the love-affairs can move to their happy conclusion, enriched by the emotional turmoil the characters have suffered and the lessons they have learned.

The second antithesis imported by Shakespeare is between love and hate. In the world of Belmont, love is paramount. People's behaviour towards one another is warm and positive, and intruders such as the princes of Morocco and Aragon, whose love is inward-looking and self-centred, are smilingly but quickly rejected. The world of Venice, by contrast, is one of hate: unloving, authoritarian and sterile. The older generation rules, sanctioning its control by contracts and arbitrating it not by amicable discussion but in court. Shylock's love for his daughter, like Antonio's for Bassanio, is possessive, and symbolizes the whole society. In fact, Shakespeare goes to some trouble to show Antonio and Shylock not as chalk and cheese but as figures of similar confusion and similar sternness. One is led to feel that if the agreement between them had been the other way round, Antonio might have been in court just as eagerly and implacably as Shylock, demanding a pound of his 'hated' creditor's flesh.

So far, the morality of the play is as explicit as its poetry, the ethics as fascinating as the games of love are enchanting. But Shakespeare stirs in another major ingredient, Shylock's religion. His treatment of this, and the anti-semitism it arouses in other characters, have stolen attention from the rest of the play from the very first production onwards. *The Merchant of Venice* was first performed six years after Marlowe's virulently anti-Jewish play *The Jew of Malta*, and in the shadow of a recent political scandal involving the queen's physician, Roderigo Lopez, a Portuguese Jewish immigrant executed for plotting to poison his employer. In such an atmosphere, Shylock may well have been played as the gloating miser, the Devil disguised as Jew familiar from medieval literature – a tradition followed in most productions of the succeeding three hundred years. By contrast, more recent productions, and particularly those in the second half of the twentieth-century, have turned this tradition on its head, making Shylock the innocent victim of persecution in a vicious and morally bankrupt society.

Nothing whatever is known about Shakespeare's own attitude to Jews and their religion. The practice of Judaism was illegal in Elizabethan England, and he may have had little personal experience. Some of the language (for example Gratiano's snarling in the trial scene) is uncomfortably anti-semitic, though it falls far short of the ranting in *The Jew of Malta*. Money and love, not Judaism and Christianity, are the major antitheses of the play, and from that perspective, give or take a few changes in the dialogue, it would be possible to play Shylock as of any nationality, and any faith.

In performance

After the play's initial performances, it was revived twice at court in 1605, but then vanished from the stage until 1741. From that date on, however, it has been one of Shakespeare's most popular plays, the part of Shylock attracting almost every leading actor of note, and being played in every conceivable way from melodramatic villain to dignified merchant banker, from orthodox fanatic to farce clown. Productions attacking the race-issue head-on range from the version of Charles Macklin (who played it as ranting anti-semitic melodrama in the late 1700s) to Bill Alexander's RSC production of 1987, where Venice was shown as a cauldron of religious hatred, Christians and Jews equally bigoted and at one another's throats. Well-respected Shylocks include Edmund Kean, Edwin Booth and Henry Irving in the nineteenth century, and in the twentieth century, Walter Hampden, George Scott, Laurence Olivier and Anthony Sher. Portia, likewise, has attracted a galaxy of stars, ranging from Sarah Siddons in the eighteenth century and Fanny Kemble and Ellen Terry in the nineteenth, to Sybil Thorndike, Katharine Hepburn, Peggy Ashcroft, Geraldine James and Janet Suzman in the twentieth.

SHYLOCK

    Signior Antonio, many a time and oft
    In the Rialto you have rated me
    About my money and my usances.
    Still have I borne it with a patient shrug
    For sufferance is the badge of all our tribe.
    You call me misbeliever, cut throat, dog
    And spit upon my Jewish gaberdine
    And all for use of that which is mine own. [I, iii]

The Merry Wives of Windsor

☞ Source

Original.

☞ Story of the play

In Windsor, Justice Shallow demands that Falstaff pay back money he has embezzled. Falstaff plans to enrich himself by love-affairs with the wives of two rich citizens, Ford and Page. He writes identical love-letters, and gives them to Nym and Pistol to deliver. Nym and Pistol take the letters to the husbands. Further complications are caused by the fact that three people are courting Page's daughter Anne: Shallow's cousin Slender (aided by the Welsh schoolmaster Sir Hugh Evans), Doctor Caius the peppery French physician and Fenton, a young gentleman from London.

Although the genial Page doesn't believe his wife is having an affair, Ford is convinced about *his* wife. Raging with jealousy, he disguises himself as 'Master Brook', tells Falstaff he loves Mistress Ford to distraction, and offers him cash to woo her on his behalf. Falstaff says that he has arranged a clandestine meeting with Mistress Ford. Meanwhile, Caius challenges Sir Hugh to a duel, and the landlord of the Garter Inn has considerable trouble in patching up their quarrel.

The wives trick Falstaff. He arrives to court Mistress Ford, and Mistress Page hurries in to say that Ford is outside. They hide Falstaff in a laundry basket and dump him in the river. A second meeting is arranged, and the same thing happens, except that this time Falstaff disguises himself as an old woman, 'the witch of Brainford', and Ford thrashes him and throws him out. The husbands and wives are reconciled, and Mistress Page suggests a third trick on Falstaff. Mistress Ford arranges to meet him at midnight in Windsor Forest (where he must be disguised as Herne the Hunter) -- and children, disguised as fairies, will 'haunt' him and torment him. Page arranges that under cover of this confusion, Anne (dressed as a fairy) will elope with Slender, Mistress Page arranges that she will go (similarly disguised) with Caius, and Anne herself makes plans to elope with Fenton.

In the Forest, Falstaff is duly tormented, and all is revealed. Caius and Slender unmask the fairies they have eloped with, only to find that neither is Anne. She and Fenton have slipped away, and return to say that they are married. Page and his wife accept this cheerfully, and Page asks everyone back to his house to celebrate.

Characters

Sir John Falstaff	**Fenton,** *in love with Anne Page*
Bardolph, Nym, Pistol, Robin,	**Robert Shallow,** *country justice*
his companions	**Abraham Slender,** *his cousin*
Frank Ford, *citizen of Windsor*	**Sir Hugh Evans,** *Welsh parson*
Mistress Alice Ford	**Doctor Caius,** *French physician*
George Page, *citizen of Windsor*	**Host** *of the Garter Inn*
Mistress Margaret Page	**Mistress Quickly, Rugby,**
Anne Page, *their daughter*	**Simple,** *and other servants*
William Page, *their young son*	**Children, Dancers, Musicians**

FALSTAFF The Falstaff of this play is a different man from the character in *Henry IV*. Disconnected from the processes of history (he no longer has a royal patron), he is desperate for cash, and his attempts to solve this problem lack all dignity. Like Sir Epicure Mammon in Jonson's *The Alchemist*, he is the personification of excess, a figure from farce not comedy. None the less, even at his most preposterous (in Act Five, alone in Windsor Great Park, disguised as Herne the Hunter and about to be humiliated and tormented), he is honoured by his creator with a wonderfully orotund and touching self-regard: 'The Windsor bell hath struck twelve; the minute draws on. Now the hot-blooded gods assist me! Remember, Jove, thou wast a bull for thy Europa, Love set on thy horns – O powerful love that in some respects makes a beast a man, in some others a man a beast! . . .' At such moments he embodies all the awkwardness and bravura of physical appetite; he is heroically ludicrous.

THE MERRY WIVES Mistress Ford and Mistress Page are two of Shakespeare's most realistic and shrewdly-observed female characters: no longer 'in the holiday time of [their] beauty' but wise, spirited, resilient and funny. Of the two, Alice Ford (the sexy Wife) takes the lead in the intrigues, making all the dates with Falstaff and inventing the scheme of the laundry basket and his disguise as the Old Woman of Brainford. But her part in the action is more than farcical. Married to the insanely jealous Ford, she is teaching him a lesson about trust in love, and this gives her depth as well as sparkiness.

Her friend Margaret Page is the maternal Wife: her main concern is for her children. She happily plays her part in fooling Falstaff, breaking up his trysts with Mistress Ford each time by rushing in to say that Ford is at the door. She devises the third trick, drawing Falstaff to Windsor Forest and choreographing the fairy dance of the children. Like Alice Ford, she has a second, private agenda, which this is intended to support: allowing her daughter Anne to slip away with Doctor Caius. But when Anne marries Fenton instead, she is quite happy: her interest is more in her daughter's happiness than in any particular choice of husband.

THE HUSBANDS Frank Ford is a middle-class Leontes, racked by suspicion and jealousy. His scheme to disguise himself as Master Brook and act as Falstaff's go-between with his wife Mistress Ford is both ludicrous and pathetic, making his self-torment worse instead of better, and he is fooled, no less than Falstaff, by the ploys of the laundry basket and the Old Woman of Brainford. Then, at the end, when he discovers that his wife was faithful after all, clouds turn to sunshine and his happiness lights up the play.

George Page, by contrast, is cheerful throughout, and at the end he abandons his preoccupation with finding the right match for his daughter Anne and accepts her elopement with rueful pragmatism: 'Well what remedy? Fenton, Heaven give thee joy. / What cannot be eschewed must be embraced.' His easiness of manner not only contrasts with Ford's brooding but is magnificently paired with the bubbliness of his wife Margaret. They are happy people, solid citizens, and their warm-hearted humanity contributes much to the atmosphere of this most genial of plays.

ANNE PAGE AND WILLIAM PAGE Anne is a lively girl in her mid-teens, pretty, pert and flirtatious with Slender, and then movingly, suddenly overwhelmed with real emotion when she sets eyes on Fenton. Their love-scenes are charming and touching, a grace note to the play.

William Page is a small child, perhaps about eight years old. He features in the scene where Evans tests him on his Latin grammar, and Mistress Quickly, overhearing, makes wild *double-entendres* from every case and participle. In this scene all William has to do is stand there and say his lines; later he is compensated by being allowed to dress up as a fairy, go the Windsor Forest at midnight and torment Falstaff.

FENTON Fenton's rivals for Anne Page's hand (especially Slender) mock the romantic young gentleman from London for his big-city ways and turns of phrase, but none the less he gets the girl. The landlord of the Garter Inn sums him up exactly: 'He capers, he dances, he has eyes of youth, he writes verses, he speaks holiday, he smells April and May . . .'

SLENDER Shallow proposes that his brainless country cousin Slender should marry Anne Page; that way, the Pages will gain aristocratic connections, and Shallow will have access to Anne's seven hundred pounds a year. For his part, Slender is more interested in horses and greyhounds than women, and although he is happy for Sir Hugh Evans to woo Anne on his behalf, he is even better pleased when Anne runs off with Fenton and the match is abandoned.

CAIUS Caius is the archetypal farce Frenchman, torturing the English language, falling in love with the prettiest girl in sight (Anne Page) and proposing to fight duels with anyone who crosses him – or if no one else obliges, with his long-suffering servant Rugby. He is the descendant of the bragging soldier of ancient Roman comedy, and the ancestor of a long line of funny-foreigner parts in later farce. Giving him rivalry, to the point of fighting a duel, with the equally peppery, equally linguistically-challenged Evans doubles the fun at a stroke, farce-craftsmanship of genius.

SIR HUGH EVANS Evans is a man of some importance in the community, a parson and schoolmaster. He is called on to act as arbiter in the quarrel between Falstaff and Shallow, and later to speak for Slender in the wooing of Anne Page. (This is what causes his quarrel, and his duel, with Doctor Caius who is also pursuing Anne.) He may have been played by the same actor as Fluellen in *Henry V* – in Falstaff's phrase, he 'makes fritters of English' in a very similar way – and he was perhaps Shakespeare's deliberate parody of a well-intentioned but long-winded Welshman at Queen Elizabeth's court, her Sergeant-at-Arms Lewis Lloyd.

PISTOL AND NYM Pistol and Nym are Falstaff's hangers-on, and when he sacks them because they won't deliver his love-letters to Mistress Page and Mistress Ford, they tell the husbands instead. Pistol is explosive and sudden, a soldier whose name suits him exactly. Nym is a dolt pretending to be deep and wise, uttering complete gibberish and, if challenged, brushing explanation aside with 'That's my humour'.

☞ *About the play*

The Merry Wives of Windsor is one of the best-constructed farces in the business. In the past, scholars unsympathetic to farce, and seduced by the main character's name into making invidious comparisons with the infinitely more layered comedy of the Falstaff scenes in *Henry IV*, used to condemn it as 'mechanical' and 'uninspired'. It also has the melancholy distinction of being the only one of Shakespeare's plays to have inspired a greater work in another form: Verdi's *Falstaff*. But although it lacks the powerful interrogations which characterize Shakespeare's greatest plays, its busy plot, good-humoured gusto and 'company' style all work superbly well on stage, and it has always been one of his most popular comedies in performance.

The panache of the writing, craftsman's skill becoming an object of pleasure in its own right, masks two of the play's most innovative features. It is one of the first bourgeois farces ever written in English, set not among world-weary, games-playing aristocrats or slapstick yokels but in the rising middle-class to which Shakespeare himself belonged. With a kind of affectionate wryness, it portrays and gently mocks the dominant preoccupations of that class: money, property, education and community. It is written in sturdy, fluent prose – with the engaging exception of scenes involving the amorous young aristocrat Fenton and those who mock or flatter him.

It is a common theme in Shakespeare's histories that bourgeois values are a bulwark against the predatory instincts of the aristocracy, and here it is given a farcical spin, starting from the fact that the 'aristocracy' in question, however sympathetic, is a fat, lecherous and gullible fool. But Shakespeare is careful to show that bourgeois values do not guarantee immunity from folly, and in the end even they give way to the triumph of romantic love. (This theme is treated in a less light-hearted manner, and in a more aristocratic context, in *The Merchant of Venice*, written at the same time.)

The play's social point is made explicit in the last act, when the corrupt aristocratic sinner undergoes purgation by fire and ridicule, staged by new money but dressed up as old English folk custom in the royal hunting park in Windsor. New intimacy with royalty (the park is the monarch's but it also belongs to the citizens) is supported by a deliberately bastardized and sceptical version of folk beliefs: it is as if *A Midsummer Night's Dream* were being deconstructed as a piece of amateur theatre, with local children playing fairies and Mistress Quickly dressed up as Titania.

The second innovation is the role in the plot of the merry wives themselves. As dramatic characters, Alice Ford and Margaret Page are among the first English examples of what was to become a glorious tradition, women as the driving force in social comedy, and their revenge on Falstaff exhibits a kind of pragmatic self-confidence quite different from the imperious upper-class games-playing of (for example) Beatrice, Portia or Helena. Their actions, and the complicity between them, are domestic and intimate, typical of the spirit which was enabling their class increasingly to take possession of the heart of England.

The Merry Wives of Windsor is populated by some of Shakespeare's most brilliantly imagined minor characters: the servants Rugby, Simple, John and Robert, Falstaff's page Robin, the genial Evans and the tough, good-hearted Host of the Garter Inn. Of the characters carried over from *Henry IV*, Mistress Quickly is cleverer and younger, Pistol and Bardolph less extravagant and more to the point, while Falstaff is the victim of intrigue rather than its master. The effect of these importations, and these changes, is both wide-ranging and highly specific: it is as if all the panoramic skills on display in *Henry IV* had been focused on one emblematic small town.

☞ In performance

Tradition claims that Queen Elizabeth so enjoyed *Henry IV* that she commissioned another play in short order, 'showing Falstaff in love'. The first performance may have been a gala Windsor occasion on 23 April 1597, part of celebrations to honour newly-created Knights of the Garter. Ever since then *The Merry Wives* has been one of Shakespeare's most frequently-performed plays, both in English and – thanks to the relative ease with which its prose can be registered in translation – throughout the world. It has been filmed twice (both times in the silent era), and has inspired several operas of which the finest are Nicolai's *The Merry Wives* (bustling farce) and Verdi's *Falstaff* (autumnal seriousness blended with rumbustious comedy).

MISTRESS PAGE What, have I scaped love letters in the holiday time of my beauty, and am I now a subject for them? [II, i]

FALSTAFF By the lord, a buck-basket. Rammed me in with foul shirts and smocks, socks, foul stocking, greasy napkins, that, Master Brook, there was the rankest compound of villainous smell that ever offended nostril. [III, v]

A Midsummer Night's Dream

🖙 Source

Original. The story of Pyramus and Thisbe comes from Ovid's *Metamorphoses*.

🖙 Story of the play

In Athens, Duke Theseus is about to marry the Amazon queen Hippolyta. One of his lords, Egeus, complains that his marriage-plans for his daughter Hermia (betrothed to Demetrius) have been upset by Lysander, who has bewitched Hermia into loving him instead. Theseus tells Hermia to marry Demetrius or become a nun. Hermia and Lysander plan to meet the following night in a magic wood outside Athens, and elope. Hermia tells her best friend Helena, who in turn tells Demetrius (the man she hopes will marry *her*).

The wood is crowded. A group of workmen, led by Nick Bottom the weaver and Peter Quince the carpenter, is rehearsing a play to perform in honour of Theseus and Hippolyta's wedding. The fairy kingdom is in turmoil. King Oberon and Queen Titania have quarrelled over a 'beautiful changeling child', and Oberon now sends his mischievous acolyte Puck to fetch the juice of a magic plant: if sprinkled on people's eyelids as they sleep, it will make them dote on whatever they first see when they wake up. Oberon squeezes the juice on Titania's eyes, and Puck, ordered to do the same to Demetrius (to make him love Helena), sprinkles Lysander's eyes instead.

During a lull in the play rehearsal, Puck gives Bottom an ass's head, and the others run in terror. Bottom is mystified – and even more so when Titania, waking up, falls in love with him and tells her fairies to 'do him all courtesy'. Meanwhile Oberon has tried to make up for Puck's mistake with the lovers by squeezing love-juice into Demetrius' eyes, with the result that Lysander and

Demetrius are both in love with Helena, much to Hermia's annoyance.

Everyone in the wood falls at last into exhausted sleep. Oberon (who by now has possession of the changeling) releases them all from the love-spell, and Puck removes the ass's head from Bottom. The lovers, their differerences sorted out (Lysander now paired with Hermia, Demetrius with Helena) go to Athens for the wedding, and the workmen perform their play. As the day finishes, Puck leads the fairies in a torchlight procession through the palace, blessing all the brides and grooms and promising lifelong happiness.

 *Characters*

AT COURT
Theseus
Hippolyta
Hermia (*loves Lysander*)
Helena (*loves Demetrius*)
Lysander, Demetrius (*both in love with Hermia*)
Egeus, *Hermia's father*
Philostrate, *master of the revels*

FAIRIES
Oberon
Titania

Puck
Peaseblossom, Cobweb, Moth, Mustardseed

'MECHANICALS'
Peter Quince, *carpenter*
Nick Bottom, *weaver*
Francis Flute, *bellows-mender*
Tom Snout, *tinker*
Snug, *joiner*
Robin Starveling, *tailor*

Fairies, Lords, Ladies

THE FAIRIES Titania and her attendants are like characters from masque, given a minimum of lines and a maximum of formality. At first, quarreling with her husband over the 'little changeling boy' ('Set your heart at rest. / The fairyland buys not the child of me'), Titania is powerful, mysterious and proud – attributes which increase our surprise when, made to dote on Bottom in his ass's head, she becomes sexually voracious and almost girlish, almost 'human', in her gush and passion ('Thou art as wise as thou art beautiful'). The Fairies are characterized chiefly by their elegant group singing and dancing, and by their cheekiness to Bottom in his ass's head – an impression greatly increased, one imagines, when they were played by small boys as in Shakespeare's theatre.

Neither Titania nor the Fairies have much opportunity, or need, to reveal depth of character. In the fairy kingdom, this is reserved chiefly for Oberon and Puck. At first, when Oberon rages over the changeling boy, he is as icily melodramatic as a demon in panto-mime. But as soon as Puck begins to muddle up the instructions for the magic eye-juice, and he has had his revenge on Titania, he sheds his coldness and becomes both more human and more fully regal. Puck, Robin Goodfellow, is the embodiment of fairy amoral-ity. He is often imagined as a light and delicate being, but period woodcuts show a being of a different and far more sinister kind: a satyr-like wood-sprite with beard, horns and phallus. He is sub-version incarnate, and for all the poetry Shakespeare gives him – the most delicate songs and speeches in the play – his presence gives jaggedness to the proceedings whenever he is on stage.

THE COURT The marriage between Theseus, the monster-slaying hero and friend of Hercules, and the Amazon archer-queen Hippolyta was one of the most glittering events of ancient myth, a favourite subject for elaborate poetry and fine art, and Shakespeare follows the formality of this tradition. But behind their dignity and sophistication, and despite their few lines, Theseus and Hippolyta show genuine character. She is dignified and independent, he is the model of an enlightened, modern ruler. Philostrate, ostensibly a stiff official, melts deliciously into giggles at the workmen's play. And, adding crucial roughage, Hermia's father Egeus remains hurt and angry by his daughter's disobedi-ence – he is not softened by what happens, and gives way only because Theseus orders it.

THE LOVERS The lovers' attitudes and sufferings mirror human experience. The women – fiery Hermia, willowy Helena – are confronted by all the toughness their world can offer. Hermia disobeys her father by running away from court, while Helena follows her in pursuit of Demetrius. At once their world seems to collapse into chaos all round them: they are (as they think) mocked and betrayed, and their sisterly friendship is threatened by forces they have never previously experienced. The men – romantic Lysander, cynical Demetrius – initially seem to be cut from traditional aristocratic cloth, but their experiences in the wood humanize and sensitize them before our eyes.

As a group, the quartet is beautifully balanced, and Shakespeare plays sophisticated games with it, breaking and reforming it in a dozen different patterns. All four characters confront themselves individually, the confrontation changes them – and we, the audience, are shown the inherent mutability of young love. We fall in love not only with these individuals, but with the idea of love itself, and with the way the lovers learn to balance the often confusing biological urge of Nature with the intellectual, romantic notion of 'true love' proclaimed and reinforced by convention.

THE 'MECHANICALS' Bottom is ambitious, upwardly-mobile – and, as an amateur actor, every director's nightmare. He wants to play all the parts, fusses and frets about inessentials (for example the kind of beard Pyramus should have), garbles his lines in rehearsal and plays one of the most over-the-top death-scenes ever seen on stage. In real life, he is entirely different. His soliloquy when he describes his fairy transmutation is full of a plain man's honest wonder – 'The eye of man hath not heard, the ear of man hath not seen, man's hand is not able to taste, his tongue to conceive nor his heart to report what my dream was . . .' – and his innate good-heartedness is shown when he thinks he is king of the fairies and sinks into the part with touching and delightful geniality: *Mustardseed*: 'What's your will?' *Bottom*: 'Nothing, good Mounseer, but to help Cavalery Peaseblossom to scratch . . .' *Titania*: 'What, wilt hear some music, my sweet love?' *Bottom*: 'I have a reasonable good ear in music. Let's have the tongs and bones.'

Quince, the author, director and producer of *The Most Lamentable Comedy and Most Cruel Death of Pyramus and Thisbe*, is a walking compendium of creatorly neurosis, pedantic and patient in rehearsal and in performance gloriously twitchy for the success of his masterpiece and his actors. Flute, cast as the hapless heroine Thisbe, is self-conscious and embarrassed – 'Nay, faith, let me not play a woman; I have a beard coming' – but does his gawky best.

Snout plays Wall with great dedication but no skill whatever, grunting out his lines and hurrying offstage as soon as he decently can. Snug plays Lion, and despite rehearsal nerves (which lead to a string of anxious suggestions for business and refinements) and stage-fright at the performance, roars with such conviction (and apologizes with such seriousness for frightening the ladies) that he earns enough courtly approval ('Well roared, lion!') to make him a thespian for ever. Starveling, the twitchy tailor entrusted with the part of Moonshine, is so fazed by remarks from the spectators that he steps out of character and explains, with magnificent literal-mindedness, exactly what is going on: 'All that I have to say is, to tell you that the lantern is the moon, I the man in the moon, this thornbush my thornbush, and this dog my dog.'

None the less, and although Shakespeare's actors must have revelled in sending up the lack of sophistication of their amateur counterparts, these 'mechanicals' are serious members of society. Shakespeare's Athens is nothing like his ancient Rome, where workers are anonymous members of an urban mob. Bottom and the others are craftsmen, with a stake in the society they live in, some control over how they spend their free time, and (relatively) free access to and intimacy with the ruling class. Their perform-ance at Theseus' wedding is a farcical, but believable, projection of Shakespeare's own relationship with his patron and, ultimately, his monarch.

☞ About the play

A Midsummer Night's Dream was probably written for celebrations of a lavish aristocratic wedding, and is patterned like an elaborate dance or masque. The court scenes book-end the action, and in between them scenes showing the three worlds of lovers, fairies and mechanicals are organized with symmetry and balance, all coming together for the triple wedding-celebration and torchlit procession which end the show.

For all the play's formality and sophistication, it seems to hark back to a more innocent age, and is full of simple, realistic human detail. At its centre is the glorious image of the Fairy Queen and her dazzling courtiers – the queen whom Spenser, in his *Faery Queen* (published five years earlier) had specifically linked with Elizabeth I and her real-life court. Deep down, and for all her regal glory, Titania/Elizabeth is alone and lonely. There is no consort in attendance, and her rupture with Oberon has caused all too real problems of bad harvests and rural discontent. And in the same way that Elizabeth, when pressed about her marriage prospects, replied that she was already married 'to the people of England', so Titania meets and falls in love with Bottom the weaver, an upwardly mobile artisan.

In sugary stagings of the play, the escape from convention and anarchy which the fairy kingdom represents is shown as a kind of permanent, English bank holiday during which nothing – not even Titania's obsession with Bottom as an ass or Puck's malicious tricks – is serious and there is neither hurt nor risk. But Shakespeare's fairies are not creations of gossamer and dew. They are either the harder, harsher 'little people' of Celtic myth or a version of the (real) courtiers of Elizabeth, the (real) 'Faery Queen', and their anarchic amorality can be cruel and dangerous. *A Midsummer Night's Dream* is, in part, an exploration of four different kinds of 'innocence' – court convention, young love, the supernatural and the world of 'honest toil' – and all the first three, including the fairies, are shown to be incomplete and unsatisfactory, the more so when they collide with one another. It is only with the intervention of the mechanicals that the divisions can be momentarily healed.

It is one of the delights of *A Midsummer Night's Dream* that all such seriousness is masked throughout, that the whole thing is merely, as Puck's epilogue reminds us, a dream. The play's dark depths lurk beneath a moonlit surface of ravishing charm. It is a piece of glint and echo, suggestion and impression, and exists, dreamlike, simultaneously on several planes of understanding. This is one reason why it seldom fails to please: one of the central images of the play, for example, Titania caressing Bottom transmuted into an ass, is both the presentation of some dark, psychosexual attraction to phallic monstrosity and a charming fantasy in which a comedian turns into a donkey and the queen of the fairies falls in love with him.

☞ In performance

There was a total absence of performances between a 1662 London production (seen by Pepys, who thought the piece 'the most insipid, ridiculous play' he'd ever seen) and the 1827 German production for which Mendelssohn wrote incidental music. In between, the play was regularly plundered and reworked, usually as a musical farce in which a group of inept amateur thespians become entangled with a group of delightful fairies. Music and gossamer charm (largely inspired by Mendelssohn's music) continued to be the keynotes of productions well into the twentieth century: Reinhardt's 1935 film, starring James Cagney (Bottom), Mickey Rooney (Puck) and with a troop of fairies materializing and dematerializing among gauzy, mist-enshrouded trees, is typical. Another tack, taken by directors as different as Granville Barker (1914), Tyrone Guthrie (1937) and Peter Brook (1970), explored the magic not of the fairy world but of theatricality, somewhat short-changing the play's poetry in the process. By and large, the less pretentious the interpretation, the more successful: the range is from a 1929 Old Vic production in the style of a masque from Shakespeare's time to innumerable local-theatre productions, indoor and outdoor. There have been half a dozen films, operas by Purcell (*The Fairy Queen*), Orff and Britten, and a 1939 jazz version (*Swingin' The Dream*) with the 'mechanicals' replaced by the Benny Goodman Sextet and with Louis Armstrong as Bottom.

LYSANDER

    Ay me, for aught that ever I could read
    Could ever hear by tale or history
    The course of true love never did run smooth [I, i]

STARVELING

    All I have to say is to tell you that the lantern is the moon, I
    am the man i'th'moon, this thorn bush my thorn bush, and
    this dog my dog. [V, i]

Much Ado About Nothing

☞ Sources

Shakespeare adapted the love-affair of Claudio and Hero from an Italian tale published in 1554, interweaving his own story of Beatrice and Benedick being tricked into falling in love despite themselves.

☞ Story of the play

Don Pedro has defeated his brother Don John in battle, and pardoned him. In Sicily, they are welcomed by the governor Leonato, and Don Pedro woos Leonato's daughter Hero on behalf of his young follower Claudio. Jealous of Claudio, Don John sets out to prevent the marriage. Hero's friend Beatrice begins a contest of witty remarks with another of Don Pedro's followers, Benedick.

At a masked ball, Don Pedro, Claudio and Hero plan to trick Beatrice and Benedick into falling in love. Don John plots against Hero and Claudio. His henchman Borachio will persuade Hero's maid Margaret to flirt with him at night on Hero's balcony, dressed as Hero, while Don John lets Claudio overhear. The plot works, but the constable Dogberry hears Borachio boasting about it and arrests him. During all this, the business between Beatrice and Benedick has been progressing, hints being dropped to Benedick that Beatrice secretly loves him, and vice versa.

At Claudio's and Hero's wedding, Claudio abruptly rejects Hero. She faints, and he takes her for dead and leaves. Leonato agrees that they should keep pretending she is dead until matters are sorted out. Beatrice demands that Benedick prove his love by killing Claudio. Benedick challenges Claudio to a duel, but Dogberry brings in Borachio and Don John's plot is revealed. In penance for (as he thinks) causing Hero's death, Claudio agrees to marry Leonato's hitherto unseen niece – and only when he unveils his bride does he find out that she is Hero. Benedick is now headlong in love with Beatrice, but she is still wary, and it is not till he stops her witticisms by kissing her that the musicians can strike up the wedding dance.

'NOTHING' AND 'NOTING' The title *Much Ado About Nothing* is a multiple pun. The meaning we understand today was enhanced in Elizabethan times by the facts that 'nothing' was pronounced 'noting' (or 'no-thing'), and 'noting' in slang had three meanings: eavesdropping (one of the plot's main ingredients), striking sparks off someone with repartee, and sex. 'Nothing' was also slang for the vagina, as 'something' stood for the penis.

☞ *Characters*

Don Pedro, *Prince of Aragon*	**Borachio, Conrad**, *Don John's*
Benedick, Claudio, *lords*	*henchmen*
Don John, *Don Pedro's brother*	**Constable Dogberry**
Leonato, *governor of Sicily*	**Antonio, Attendants, Boy, Friar**
Hero, *his daughter*	**Francis, Messenger, Sexton,**
Beatrice, *his niece*	**Watchmen**
Margaret, Ursula, *Hero's maids*	

BEATRICE Beatrice is set against marriage, and makes merciless fun of would-be suitors. As the play proceeds, however, it becomes apparent that she uses her dazzle of words to shield herself from genuine feeling and communication, particularly with Benedick, and Shakespeare lets us see that the match between them is nevertheless inevitable. The pivotal moment comes after the trick against Hero is played and the wedding broken off. Beatrice's subsequent instruction to Benedick to 'kill Claudio' has devastating emotional irony. She means it literally, dreadfully – but her desperation is less for Hero than about her own longing that Benedick should prove that he loves her as irrevocably as she loves him.

BENEDICK Benedick is vain, and much of the comedy in his character arises from the clash between this vanity and the increasing seriousness of his emotional situation: against expectation, he falls in love. He has no opportunity to do anything about it – his relationship with Beatrice is interrupted by Don John's plot against Claudio – until after the first wedding-scene, when Benedick accepts Beatrice's demand that he 'kill Claudio'. Even after this, they still find it hard to express true feelings unencumbered by wit, and it is not till Benedick gives up words for actions altogether, and kisses Beatrice, that they find at last the happiness we have longed for them.

CLAUDIO In Shakespeare's company, the actor playing Claudio need have been no older than thirteen or fourteen. This explains Claudio's callowness and pliability – and it also affects the play's whole emotional balance, making the melodramatic lovers no more than shadows of Benedick and Beatrice, and letting the adults' passion and ironical unpredictability dominate the action. Then, Claudio blossoms. His journey through pain, then ecstasy (at the moment when Hero suddenly whispers in his ear that she loves him) and self-loathing (when he thinks he has killed her) gives him insight into his own emotions, and he grows into adulthood before our eyes.

HERO Hero's character – that of a bright, innocent child – is wonderfully displayed in the Act Three conversation with Ursula which Beatrice overhears, the tale that Benedick is secretly and desperately in love. Intellectual high spirits combine with innocence to make this scene, and contrast entirely with the first wedding-scene which follows. Here she says little (chiefly a short speech defending herself against Claudio's charges), and the impression is of someone reeling with shock, of the child of the earlier scenes being forced to grow up in an instant. Finally, when Hero unmasks herself in the second wedding-scene, Shakespeare gives her moments of real power and mystery. She has made the journey from innocence to a kind of authority and responsibility, and her lines have a quality of dignified wonder which illuminates the play.

DON PEDRO For a noble and heroic prince, Don Pedro is unexpectedly eager to involve himself in japes and charades of all kinds. He takes part in the tricking of Benedick and Claudio, woos Hero on Claudio's behalf and then, when Beatrice rejects his own unexpected proposal of marriage, suggests tricking her into thinking that Benedick is in love with her. In short, he is not merely prince and warrior, but a gamesome young bachelor on the lookout, and explains it by saying that now the wars are done, he has decided to play Cupid instead of Mars. The contradiction between being prince of the great state of Aragon and playing the mischievous Cupid is central to his makeup.

LEONATO Leonato is that favourite Shakespearean character, a genial middle-aged man enjoying himself with jokes and ironies at the world's expense. As governor of Messina, he is required to keep up the formal façade, but entertains himself none the less by arranging masked balls, charades and all kinds of 'games and sports'. However, when Don John's plot succeeds and he thinks that Hero is guilty of deceit, he shows true feeling, true despair – 'Wherefore? Why doth not every earthly thing / Cry shame upon her?' But that is swept away by another piece of ironical play-acting, remarkable in the circumstances, when he agrees, after Claudio breaks off the wedding with Hero, to let the young man think that Hero is truly dead. This edge of darkness in Leonato's character deepens his play-acting, and can make us think about the nature of all the other pieces of deception in the whirlwind of ploys, tricks and ironies which fill the play.

About the play

Nowadays, largely thanks to Shakespeare, we are used to the intermingling of disparate dramatic styles in the same play. But in its own day, *Much Ado* must have seemed daringly experimental, blending two apparently irreconcilable genres, high comedy and melodrama, giving each its own distinctive language (prose and verse), and moving between them not only scene by scene but even speech by speech and line by line.

The verse/prose distinction is vital to the play. Until Shakespeare's own work, the language of drama was almost exclusively verse. Prose was reserved for holy scripture, learned argument, folk-tale and such (literally) 'prosaic' communications as legal documents; it seemed inappropriate for the stage. In those parts of *Much Ado* dealing with Claudio and Hero, Shakespeare used the formality of verse to characterize both the lovers and the villains who set out to destroy them. By contrast, he used prose for such 'ordinary' characters as the Watchmen, and – crucially – for the verbal sparring between Beatrice and Benedick. The contrast of linguistic forms and styles articulates psychological difference without ever stating it. When Claudio speaks of his love in verse, his emotion seems conventional and unconvincing; when Benedick tells of his love in prose, he leaves no doubt about the depth and 'reality' of his feelings. Style makes the point: 'romance' (in the medieval, sentimental sense) is dead, long live true love.

Entwining the actual plots posed few technical problems. Shakespeare put characters from each story into the other, and instead of telling two separate tales with different locations, showed two intrigues proceeding step-by-step in the same setting. The joining of the stories also allowed him such superb dramatic strokes as the moment when Benedick declares his love to Beatrice, asks her what he must do to prove it, and Beatrice (who has just heard what has happened to Hero) takes his and our breath away by answering 'Kill Claudio' – a no-nonsense ramming-together of the two plots, but also a moment of dazzling psychological perception. Shakespeare also bound the plots with his own personal brand of rustic-farce alchemy, making Dogberry and his Watchmen the agents who discover Borachio's treachery and bring the whole intrigue to light.

Not every critic enjoyed the mingling of genres: Shaw, for example, called *Much Ado* 'a hopeless mess'. But genre-interaction is vital to the play's effect. The Hero/Claudio story, however implausible, is serious, full of pain, unironical and unequivocal – factors which allow it to provide a context and a contrast for the feelings expressed by Beatrice and Benedick, a hint of the darkness and obsession which underlie their frivolity. In turn, their gaiety, inconsequentiality and the dance of their language, while leaving intact the energy of the Hero/Claudio plot, undercut its absurdities and make it seem less doom-ridden.

Shakespeare enhances this cross-fertilization by consistently refracting the same events or ideas from different points of view. The trick played on Hero and Claudio (setting someone up to eavesdrop on a stage-managed conversation) is paralleled by the scenes where Beatrice overhears people saying that Benedick loves her, and he hears that she loves him. There are two pairs of lovers, two villains, two aristocratic old men, two maidservants, two Spanish lords (one noble, one villainous). Even the Watchmen parallel the 'main' characters, Dogberry's linguistic manipulations reflecting Beatrice's and Benedick's witshafts, Verges mirroring Leonato's doddering brother Antonio, Oatcake and Seacole matching such 'main-action' characters as Conrad (Borachio's fellow-conspirator) and Hero's maid Ursula.

Throughout the play, Shakespeare uses the interaction between styles to round out characters who might otherwise have remained two-dimensional. Hero is not the innocent, put-upon child of the original story, but acquires adult understanding and mystery before our eyes, in a way entirely dependent on the softening and deepening effects of comedy. As the play develops, we see the layers of Leonato's character peeled away like onion-skins, until he loses his early blandness and becomes a complex and sympathetic human being. Borachio moves from the shadows of melodrama to a last-act repentance of resonant nobility.

The richness of lesser parts in *Much Ado* was another innovation. The play fully displays one of the glories of Shakespeare's art: the way he uses minor characters to give a human context, a relevant if at times unexpected background to the main action. Don John is not merely a melodramatic scoundrel; he is dignified by the eloquence of his language (a mirror of the word-dancing of the main characters) and by his delight in his own malevolence. Conrad is a nobleman in decline, and his journey reverses that of Borachio, a braggart happy to try any means of social advancement. Antonio is not just a *commedia dell'arte* greybeard, but a loyal brother to Leonato and uncle to Hero. Each of the Watchmen is sharply characterized, and Hero's maids are two of

Shakespeare's most adroit creations: the sparky, ambitious and sexually lively Margaret, and the more mature and sensible, but still fun-loving Ursula.

For all its excellences, *Much Ado* is by no means Shakespeare's comic masterpiece. Both plot and language can seem over-artificial, lacking in the mysteries and profundities which make some of his other comedies so haunting. Its importance in the canon of his work comes from the fact that the people who triumph in it are those who speak in an idiom we all understand and can claim as our own. It plays a central part in the demystification and democratization of language and behaviour which is so much a part – if so seldom sung a part – of Shakespeare's artistic achievement. For audiences, it lives because of its blend of gossamer lightness and emotional resonance, and because its characters and intrigues are so engaging.

🖝 In performance

Much Ado has been popular almost from the day it was written. Performers who made a particular mark in it include Robert Armin (the original Dogberry), David Garrick (who played Benedick every year for thirty years), Helen Faucit (who played Beatrice from 1836 until her retirement in 1879), Ellen Terry, Lewis Casson and Sybil Thorndike, John Gielgud (who directed half a dozen productions in the 1930s to the 1950s), Katharine Hepburn and Alfred Drake, Judi Dench and Felicity Kendal.

The play resists translation into other media. Only Berlioz's opera *Beatrice and Benedick* (1862) is anything like as 'magical' as the original. Early stage writers had a mania for adapting it, and their efforts lie well towards the lunatic fringe of Shakespeare on stage. In 1662 William Davenant stitched it to *Measure for Measure*, added songs and delighted Pepys, and in *Love in a Forest* (1723) Charles Johnson stirred in scenes from *Twelfth Night*, *A Midsummer Night's Dream*, *As You Like It* and *Love's Labour's Lost*. Updatings, by contrast, often work well. Among the best have been J. J. Antoon's 1972 production set in 1920s America, with Dogberry and Co. as Keystone Cops, and John Barton's 1976 RSC production set in India during British Imperial rule.

LEONATO Well, niece, I hope to see you one day fitted with a husband.

BEATRICE Not till God make men of some other metal than earth. Would it not grieve a woman to be over-mastered with a piece of valiant dust? To make an account of her life to a clod of wayward marl? No, uncle, I'll none. Adam's sons are my brethren, and truly, I hold it a sin to match in my kindred. [II, i]

DON PEDRO Out of question, you were born in a merry hour.

BEATRICE No, sure, my lord. My mother cried, but then a star danced, and under that I was born. [II, i]

BENEDICK She speaks poniards and every word stabs. If her breath were as terrible as her terminations, there were no living near her – she would infect to the North Star. [II, i]

DOGBERRY Well said, i' faith, neighbour Verges. Well God's a good man. An two men ride of a horse, one must ride behind. [III, v]

CLAUDIO
There, Leonato, take her back again.
Give not this rotten orange to your friend. [IV, i]

BEATRICE You have stayed me in a happy hour. I was about to protest I loved you.

BENEDICK And do it with all thy heart.

BEATRICE I love you with so much of my heart that none is left to protest.

BENEDICK Come bid me me do anything anything for thee.

BEATRICE Kill Claudio.

BENEDICK Ha. Not for the wide world.

BEATRICE You kill me to deny it. Farewell. [IV, i]

Othello

🖙 Source

Geraldus Cinthio, *Hecatommithi* (1565).

🖙 Story of the play

Iago, an ensign risen from the ranks, expects his general, Othello, to promote him to lieutenant, but Othello gives that post to the aristocratic Cassio. Iago plots revenge on both of them. Knowing that Othello has been paying court to Desdemona, young daughter of the Venetian senator Brabantio, Iago tells Brabantio that they have slept together. Brabantio arraigns Othello before the court, but Othello demonstrates that their love is innocent and Brabantio reluctantly allows the marriage.

Othello's troops go to defend Cyprus against the Turks. Othello and Desdemona are to follow later. Iago puts his plan into action. He gets Cassio drunk, and organizes a brawl which climaxes just as Othello steps on to the quay. Othello strips Cassio of his commission. Iago suggests to Cassio that he ask Desdemona to plead for him – and at the same time begins hinting to Othello that Cassio and Desdemona are lovers. Iago acquires a handkerchief which Othello gave to Desdemona and she accidentally lost, and he hides it in Cassio's room. Iago then tells Othello that he kisses it and dreams of Desdemona. Othello asks Desdemona for the handkerchief, and she says in all innocence that she doesn't know where it is. Cassio, finding it, equally innocently gives it to his mistress Bianca.

Othello is now so eaten with jealousy, and Iago's insinuations, that he swoons. Iago takes him to watch himself and Desdemona laughing together – in fact about Bianca, though Othello takes it to be about Desdemona. Othello tells Iago to kill Cassio, and plans himself to murder Desdemona. Visitors arrive from Venice, and are horrified when at the formal dinner of welcome Othello first insults Desdemona in public, then strikes her.

Iago tries to persuade Roderigo, a foolish lover of Desdemona, to kill Cassio, and when Roderigo bungles it, Iago murders him to stop him telling. Othello smothers Desdemona with a pillow, and Emilia (her maid and Iago's wife) finds the body and tells Othello the truth: that she, Emilia, found the handkerchief and gave it to Iago. Iago kills her for this, and Othello wounds him. The whole story is revealed, and Othello commits suicide in front of the Venetian envoys. Cassio is made governor of Cyprus, and Iago is taken to Venice for punishment.

🖐 Characters

Othello	**Brabantio,** *Desdemona's father*
Desdemona, *his wife*	**Gratiano,** *his brother*
Cassio, *his lieutenant*	**Lodovico,** *their cousin*
Iago, *his ancient (ensign)*	**Montano,** *former governor of*
Emilia, *Iago's wife*	*Cyprus*
Bianca, *Cassio's mistress*	**Clown, Musicians, Servants,**
Roderigo, *in love with Desdemona*	**Senators, Soldiers, Sailors**
Duke of Venice	

OTHELLO Othello is a successful man, and proud of it. An African prince who has chosen to accept Venetian ways and standards and has risen to the top of that society by merit, he keeps reminding himself of who he is and what he has done. Only one thing makes him vulnerable: his marriage. It disturbs the balance in a rigidly conventional society, and awakens latent Venetian racism. He deals with this problem by ignoring it – a fatal miscalculation – and the reason is that he is obsessively in love, a mature man captivated by a teenage girl.

Iago uses Othello's own pride to destroy him. When, thanks to his insinuations and stage-management of events, Othello begins to think that Desdemona is having an affair with Cassio, Othello's doubts are almost immediately not about the relationship but about himself: 'Haply, for I am black / And have not the soft parts of conversation / That chamberers have, or, for I am declined / Into the vale of years (yet that's not much) / She's gone, I am abused, and my relief / Must be to loathe her ...' Such self-loathing is psychologically devastating, and every new piece of 'evidence' merely increases it, until, at the end of the handkerchief scene, Othello is so overwrought that he collapses both mentally and physically: 'Lie with her! Lie on her! We say lie on her when they belie her. Lie with her! That's fulsome. Handkerchief . . . confession . . . handkerchief . . . (*He swoons*)'

For such a man as Othello, the only way to recover from such a situation is violence. He kills Desdemona – not hysterically but gently, almost lovingly ('I'll not shed her blood / Nor scar that whiter skin of hers than snow . . .') – and then, when Iago's deceit is finally made clear, turns on himself and commits suicide, quietly, almost ceremonially, as if it were some necessary religious ritual.

IAGO Iago is the arch-villain of Jacobean theatre, adding spice to his malevolence by self-admiring soliloquies which announce to the audience every stage of his intrigue in advance. He loves his work: playing games with the fool Roderigo, being taken by everyone for the 'honest ancient' he is not, revelling in the success of his 'medicine' on Othello's mind in the handkerchief scene.

In fact Iago plays games even with the spectators, pretending that his motives for destroying Othello are far more complex than they are. His real reason is revenge (because he has not been given the promotion he deserves), but he adds, or pretends to add, to this a general hatred of his social superiors, a kind of muted racism, even the accusation that Cassio has had an affair with Emilia.

There is a fatal dissociation between the the slightness of Iago's motives and the catastrophe he unleashes. In snaring Othello he shows all the desperate attention to detail of the second-rate mind. In him we see, perhaps, in Hannah Arendt's description of the career and mind of Adolf Eichmann, the true 'banality of evil'.

DESDEMONA Desdemona is nowadays most often played as a mature woman, but in Shakespeare's day she was more probably portrayed as someone in her early teens, about the same age as Juliet. Captivated by Othello and his traveller's tales, she either falls in love with him personally or imagines she does, and marries him without the slightest regard for her father's wishes or feelings. This is both brave and touchingly naive. In Cyprus she enjoys her grown-up role as the new Governor's wife, is sure of her influence over Othello (when she pleads with him for Cassio), and then, when things go fatally wrong, is utterly and completely bewildered, a child again: 'Why I should fear I know not / Since guiltiness I know not, but yet I feel fear.' At the end she gains genuine tragic pathos, moving into a serene, otherworldly acceptance of her fate and blessing Othello with the last bestowal of the only gift she has ever been able to give him, her love: *Emilia*: 'O, who hath done/This deed?' *Desdemona*: 'Nobody. I myself. Farewell. / Commend me to my kind lord. O, farewell.'

EMILIA Emilia has less power than almost anyone in the play – a fact which, paradoxically, gives her enormous moral authority. She is a matter-of-fact soul who depends entirely on her husband Iago but reserves her love for her mistress Desdemona, and Iago's and Othello's behaviour drive her to furious disgust at what men do to women. Her death-scene is one of the most touching in all Shakespeare.

About the play

Othello was produced at court on 1 November 1604. Shakespeare took the plot from a melodramatic Italian story, streamlining the action, giving Othello complexity and nobility of character (both missing in the original), and making the whole play a study in suspicion, mistrust and jealousy. Crucially, he also added depth to the part of Iago. In the original story Iago is merely devilish, so obviously evil that the other characters seem fools not to notice, but in Shakespeare he seems to everyone the model of a loyal soldier and friend, and it is only we, the audience, who share his secret (thanks to the saturnine soliloquies which are one of the glories of the part – a characteristic of Shakespeare's finest villains).

Othello is the most domestic of Shakespeare's tragedies. Its focus is not on the fall of a king, the collapse of a nation, the agony of a prince or the contradiction between love and duty. Rather, it is about the end of a marriage and a husband's murder of his wife. It is intimately concerned with the details of sexual jealousy: how it is sparked, how the flames are fuelled and how it brings down catastrophe on the protagonists' shoulders. Shakespeare focuses on details: the erotic intimacy of the mutual attraction between Othello and Desdemona; the particularities of Iago's tactics; the irony of Desdemona's pleading for Cassio; the story of the handkerchief; Desdemona's elaborate preparations for bed; the methods of Othello's murder of Desdemona; Othello's suicide. Locations are drawn so as to give a uniquely realistic atmosphere: the back alleys of Venice, the Doge's palace, the garrison in Cyprus, Desdemona's bedroom. The surface is almost lovingly naturalistic, full of vernacular turns of speech and references to everyday objects, the dramatic equivalent of a Vermeer painting.

This is not, however, style for its own sake. The objects carry meaning, but the realism of the world in which Shakespeare's characters live defies transcendence. His Venice and his Cyprus are without romance and without forgiveness. They are worlds in which people are only as good as their reputation, class-division is explicit and relentless, girls are sexually exploited, a good-looking and well-spoken junior officer can almost automatically be presumed to be having an affair with his commander's wife, a pathetic fool like Roderigo can, almost unnoticed, be killed in a brawl. For all its tragedy, the play's world is allied to that of the cruel and violent *commedia dell'arte*, in which the only motive forces are sex and money. For underneath the farce of *commedia*, its vision is bleak: ideal ground for a domestic, sexual tragedy.

Shakespeare's masterstroke is that he introduces into this world two central characters who stand for everything which Venice, and *commedia*, utterly reject: respectively, heroism and innocence. Othello and Desdemona are outsiders, he by virtue of his birth, his magnificent self-imagining and the rolling, rhetorical language in which he dresses it, she because she has betrayed her origins by choosing a Moor as husband. If convention had ruled, she would have married Cassio, and everything might have been well. Her liaison with Othello is domestically explosive – and the issue is put aside, rather than resolved, because of the greater political emergency. But it contains the seeds of its own destruction: together, Othello and Desdemona soar, but they must also crash. Their tragedy is that in the heartlessly materialist world they live in, they themselves become like objects, as meaningless and disposable as everyone around them. She is treated as a whore, he is made to behave like a cuckold in a farce, she is meanly stifled by a pillow, he kills himself almost casually, sordidly stealing away his own dignity. In this dark world, their light is indeed 'put out'.

Othello is one of Shakespeare's most tightly constructed plays. The action involves only half a dozen main characters, and the issues of possession/jealousy and honour/treachery are pursued with such concentration that there is no time for sub-plots or diversionary scenes. Othello's personal grandeur and Desdemona's unquestioning and unquestioned innocence drive the play inexorably from bliss through crisis to catastrophe. As with Romeo and Juliet and Troilus and Cressida, we are left both dazzled by their relationship and feeling that if love like theirs is to be possible, the world must be better constructed. Significantly, the play ends not with grandeur but with mediocrity. Its last words are spoken by the nonentity Lodovico, and are full of suitably half-baked rhetoric: '(*to Iago*) O Spartan dog / More fell than anguish, hunger or the sea . . . / This is thy work . . . / Myself will straight aboard, and to the state / This heavy act with heavy heart relate.'

The poetry and formal control of *Othello* make it as organized as a symphony: scholars rightly talk of 'the *Othello* music'. In particular, this quality is signalled by the soaring language which Othello, and Othello alone, is given to speak – in marked contrast, for example, to Iago's style, which is witty, ironical, matter-of-fact and ruthless. Lack of accommodation between the play's two worlds is symbolized by the collision between the two main characters – one reason why it has always been popular for pairs of leading actors to alternate the parts on different nights of the same production.

☞ *In performance*

Right from the time of Shakespeare's colleague Richard Burbage, the Moor has been most often played by white leading actors. It was not till the twentieth century that actors of colour regularly began to make their names in the part. Paul Robeson, for example, first played Othello in 1930 when he was 32, and went on doing so for the next thirty years, and in the 1996 film Laurence Fishburne used the part to explore particularly twentieth-century areas of psychological devastation and collapse. Although the play is largely free of the racist outbursts of other works from the same era (such as Marlowe's *The Jew of Malta*), it nevertheless depends on the covert assumption that people who are 'different' are exotic, sexually attractive and potentially dangerous.

Many actors have been wary of playing Othello – and some of those who did, notably Garrick, Macready, Irving and Booth, had more success as Iago. Exceptions include Edmund Kean in the 1810s (whose final speech, according to the critic Hazlitt, was like 'the sound of years of departed happiness'), Paul Scofield in the 1960s, and two who disconcerted some spectators by playing Othello's ethnic origins head-on: Edwin Forrest in the 1870s (who also played him like a 'huge, tormented bull') and Laurence Olivier in the 1960s (the finely-spoken performance later filmed).

Works based on *Othello* range from the sublime (Verdi's opera) to the bizarre (*Catch My Soul*, a 1960s rock musical), from the savage (Phil Wilmott's 1972 play *Iago*) to the far-fetched (the 1947 film *A Double Life*, in which an actor playing Othello finds the part taking over his real-life existence). Dvořák's *Othello* overture of 1892 is a musical reinvention of Shakespeare's text.

> IAGO   O beware my lord of jealousy.
>   It is the green-eyed monster which doth mock
>   The meat it feeds on. [III, iii]

Pericles, Prince of Tyre

🖎 Sources

John Gower, *Confessio Amantis*, itself based on an anonymous story from classical times, the tale of Apollonius of Tyre.

🖎 Story of the play

Gower, as Chorus, introduces each act and reminds us of the passing of time – the play's action spans sixteen years.

King Antiochus of Antioch poses a riddle to his daughter's suitors, and Pericles, prince of Tyre, solves it. But the answer involves revealing that Antiochus and his daughter have committed incest, and although Pericles prudently leaves Antioch, Antiochus sends an assassin to track him down. Not safe even in his own kingdom, Pericles leaves his deputy Helicanus to govern Tyre and wanders the world. In Tarsus he helps the governor Cleon and his wife Dionyza to relieve a famine. In Pentapolis, saved by fishermen from shipwreck, he takes part in the birthday tournament for Princess Thaisa, and marries her.

Some months later, Antiochus and his daughter die (struck by a thunderbolt), and Pericles and Thaisa set sail from Pentapolis to return to Tyre. Thaisa is pregnant, and in a storm during the voyage she gives birth to a child (Marina) and dies. The sailors put her body in a chest and throw it into the sea to placate the storm-gods. The chest is washed up in Ephesus, where the physician Cerimon brings Thaisa back to life. She becomes priestess of the Temple of Diana. Pericles, meanwhile, has given Marina to Cleon and Dionyza to bring up in Tarsus, and gone home to Tyre.

Sixteen years pass. Dionyza, angry that Marina is more popular than her own son Philoten, plots to have her killed, but Marina is captured instead by pirates and sold to a brothel in Mytilene. Cleon and Dionyza tell Pericles that she is dead. In Mytilene, Marina's determination to stay a virgin so terrifies the brothel's customers that the owners give her to Lysimachus the governor. By now, Pericles, maddened by grief for Marina's loss, has begun his wanderings again. He comes to Mytilene, where Marina sings and restores his wits. In a dream, the goddess Diana orders him to Ephesus, where he tells his adventures to the priestess. The priestess then reveals that she is Thaisa. Marina and Lysimachus become king and queen of Tyre, Pericles and Thaisa live on in Ephesus, and everyone lives happily ever afterwards.

👉 *Characters*

Gower, *as Chorus*	**Lysimachus,** *governor of Mytilene*
Pericles, *Prince of Tyre*	**Cerimon** (*of Ephesus*), **Escanes**
Simonides, *King of Pentapolis*	**and Helicanus** (*of Tyre*), *lords*
Thaisa, *his daughter*	**Bawd, Boult** (*servant*), **Diana**
Marina, *daughter of Pericles and*	(*goddess of chastity*), **Fishermen,**
Thaisa	**Gentlemen, Knights, Ladies,**
Antiochus, *King of Corinth*	**Leonine** (*servant*), **Lords,**
His Daughter	**Lychorida** (*Marina's nurse*),
Thaliard, *his dastardly servant*	**Marshal, Messengers, Pandar,**
Cleon, *governor of Tarsus*	**Philemon** (*servant*), **Pirates,**
Dionyza, *his wife*	**Sailors**

PERICLES For most of *Pericles* the mood and style are fairy tale, action predominates over character, and the individuals are drawn more as types than as people who change or develop to articulate the 'meaning' of the action. Pericles is a good man, an innocent who moves from sorrow to happiness. His misfortunes come on him out of the blue – the riddle he answers all but brings about his death, his beloved wife dies in childbirth, the 'friends' to whom he gives his daughter to bring up inform him that she has died. But for all this, and despite the misery which leads him to wander the world in rags, he is under Heaven's protection, and God (in the form of Diana of Ephesus) eventually restores to him the wife and daughter he thought were lost for ever.

Act Four centres on Marina's time in the brothel, and Pericles does not appear. And when he does return in Act Five, Shakespeare springs a major surprise. Pericles' cardboard nature has disappeared entirely, and he is presented as the incarnation of suffering humanity, reduced, Lear-like, to a beggar shouting at Fate in a storm. Then, again like Lear, he is redeemed before our eyes, restored to humanity by contact with pure innocence. Thanks to the quality of its verse, the scene between him and Marina moves the play into unheralded realms of transcendental beauty: 'This is the rarest dream that e'er dull sleep / Did mock sad fools withal . . .'; 'Most heavenly music! / It nips me into listening, and thick slumber / Hangs upon mine eyes: let me rest . . .'

MARINA Acts One and Two take place before Marina is born; in Act Three she is an infant. It is not until Act Four that we see her as a grown girl, innocent of life but independent-minded and determined to get her own way. (The presence of such heroines in four successive plays – Imogen in *Cymbeline*, Marina in *Pericles*, Perdita in *The Winter's Tale*, Miranda in *The Tempest* – suggests that there may have been a boy in the company able to play purity and simplicity without embarrassment.) Marina has no duplicity; she is as honest as a glass of water – so much so that modern actresses are sometimes tempted to ironize her charm, playing games with the character which would have seemed surprising in Shakespeare's time, when virtue was an absolute quality, admired without equivocation.

Even so, Shakespeare does seem to find it hard always to keep his tongue out of his cheek – for example when he describes Marina's methods of dissuading would-be customers in the brothel as 'her quirks, her reasons, her master reasons, her knees . . .' Speeches like 'I never did hurt in all my life: / I never spake bad word, nor did ill turn / To any living creature. Believe me, la / I never kill'd a mouse, nor hurt a fly; / I trod upon a worm once, 'gainst my will / But I wept for it . . .' are so off-putting to the brothel's aristocratic patrons that its owners quickly put her to other duties: sewing, singing and teaching dancing.

Like everything else in *Pericles*, Marina's purity reaches apotheosis in the last act, when it is the means of restoring her distracted father's sanity. In the scene between them, he is the one who changes; she remains as ethereal and radiant as she has been throughout the play. Technical necessity is turned into art (in the same way as happens in *Antony and Cleopatra*): the adult actor is given challenges beyond a child's capacity, and the child's innocence is left to shine through without the need of acting.

ANTIOCHUS AND HIS DAUGHTER Antiochus is pure evil, a villain who keeps his daughter for his own incestuous pleasures by killing any suitor who fails to solve an unanswerable riddle, and when by chance Pericles *does* answer it, sends a henchman (Thaliard) to murder him before he can claim his prize. Antiochus' daughter, appropriately enough for such a scenario, is characterless and speaks only two lines. The pair of them die in a suitably melodramatic, fairy-tale manner, shrivelled 'even to loathing' by a thunderbolt.

CLEON, DIONYZA, THALIARD These characters seem to have stepped straight out of pantomime: Dionyza, the wicked stepmother who tries to have Miranda killed; her doddering, hen-pecked husband Cleon who vainly tries to stop her; the villainous Thaliard, sent by Antiochus to murder Pericles and always arriving a moment too late and finding his victim gone.

CERIMON The old physician-necromancer who discovers the chest containing Thaisa's body and sets to work to bring her back to life is fond – as his name implies – of the sound of his own voice: ''Tis known, I ever / Have studied physic, through which secret art / By turning o'er authorities, I have – / Together with my practice – made familiar / To me and to my aid the blest infusions / That dwell in vegetives, in metals, stones . . .' But for all his long-windedness, he knows what he is talking about, and his potion works. In the last scene of the play, again as befits his name, he is like a master of ceremonies introducing all the characters to each other and breaking into their cries of surprise and happiness to explain exactly what has happened.

PANDAR, BAWD, BOULT The staff of a Mytilene brothel buy Marina from pirates and almost immediately start losing customers. The Pandar's tough façade masks longing for retirement:

'Three or four thousand chequins were as pretty a proportion to live quietly, and so give over . . .' His wife the Bawd, driven distracted by Marina's innocence ('Fie, fie upon her! She's able to freeze the god Priapus, and undo a whole generation'), orders her to have sex with Lysimachus 'without any more virginal fencing', and when Marina refuses tells her factotum Boult to 'crack the glass of her virginity, and make the rest malleable'. Unfortunately for the enterprise, the soft-hearted Boult is captivated by Marina and moves her to 'an honest house'.

GENTLEMEN OF MYTILENE In a wonderfully funny five-speech scene, the gentlemen of Mytilene rush out of the brothel, aghast to 'have divinity preach'd there' by Marina. 'Come, I am for no more bawdy-houses,' cries one; 'Shall's go and hear the vestals sing?' 'I'll do anything now that is virtuous,' his friend devoutly answers. 'But I am out of the road of rutting forever.'

☞ *About the play*

This *Arabian-Nights*-ish story is actually based on a much older source, *The Adventures of Apollonius of Tyre*, written in the second century when stories of lost relatives, quests, magic cures, madness and transformation were popular throughout the Middle Eastern provinces of the Roman Empire. In the thirteenth-century, perhaps influenced by similar tales in such collections as the *Decameron*, John Gower reworked Apollonius' adventures in his poem *Confessio Amantis* – and it was this retelling that Shakespeare and his collaborator drew on when they made their play. No one knows who the collaborator was, but a strong candidate is George Wilkins, who worked for Shakespeare's company in the early 1600s and in 1609 produced a novelized version of this play. Scholars suggest that he (or whoever the collaborator was) wrote the first two acts, and that Shakespeare provided the rest.

Like the original classical story, *Pericles* is a kind of shaggy-dog fairy tale, complete with tyrant king, wicked stepmother, put-upon heroine, pirates, jousts, shipwrecks, a sexually explicit brothel-scene, magic cures and a happy ending. Its form is episodic, with none of the tight plotting and narrative muscle of such comparatively recent plays as *Macbeth* or *Coriolanus*. Perhaps Shakespeare was experimenting with a new form – his next three plays, *Cymbeline*, *The Winter's Tale* and *The Tempest*, all use it, and *Henry VIII* applies it to English history – and it certainly chimed with the mood of the play-going public at the time: *Pericles* was one of his most popular plays, and as late as 1631 Ben Jonson, master of that analogous theatre form, the masque, wrote sourly that this 'mouldy' drama was stealing his audiences.

Whether or not Shakespeare was the sole author, the change of register at the start of Act Three is marked. Until then, the plot has been full of melodramatic bustle, event crowding after event in true fairy-tale style, and both characterization and language are workaday. Then, suddenly, in the storm that opens Act Three, the authentic late-Shakespearean voice is heard at last, as Pericles rails at the weather: 'Thou god of this great vast, rebuke these surges / Which wash both heaven and hell; and thou, that hast / Upon the winds command, bind them in brass / Having called them from the deep. O still / Thy deafening, dreadful thunders; gently quench / Thy nimble, sulphurous flashes . . . Thou stormest venomously: / Wilt thou spit all thyself? The seaman's whistle / Is as a whisper in the ears of death . . .' This linguistic intensity, matched by the ferocious realism of the brothel scenes, adds elements of epic to the fairy-tale plot, and Pericles' quest becomes more than a merely episodic journey. As the action proceeds, and concentration focuses on the characters of Marina and Pericles, the irradiation of poetry allows Shakespeare to use all the bizarre events and coincidences (these are the Acts with the pirates, the brothel and the magic potion) not just for their own enjoyable sake, but to articulate a moving story of loss, longing and rediscovery.

Shakespeareans who know the play chiefly from reading it tend to dismiss it as a farrago, a dramatic bran-tub which contains dross as well as jewels. (The cumulative effect of the mixture of styles and strategies reminds some of the swaggering sentimentality of such Beaumont and Fletcher 'adventure' plays as *The Maid's Tragedy* or *A King and No King*, hugely popular at the time.) On

stage, however, its dramatic logic is obvious, its events and characters are splendidly entertaining, and the switch halfway through
from comic-strip narrative to poignant, character-driven drama
makes it one of Shakespeare's most unexpectedly satisfying plays.

☞ In performance

Pericles' Jacobean popularity was followed by mixed fortunes. In
the eighteenth century it was eclipsed by a poor play (*Marina*) on
the same subject by George Lillo, and in the nineteenth century
Samuel Phelps bowdlerized and 'disinfected' it by removing the
brothel scenes and all references to incest. It was not till 1939 that
the full text was restored to the stage (by Robert Atkins), and even
since then the play has had only a handful of productions, of
which those by the RSC in 1979 and by Cheek By Jowl in 1985
were particularly admired.

BOULT How's this? We must take another course with you. If
　　　your peevish chastity, which is not worth a breakfast in the
　　　cheapest country under the cope, shall undo a whole
　　　household, let me be gelded like a spaniel. Come your
　　　ways. [IV, iv]

PERICLES
　　　O Helicanus, strike me, honoured Sir
　　　Give me a gash, put me to present pain
　　　Lest this great sea of joys rushing upon me
　　　O'erbear the shores of my mortality
　　　And drown me with their sweetness!
　　　(To Marina)　　　　　O come hither
　　　Thou that beget'st him that did thee beget
　　　Thou that wast born at sea, buried at Tarsus
　　　And found at sea again. O Helicanus
　　　Down on thy knees, thank the holy gods as loud
　　　As thunder threatens us. This is Marina. [V, i]

Richard II

☞ Source

Raphael Holinshed, *Chronicles of England, Scotland and Ireland* (1587).

☞ Story of the play

Richard and his cousin Henry Bolingbroke are both of royal descent, grandsons of King Edward III. Bolingbroke is a few months older, but Richard, son of Edward's elder son the Black Prince, has inherited the throne and rules by divine right. He is capricious and narcissistic, surrounded by flatterers and seeming not to notice that his country is slipping towards bankruptcy and civil war. The issue comes to a head when Bolingbroke appears before Richard to claim that Thomas Mowbray, Duke of Norfolk, was part of a conspiracy to murder their uncle Gloucester. Richard first decrees that the matter shall be settled by a joust of honour, then capriciously ends the fight before it begins and banishes both men. Bolingbroke's exile is to last six years, but when his father John of Gaunt dies and Richard commandeers Bolingbroke's inheritance to finance a war in Ireland, he comes back from exile – and some of Richard's lords, led by Northumberland, make him their leader in a war against the King.

Richard loses first his supporters and then the war. He takes refuge in Flint Castle, where he is finally captured. He agrees to abdicate, but refuses to read a public document detailing his crimes against the state, and is exiled to Pomfret Castle in Yorkshire. The Duke of York, Gaunt's brother and the uncle of Richard and Bolingbroke, acts as regent, but although Bolingbroke refuses the name of king, he holds royal power.

The nobles hotly debate the legality of Richard's abdication, and two churchmen and York's son Aumerle plan a revolt against Bolingbroke. This plot is discovered and the churchmen are ban-

ished. Aumerle's mother, the Duchess of York, persuades Bolingbroke to spare her son. Sir Piers Exton overhears Bolingbroke
saying 'Have I no friend will rid me of this living fear?', takes it as
an order, goes to Yorkshire and murders Richard. Bolingbroke is
crowned king (Henry IV), but blames himself for Richard's death
and plans a pilgrimage of penance to the Holy Land.

Characters

Richard II	*Other lords and courtiers:* **Berkeley,**
Queen	**Fitzwater, Ross, Salisbury,**
John of Gaunt, *Richard's uncle*	**Surrey, Willougby; Bushy,**
Duke of York, *Gaunt's brother*	**Green, Bagot; Bishop of**
Duchess of York	**Carlisle; Abbot of**
Duchess of Gloucester	**Westminster; Sir Piers Exton;**
Henry Bolingbroke, *Gaunt's son*	**Sir Stephen Scroop**
Duke of Aumerle, *York's son*	**Attendants, Captain,**
Duke of Norfolk	**Gardeners, Groom, Keeper,**
Earl of Northumberland	**Ladies-in-Waiting, Lords,**
Henry Percy, *his son, nicknamed*	**Messenger, Soldiers**
'Hotspur'	

RICHARD Richard is like one of the suffering heroes of ancient
Greek drama. He has a tragic flaw, *hubris*, the blindness to Fate
which makes mortals compare themselves to gods (in his fall, he
likens himself to Christ betrayed). Early in the play this leads him
to an action (annexing Bolingbroke's inheritance) which triggers
inexorable progress towards disaster. Each attempt to halt his
decline only makes things worse. What happens to him evokes in
us, the audience, the emotions of pity (sympathy for his suffering)
and fear (awareness that what we have seen has implications for
general moral behaviour).

Throughout the play, Richard seems almost to be performing
his life rather than living it. At the start, he surrounds himself
with an aura of omnipotence, as if his 'divine right' actually makes
him some kind of god whose actions are admirable just because he
does them. But even when Bolingbroke's rebellion succeeds and
his royal power collapses all round him, he continues to act, and
observe, his feelings and emotions. (The soliloquy 'I have been

studying how I may compare / This prison where I live unto the world' is typical.) At one point he compares himself to 'a well-graced actor' whose departure from the stage disappoints the audience.

Richard's inability to think objectively about himself is not the result of wickedness or arrogance. Instead of controlling the momentum of affairs, he is swept along by it. In a play – and a political argument – dealing with the balance between divine right to rule and fitness for the crown, the way Shakespeare uses the power of poetry to elevate his character is both an ironical conjuring-trick and central to the argument.

BOLINGBROKE At first, when all attention is on Richard, Bolingbroke seems to be just one more indistinguishable courtier. In his fractiousness, his acceptance of an outdated chivalric code (proving an accusation not in court but by fighting) and his obedience to Richard, he is as blinkered as all the others. But as civil war develops and Richard becomes ever more flamboyant and unpredictable, Bolingbroke begins to amass systematically and effectively the royal authority which is dribbling away from Richard. In the poker-game of power, he is inscrutable and unbeatable.

At the end of the play, when Bolingbroke hears that Exton has killed Richard, his certainty collapses and he begins brooding on his own moral state rather than that of the country, planning a pilgrimage to atone for regicide. In short, as King he falls prey to exactly the same fault as Richard, neurotic self-absorption – a point of considerable political pungency at the end of a century which had survived four dazzling, capricious and highly dangerous Tudor monarchs.

JOHN OF GAUNT Gaunt is a flinty guardian of tradition, with uncompromising views on honour and the duties and obligations of high position. His deathbed speech ('This royal throne of kings, this sceptr'd isle . . . / This blessed plot . . .') is typical. It is often taken out of context, as a ringing patriotic celebration of England and the English. It is actually an elegy, angry and accusing, for the way the country's honour is being bought and sold by a monarch who has betrayed his royal inheritance.

YORK An elder statesman, York shares his brother Gaunt's views on honour and duty, believes absolutely in the anointed king's 'divine right' to rule, and has no hesitation in scolding Richard when he falls short of these ideals. He is bluff and blunt, quite different from the simpering dandies (including his own son Aumerle) who are Richard's preferred courtiers.

Gaunt, however, dies before the issues come to a head; York has to temper his ideals to the momentum of history. When the anointed King is toppled, York puts his country before his feelings and swears loyalty to the usurper. When he discovers that Aumerle is plotting against the new King, he is forced to choose between loyalty to the crown and affection for a son of whom he entirely disapproves. Richard and Bolingbroke stand for the two sides of the transition from one kind of society to another; York embodies the struggle in a single individual to balance two kinds of political 'right', and the pain it can cause to come to terms with change.

✒ About the play

Shakespeare wrote *Richard II* in the flood of poetic inspiration which also produced *Romeo and Juliet* and *A Midsummer Night's Dream*. It was his fifth play using events from English history, and one of a pair of unrelated plays – the other was *King John* (1596) – on the theme of a flawed monarch. Shakespeare drew his plot (the feud between Richard and Bolingbroke) directly from history, telescoping the action into a few weeks to highlight his main dramatic theme, the character-contrast between the two men. In real life the unrest seethed for years, and was made infinitely more complex by the shifting loyalties of everyone involved.

In books, political turmoil can be described exactly, and readers can vary their pace to suit their understanding. On stage, the risk is of an incomprehensible babble of characters and points of view. Shakespeare's first histories, the *Henry VI* trilogy, were prone to this, and to some extent the same problem arises in *Richard II*: the Court and Parliament scenes, in particular, can degenerate into shouting-matches. But by and large he avoids the difficulty by making politics not the main part of the picture but the background, and concentrating on the two versions of suitability for rule presented by Richard and Bolingbroke, and the characters of the men who embody those qualities. In this scheme of multiple dramatic opposites, Richard is Abel, Bolingbroke Cain; Richard a man of ideas, Bolingbroke of actions; Richard a falling son of light, Bolingbroke a rising son of dark; Richard a throwback to feudal concepts of kingship, Bolingbroke a herald of Renaissance thought. Shakespeare structures the roles to highlight these contrasts.

Richard's personality, unvaried from start to finish, is displayed gradually, like a jewel lit first from one side then another. In the 'cracked mirror' scene, the climax of the deposition (end of Act Four, Scene One), Richard looks for a king in the mirror and finds a human being: the notion of 'the sacred king' is for ever smashed. Bolingbroke, by contrast, is mercurial and pragmatic. We never feel (as we do with Richard) that his choices are imposed or stage-managed by some external power – he is subject to no one but himself. Only at the end of the play, when he turns in on himself after Richard's murder, is he trapped and not liberated by a new situation.

It is sometimes said that Bolingbroke's character is incompletely displayed in this play, that it must be seen in conjunction with *Henry IV* – and indeed that Richard and Bolingbroke are early characters in a meditation on the nature of kingship spread over four plays and reaching its climax in *Henry V*. This may be so, but it is also true that within the span of a single evening – *Richard II* is a full-length, even lengthy, play – Bolingbroke's character is expounded clearly and sufficiently for all dramatic purposes.

Having decided to build his drama on the duality between Richard and Bolingbroke, Shakespeare further used the power of his language to illuminate their characters. Bolingbroke's speeches are brisk and unornate. For him, language is a tool for getting things done; he wastes no words. Richard, by contrast, is a man entirely of poetry. At first, when his power is unquestioned, the beauty of his language is two-dimensional, as if drawn from literature rather than life. But as things start to go wrong and his inward collapse begins, he turns more and more to lyrical fantasy, as if he were wandering in the garden of his own imagination, a place where no other person has ever followed him and which has always been more real to him than reality. The steepness of his decline is matched by an upward soaring of imagery: the more he suffers, the more finely he expresses his dilemmas and his pain.

With all dramatic weight heaped on the two main characters, the other participants have shorter shrift. A few high-ranking lords (Gaunt, York, Aumerle) have meaty roles, articulating the play's politics as the main characters articulate its underlying theme. The women, notably Richard's pathetic, put-upon Queen, are given powerful cameo scenes. But the other grandees are ciphers, chiefly there to point a moral or swell a scene. In modern productions, their parts are often doubled or trebled, to attract actors of the calibre the language demands: a typical combination is Mowbray (Bolingbroke's whimsical, valiant opponent in the joust who vanishes after Act One) and Carlisle (who has, after Richard, some of the play's most exquisite poetry).

In a drama so concerned with high politics that most walk-on roles are for lords and knights, there is little scope for the 'common-people' scenes of which Shakespeare was such a master – perhaps another reason why *Richard II* can give such an otherworldly, remote impression. However, Shakespeare does give commoners pride of place in two scenes, each crucial to the action. In Act Three, gardeners discuss the state of the country by drawing metaphors from their profession: an interlude in the more sonorous rhetoric as refreshing as a shower in summer. In Act Five, just before Exton and his soldiers burst in to murder Richard, the dungeon-keeper brings food. Richard beats the man for refusing to taste it (the first time this has happened), and then Exton and his soldiers enter with axes. In a Greek tragedy, the King's death would have happened offstage and been reported by a messenger. Shakespeare sets it before our eyes, in fewer than a dozen lines, and uses the Keeper's defection – Exton has forbidden him to taste the food, and he obeys the upstart instead of his true master – to show the absolute aloneness of the King's position. In a context in which Richard has already compared himself to the deserted Christ, this is a powerful moment – and it is made even more so, in a way characteristic of Shakespeare's dramatic skill throughout this play, by being shown and not described.

☞ In performance

On 8 February 1601, Shakespeare's actors performed *The Play of Deposing Richard II* for a private party of aristocrats – and the following day the same lords supported the Earl of Essex in his attempt to depose Queen Elizabeth and many paid with their heads. (The Queen famously identified herself with Richard.) The incident raises questions about why Shakespeare's actors accepted such a risky engagement in the first place, why they were spared, and what Shakespeare's own political sympathies may have been. The second recorded performance of the play is, in its way, equally extraordinary: by the officers of a Royal Navy ship off Sierra Leone in 1607.

For the next two hundred years *Richard II* was treated less as drama than spectacle, the joust and Parliament scenes in particular sending designers and managers well over the top. (One 1850s production used fifty horses.) In the twentieth century the original text was restored, and due attention was given to the poetry. Notable Richards included John Gielgud, Alec Guinness, Ian Richardson and Richard Pasco (who alternated Richard and Bolingbroke on successive nights). The 1995 Royal National Theatre production, starring Fiona Shaw as Richard, stirred sexual ambiguity into the King's relationship with Bolingbroke (David Threlfall), a startling effect.

> RICHARD
> Not all the water in the rough rude sea
> Can wash the balm from an anointed king. [III, ii]

Richard III

🕮 Sources

Thomas More, *History of King Richard III*, quoted in Richard Hall, *The Union of the Two Noble and Illustrious Families of Lancaster and York*. Raphael Holinshed, *Chronicles*.

🕮 Story of the play

Richard Duke of Gloucester is determined to become king. He has already personally murdered Henry VI and Henry's son Edward. Now he woos Edward's widow Anne (during Edward's funeral procesion) and tells his own elder brother, King Edward IV, that their other brother Clarence is plotting against him. Clarence is imprisoned in the Tower of London, and Richard sends murderers who stab him and drown him in a barrel of wine. He tells the sick Edward of Clarence's death, and Edward dies of guilt. (In fact he had pardoned Clarence, but Richard had held back the pardon until after Clarence's murder.)

Edward's death means that two children are next in line to the throne: his sons Edward Prince of Wales and Richard Duke of York. Their uncle Richard welcomes them to London for the coronation, houses them in the Tower – and arranges for his henchman Buckingham to spread the rumour that they, and their father Edward before them, were illegitimate. The Lord Mayor of London offers him the crown in their place, and he accepts with a show of reluctance. The royal women Queen Anne, Queen Elizabeth (the widow of the dead King Edward) and Queen Margaret (the widow of Henry VI), curse Richard comprehensively, but are unable to stop his progress towards royal legitimacy. He arranges for Sir James Tyrell to murder the princes in the Tower and makes plans to poison Queen Anne and instead marry Princess Elizabeth, daughter of his dead brother King Edward.

Amid the hurly-burly of plotting and assassination, Buckingham asks for the Dukedom promised him as a reward for helping Richard to the throne, and Richard refuses. Buckingham starts a revolt against him, and it is joined by the Earl of Richmond, newly returned from France. The rebels meet Richard's army at the battle of Bosworth. The night before, Richard has dreamed of the ghosts of all the people he has murdered; Richmond's dreams have all been of victory. During the battle Richard's men desert him. Richmond kills him, takes power as King Henry VII and announces that he will end civil unrest in England by marrying Princess Elizabeth.

☞ Characters

King Edward IV
Richard of Gloucester, *his brother,* *later* Richard III
George Duke of Clarence, *their brother*
Duchess of York, *their mother*
Elizabeth, *queen of Edward IV*
Woodville, Rivers, *her brothers*
Dorset, Grey, *her sons*
Lady Anne
Margaret, *widow of Henry VI*
Earl of Richmond, *later Henry VII*
Archbishops of Canterbury, York
Bishop of Ely
Dukes of Buckingham, Norfolk
Earls of Derby, Oxford, Surrey
Lords Hastings, Lovel
Sir James Blount, Sir Robert Brakenbury, Sir William

Brandon, Sir William
Catesby, Sir Walter Herbert, Sir Richard Ratcliff, Sir James Tyrell, Sir Thomas Vaughan, *knights*
Edward, Richard, *the Princes in the Tower*
Edward, Margaret, *Clarence's children*
Attendants (*including* Berkeley, Tressel), Aldermen, Bishops, Citizens, Gentlemen, Ghosts, Keeper of the Tower of London, Lord Mayor of London, Lords, Messengers, Murderers, Page, Priest (Christopher Urswick), Pursuivant (Messenger), Scrivener, Sheriff of Wiltshire, Soldiers

RICHARD Richard is presented as monstrous, satanic and unnatural, the terrifying wild boar of Lord Stanley's dream. His brilliant and irresistible theatricality is the posturing of power. He knows how wicked his deeds are, but does them anyway. Save that he is less profoundly engaged with evil, and far less racked by conscience, he is a prototype Macbeth.

Richard's opening monologue, the prologue to the entire action, superbly establishes the three cardinal points we need so that we can savour the play to come: Richard's complicity with the audience, his gloating relish for evil-doing and his attitude to his own deformity, the hunchback which is a metaphor for his moral disablement. 'I am not shaped for sportive tricks / Nor made to court an amorous looking-glass ... / ... I, in this weak piping time of peace / Have no delight to pass away the time / Unless to spy my shadow in the sun / And descant on mine own deformity. / And therefore, since I cannot prove a lover ... / I am determined to prove a villain.'

From that moment on, we are disappointed neither in what Richard does nor in the way he 'frames' each event for us, announcing it in advance, commenting while it happens and reflecting on its success. He moves straight from the first speech to seduce a grieving widow during her husband's funeral. He murders anyone in his way to power: not merely strangers, but his brother, his wife, his nephews – blood relatives have seldom been so aptly named. He tricks, lies, boasts, jeers and laughs, delighting in his malignancy and making us the mirror of his vanity.

And then, spectacularly, he falls. Richmond returns from France and takes the initiative, and the hunchback metaphor once again becomes meaningful: only Richard's mind can soar, since he is hobbled by the physical. He fights bravely but unsuccessfully. As he loses his supporters, so he loses his self-possession, to the point where he cannot sleep and sees nightmare visions. On the field of Bosworth he is totally isolated, unhorsed and trapped. After a final despairing cry ('A horse, a horse!') he is stripped even of the capacity for speech which has served so well throughout his murderous career: his duel with Richmond and his death take place in dumb-show. His entire life has been like the performance of a trapeze artist without a safety-net, a gamble with Fate, and when he loses the effect is of grim, ironical catharsis. His death is as much a performance as everything he did in life.

BUCKINGHAM Buckingham begins as the straight man in a devilish double-act with Richard. Richard uses him as go-between with the citizens of London, and needs him to ensure that the young princes are discredited and the crown is offered, as planned, to Richard. He helps Richard to plot the downfall of Hastings. In all of this, he thinks he is Richard's equal for deviousness and astuteness, and we are persistently, ironically shown how in fact he is a dupe and a fool. The dialogue which opens Act Three, Scene Five is absolutely typical: *Richard*: 'Come, cousin, canst thou quake and change thy colour / Murder thy breath in middle of a word / And then begin, and stop again / As if thou were distraught and mad with terror?' *Buckingham*: 'Tut, I can counterfeit the deep tragedian / Speak, and look back, and pry on every side, / Tremble and start at wagging of a straw / Intending deep suspicion.' When Sir Toby nerves Sir Andrew to fight Viola/Cesario in *Twelfth Night*, Sir Andrew boasts in an almost identical fashion – and is a character of equally few brains.

Typically, Shakespeare sets up this characterization in our minds only to turn it inside-out, giving Buckingham unexpected moral scruples and making them the hinge of the action. Richard tries to co-opt Buckingham in the murder of the Princes in the Tower, Buckingham refuses, Richard punishes him by withholding the promised Earldom of Hereford, and Buckingham turns against him and raises the revolt which triggers Richmond's return to England and the collapse of Richard's reign. But Buckingham himself never lives to see that collapse. He is arrested and executed on All Soul's Day, and the soliloquy of remorse Shakespeare gives him, a chance to achieve final moral dignity, is undercut by being as platitudinous as everything else he says throughout the play. For all his presence in great events, to the end he remains one of the most magnificently futile people Shakespeare ever created. (*Buckingham*: 'This is All-Souls' Day, fellow, is it not?' *Sheriff*: 'It is.' *Buckingham*: 'Why then, All-Souls' Day is my body's doomsday. / This is the day which, in King Edward's time / I wished might fall on me when I was found / False to his children and his wife's allies. / This is the day wherein I wished to fall / By the false faith of him whom most I trusted. / This, this All-

Souls' Day to my fearful soul / Is the determined respite of my wrongs . . .')

EDWARD AND RICHARD (the Princes in the Tower) – Edward Prince of Wales is a young teenager – in history he was thirteen – and his brother Richard is half a dozen years younger. When they arrive in London for Edward's coronation, prince Richard plays prettily with his uncle Richard's dagger and sword, and then asks, 'because I am little, like an ape', if he can ride piggy-back on Richard's shoulder; Edward, by contrast, asks pointedly why there are not 'more uncles here to welcome me'. When the children are taken to the Tower, Edward counters his younger brother's only-too-accurate foreboding ('I shall not sleep in quiet at the Tower') with equal sharpness, telling him he should be afraid of living uncles, not dead ones. The boys' second appearance is as ghosts, haunting Richard on the night before Bosworth.

MARGARET, ELIZABETH AND ANNE *Richard III* is hardly crammed with female roles, but Shakespeare makes up for it with these three powerful cameos: Margaret, widow of Henry VI, Elizabeth, widow of Edward IV and Lady Anne, widow of the Edward Prince of Wales whom Richard murdered in *Henry VI, Part III*. All three have good reason to hate Richard, and denounce him both individually and in a scene of antiphonal rage and grief as powerful as the set-pieces for avenging Furies in ancient tragedy.

About the play

Richard III is the first of Shakespeare's plays to strike the authentic tragic note. Its atmosphere has the grandeur of myth: primitive, massive, like Greek tragedy. It also brings Shakespeare's Wars of the Roses tetralogy to a triumphant, trumpets-blaring conclusion in which the arrival of the Tudor dynasty (in the shape of the Earl of Richmond) ends decades of bloody chaos in English politics and stabilizes the throne. As such, the play marks the beginning of Shakespeare's mythologizing of the modernization of England.

'Mythologizing' is a key word here. Shakespeare's propagandist scenario, reflecting the bias of his sources, requires that if the Tudors are to seem all-good, Richard himself must be presented as all-bad and his reign a procession of tyranny and disaster. Shakespeare succeeds so well at this that people have argued with his approach as if it were 'true' history. The real Richard is now thought to have committed none of the murders Shakespeare attributed to him, to have ruled wisely, not even to have been humpbacked – but where is the play in that? Shakespeare's decisions about Richard were not historical but dramatic. As a dramatic character, Richard suddenly begins to leap from the surrounding throng in *Henry VI, Part II*, acquires his saturnine menace, hypnotic sexuality and ironical stance to the audience in *Henry VI, Part III* and reaches apotheosis in this play, its author's first calculated masterpiece.

Liberating Richard from historical accuracy creates him. The play's effectiveness would be undiminished, perhaps even enhanced, if all the characters had neutral names, peripheral to English history – as happens in *Lear* or *Cymbeline*. Because the *Henry VI* cycle is still shackled to reality, the plays offer a plethora of barely distinguishable schemers, motives, events and come-uppances. By focusing *Richard III* on the political and psychological 'journey' of a single character, Shakespeare trims away all such undergrowth: the cast of *Richard III* is as large as that of *Henry VI, Part III*, but it is always perfectly clear who everyone is and who is doing what to whom. This is partly because Shakespeare also treats Richard as a kind of Chorus or master-of-ceremonies, constantly allowing him to make us complicit in his plans, to 'work' us as a comedian 'works' the house or confidence-tricksters 'work' their dupes. His soliloquies, oozing with relish and ironical self-satisfaction, frame the action and are the play's enduring glory.

In writing the part, Shakespeare drew on one of the most popular traditions of earlier drama: the character 'Vice' in the old morality plays. Vice, embodying all the evils which afflict the human race, was presented as a kind of malign master-of-ceremonies, a deformed jester like the demons in Bosch's paintings of Hell. Vice was the turn everyone waited to see, and in surviving scripts he has all the best lines. Shakespeare's inspiration was to give this interesting but two-dimensional figure not the preachiness of morality plays but the deviousness and cut-and-thrust of political intrigue, and to enrich the character with human feelings and reactions. The unexpected collision of two theatrical genres, morality and history-play, allowed him to spring all kinds of surprises. History, in short, turns into drama before our eyes.

☞ *In performance*

From its first performances on, *Richard III* has been a crowd-puller, Richard's wit and his spectacular downfall guaranteeing popularity. For over 150 years the play was known not in Shakespeare's text, but in a version written in 1700 by Colley Cibber which cut the original by half, added new material by Cibber himself (including the line 'Off with his head – so much for Buckingham', still sometimes interpolated in Shakespeare's own text), and used speeches and songs from other Shakespeare plays. Even after Shakespeare's text was restored to the stage (by Samuel Phelps in 1845), it was half a century before it finally triumphed over Cibber.

Beginning with Richard Burbage in the original production, Richard has been played by almost every leading actor of note. Famous for melodramatic intensity were Edmund Kean, Edwin Booth and Henry Irving in the nineteenth century and Donald Wolfit, Laurence Olivier and Anthony Sher in the twentieth. Psychologically more complex Richards were created by David Garrick in the eighteenth century, William Macready in the nineteenth and John Barrymore, Alec Guinness and Ian McKellen in the twentieth. In 1913, *Richard III* was one of the first Shakespeare plays ever filmed, the actor Frederick Warde claiming that he had to 'suppress all sense of the ridiculous' to undertake the project. Laurence Olivier directed himself on film in 1955, and Ian McKellen starred in a chilling film version, updated to a modern fascist state, in 1996.

Romeo and Juliet

☞ Sources

Arthur Brooke, *The Tragical History of Romeus and Juliet* (1562). The story came to England from Italy via France, and was popular: apart from Brooke's poem, several plays, masques and other retellings were in circulation in Shakespeare's youth.

☞ Story of the play

There is a feud between two of the most powerful aristocratic families in Verona, the Montagues and the Capulets. The Prince of Verona orders it to stop, and Old Capulet, to show his good faith, agrees that his daughter Juliet can marry the prince's nephew Paris, and arranges a masked ball to celebrate the engagement. Romeo Montague and his friends (including the witty Mercutio), go to the ball, where Romeo and Juliet fall in love. They meet that night, and arrange that next morning when Juliet goes to confession her priest Friar Lawrence will marry them; he and Juliet's nurse will act as witnesses.

The wedding takes place, but any further plans are prevented by an upsurge of violence between the two families. Mercutio fights Tybalt, Juliet's fiery cousin and 'prince of duellists', who kills him. Romeo kills Tybalt, and the Prince punishes him by exiling him from Verona. Capulet tells Juliet that her marriage with Paris must go ahead as soon as possible. She asks Friar Lawrence's help, and he advises her to pretend to agree to the wedding, but to take a sleeping-draught which will make her seem dead for forty-eight hours. She will be laid to rest in the family vault, and Romeo can come secretly and steal her away from there.

The plan works well, except that Friar Lawrence's message to Romeo, explaining the situation, is not delivered, and Romeo hears instead that Juliet is dead. He goes secretly to the vault. He is grieving over the body when Paris arrives with flowers; they fight and Romeo kills Paris. After another outburst of grief over Juliet, he takes poison and dies. Juliet recovers consciousness, finds Romeo's body and stabs herself. Friar Lawrence explains the whole mess to the heads of the Montague and Capulet families, and the Prince insists that from now on they end their feud.

 ## Characters

Chorus	Tybalt, *her cousin*
Escalus, *Prince of Verona*	Juliet's Nurse
Mercutio, Paris, *his kinsmen*	Friar Lawrence, Friar John
Old Montague, *Romeo's father*	Abram, Balthasar, Gregory,
Lady Montague	Peter, Potpan, Sampson,
Romeo	*servants*
Benvolio, *his cousin*	Apothecary, Attendants,
Old Capulet, *Juliet's father*	Citizens, Guards, Guests,
Lady Capulet	Horatio, Musicians, Officer,
Juliet	Pages, Petruchio, Watchmen

ROMEO At the start Romeo is characterized as one of the leaders of a group of overbred young men with too much time on their hands and under-occupied brains. When he talks to Benvolio of the love he feels for Rosaline, it is more like under-graduate showing-off than true feeling: 'Love is a smoke raised with the fume of sighs; / Being purged, a fire sparkling in lovers' eyes; / Being vexed, a sea nourished with lovers' tears. / What is it else? A madness most discreet . . .' and so on). He decides to go to the Capulets' masked ball out of pure bravado, the threat of discovery adding spice to what is little more than a student prank.

As soon as Romeo meets Juliet, however, he changes. Instead of merely phrase-making about love, he begins to devote his whole being and his intelligence to it and to its object, Juliet. This is a tragic fixation – and his tragedy is that he is not, in fact, the innocent adolescent he would like to be. He is old enough to have finished university education, has some understanding of the world and makes each choice of action knowing that there will be consequences. Like Richard in *Richard II*, he is a victim assenting in his own delirious fall – and this turns the melodrama of the original tale to tragedy.

JULIET Like Romeo, Juliet utterly changes as soon as they meet and fall in love. Until then, she is spoiled, spirited and bored: when she grows up, one imagines her becoming a version of her mother. But love suddenly projects her into adulthood, and at the same time fills her with a tremulous rapture which reveals the essential innocence of her character: 'O gentle Romeo / If thou dost love pronounce it faithfully / Or if thou thinkst I am too quickly won / I'll frown and be perverse and say thee nay / So thou wilt woo . . .'

In the scene in Juliet's room, before she goes to the tomb (Act Four Scene Three), Shakespeare marvellously exploits the way youth, innocence and new-found maturity coexist in her. She is suddenly brought up against the possibility of death, in all its grimness, and her determination to go forward with her plan nevertheless is balanced by simple, childish terror: 'I have a faint cold fear thrills through my veins / That almost freezes up the heat of life. / I'll call them back again to comfort me. / Nurse! What should she do here? / My dismal scene I needs must act alone. / Come, vial . . .'

FRIAR LAWRENCE Lawrence is one of the play's most equivocal characters. Viewed in one light, he is a dangerous meddler. It is thanks to his advice, his actions, and his bumbling, however well-meant, that disaster happens. Shakespeare allows him no morality whatever, apart from that implied by his position as a churchman, and he shows awareness of the meaning of his actions only after the lovers are discovered dead.

On the other hand, from his first entrance onwards ('The grey-eyed morning smiles on the frowning night . . .'), Lawrence is the character most in touch with Nature and the natural world. He is humane, knowledgeable and gentle, Romeo's surrogate father (as the Nurse is Juliet's surrogate mother). Everyone treats him with affection and respect – and in this light, when he realizes and proclaims his guilt in the play's final scene, he shares in the lovers' tragedy, and thus the defeat of true love by circumstances is also the destruction of Nature by man-made convention.

NURSE The Nurse is sometimes played as a foolish, earthy old woman, a kind of attractive but addle-pated bawd. This is quite possibly false to Shakespeare. She was Juliet's wetnurse only eleven years before the play opens, and therefore (since wetnurses were often recruited in their teens) need be no older than her thirties. She may be self-important, but she has genuine high status, as one of the Capulets' most senior and trusted servants.

Furthermore, for three-quarters of the play the Nurse provides the warmth, human affection and dignity which the play's quarrelsome upper-class characters lack. In particular, her former role as Juliet's wetnurse makes her, in a sense, the girl's 'true' mother, and she is largely responsible for the feeling that the family environment which Juliet surrenders because of her love for Romeo is warm and close. The comic relief she provides, her earthiness puncturing the passion and rhetoric of the upper-class characters, masks the fact that she is not peripheral to the play's meaning but essential.

OLD CAPULET To outsiders such as the Montagues and their supporters (and to some extent, Prince Escalus), Juliet's father seems little more than a headstrong old fool, whose intransigent pride and persistent short fuse are two of the main reasons for the feud continuing. His own family treat him with more tolerance. He is a beloved husband (a generation or more older than his wife: their loving relationship is a small matter in the play, but interesting) and a stern but affectionate father. At the end he is so overwhelmed by grief that he can barely speak.

MERCUTIO Mercutio (named after the volatile element mercury) is Romeo's friend and belongs entirely to the world he lived in before he met Juliet: witty, bawdy, fanciful, bored and dangerous. When Romeo talks of Rosaline at the start of the play, he confects a kind of abstract, brilliant-student's list of all the attributes of love. Mercutio's talk, by contrast, is bluntly bawdy: chided by Benvolio for using Rosaline's name to 'conjure' the absent Romeo as if he were a supernatural spirit, because it might anger him, he says 'This cannot anger him. 'Twould anger him / To raise a spirit in his mistress' circle / Of some strange nature, letting it there stand / Till she had laid it and conjured it down . . . / My invocation / Is fair and honest: in his mistress' name / I conjure only but to raise him up'.

Although Mercutio is the cleverest person in the play, he is also prickly and quarrelsome – qualities which are the death of him when he insists on duelling with Tybalt. He speaks one of the best-loved speeches in all Shakespeare, a dazzling fantasy, as insubstantial as if spun from air itself, describing Queen Mab who steals magically into people's minds in dreams: 'She is the fairies' midwife, and she comes / In shape no bigger than an agate-stone / On the forefinger of an alderman . . .'

TYBALT Capulet's nephew, in Mercutio's words 'the prince of cats', is easily provoked and dangerous. He is a master-duellist, and his barely controlled ferocity is one ingredient in the lethal cocktail of overbreeding, boredom and arrogance which poisons all the young people in the play.

About the play

The underlying subject of *Romeo and Juliet* is the clash between idealism and the real world. The action sets the jewel of romantic young love in the mud of a bustling, realistically drawn society, and, with tragic inevitability, shows it being swamped. The play's social world sometimes takes second place to the lyricism and magnetism of the central pair, but it is vital to Shakespeare's purpose.

The play shows more working people than any other single work of Shakespeare: illiterate Peter, the tough lads Samson and Gregory, Antony, Abram, Potpan, Balthasar and others, the musicians who lose their fees when the wedding feast is called off, the apothecary who sells Romeo poison because his poverty leaves him no alternative, and above all Juliet's Nurse, abused and loved in equal measure, and given, in her discovery of the 'dead' Juliet, one of the most heartbreaking moments in the action.

These vividly drawn characters strikingly contrast with the powerful but shadowy aristocratic elders. These people are sophisticated and dignified, but – apart from one scene exploring Lady Capulet's relationship with her daughter – ineffectual and remote from their children. Friar Lawrence, Juliet's alternative father (as the Nurse is her alternative mother), is fundamentally unpractical and his well-meaning interventions lead only to catastrophe.

The young people are witty, volatile, out of control and doomed. Tybalt, Mercutio and Paris are typical, duelling and dying on the turn of a word or the fall of a handkerchief. Their posturing is seductive – but part of its fascination is its very tragic intensity, the fact that it is hollow and on the edge of the grave. Only the peacable Benvolio survives – and the irony is that it is his Act One advice, that Romeo should cure his lovesickness for Rosaline by finding another woman, which sets the tragic mechanism in action.

Shakespeare shows this bustle of characters in brisk, clear strokes: the language is fast and the character-drawing simple. By contrast, when we enter the lovers' presence time seems to hold its breath. The linguistic pace slows down, words and images become engorged and glorious, the very air seems to belong to paradise. In some hands – Pre-Raphaelite painters come to mind – all this might lead to sentimentality, the lovers as unreal as their own heady fantasies. Shakespeare avoids this by giving attention to practical details – masks, balconies, duels, poison-flasks, daggers and tombs – and by accentuating the lovers' reality, telling us far more about them than merely that they are young, beautiful and in ecstasy. Romeo's love steals all the frivolity out of him. At the start, he is as frivolous as Mercutio; as the action proceeds he learns intellectual and emotional self-possession; by his death he has reached true maturity. He is 'wedded to calamity', but his defiance of fate is heroic. Juliet, similarly, is not merely moonstruck, but a bright, sparky girl forced to confront the adult mysteries of love, sexuality and ultimately death when she has hardly left her wet-nurse. Potential is all she has, and it is nullified before our eyes.

In a later play, Shakespeare might have used his technique of short-cutting to trim and speed the action, varying the pace between different groups and characters. As it is, he lets the main action unroll steadily and magisterially, and the effect is to suffuse the whole play with lyricism, to let the ecstasy of the lovers' language irradiate the other characters as their affair changes the whole tenor of Veronese society.

In performance

Of the countless productions of this play, only a few made their impression because of the male stars: Charles Kemble played Romeo in the 1810s, and Mercutio a dozen years later; Laurence Olivier and John Gielgud played the two roles on alternate nights in the 1930s; Mark Rylance and Kenneth Branagh were outstanding Romeos in more reent times. The role of Juliet, by contrast, has been played by some of the most luminous stars in English-speaking theatre: they include Fanny Kemble, Helen Faucit, Adelaide Neilson, Ellen Terry, Mrs Patrick Campbell, Peggy Ashcroft (for many critics, the 'definitive' Juliet), Dorothy Tutin and Judi Dench.

The play has been regularly subject to adaptation and experiment: the range is from Thomas Otway's 1679 resiting in ancient Rome to Baz Luhrmann's 1997 film version, set in a drug-soaked contemporary US city and with a blaring heavy-metal music score. The lyricism has inspired many composers; results include Bellini's opera *The Capulets and the Montagues*, Berlioz's 'dramatic symphony' *Romeo and Juliet*, Tchaikovsky's 'symphonic fantasy' *Romeo and Juliet*, Prokofiev's ballet *Romeo and Juliet* and Bernstein's musical *West Side Story*.

ROMEO

>It was the lark, the herald of the morn
>No nightingale. Look, love, what envious streaks
>Do lace the severing clouds in yonder east.
>Night's candles are burnt out and jocund day
>Stands tiptoe on the misty mountaintops. [III, v]

The Taming of the Shrew

☞ Sources

Shakespeare took the Lucentio/Bianca sub-plot from Ariosto's comedy *The Counterfeits*. He invented the induction and main plot himself, drawing on folk tales and ballads now lost to us. There are similarities between the play and the anonymous *The Taming of a Shrew*, published in 1594; scholars think that *A Shrew* is not the original of Shakespeare's play but a version of it pieced together for publication from actors' (mis)remembrances.

☞ Story of the play

In the Induction, the drunken tinker Christopher Sly is persuaded that he is a lord and agrees to watch players performing a 'pleasant comedy'.

Old Baptista says that until his shrewish daughter Kate is off his hands, his beautiful daughter Bianca will never marry. This disconcerts Bianca's three suitors, Gremio and Hortensio and young, handsome Lucentio. Gremio and Hortensio bet with a visitor from Verona, Petruchio, that he will never woo and marry Kate. A plot is hatched and Baptista's house soon contains a fake music-master (Hortensio), a Latin teacher who knows little Latin (Lucentio) and a pretend Lucentio (Lucentio's servant Tranio, dressed in his master's clothes and wooing Bianca on Lucentio's behalf).

Petruchio ignores Kate's objections to marriage, constantly doing the opposite of what she expects. Instead of arriving at church in finery, he comes in rags. Scorning the wedding feast, he carries her off to Verona, starving and furious. He refuses to let her eat a banquet (on the grounds that the food is unworthy), rejects fine clothes for her (because honest, everyday clothes suit her better), bullies the servants till she begs him to be kinder, and brainwashes her into agreeing with anything he says (for example that the Sun is the Moon, or that a man they meet on the road is a woman).

Kate and Petruchio return to Baptista, who has agreed that 'Lucentio' (the disguised Tranio) should marry Bianca, so long as he can prove his father's intention to leave him his money. Tranio persuades a visitor to pretend to be Lucentio's father, and when his real father arrives, mayhem ensues. Lucentio marries Bianca in secret, while Hortensio, in disappointment, has married a rich widow. Lucentio, Petruchio and Hortensio argue about whose wife is more obedient – and Kate demonstrates her obedience by coming when called, and praises the duty women owe their husbands.

☞ Characters

IN THE INDUCTION
Christopher Sly, *a tinker*;
  Hostess, Huntsmen, Lord,
  Page, Players, Servants

IN THE PLAY
Baptista
Bianca and Katharina (Kate),
  his daughters
Vincentio, *an old gentleman*

Lucentio, *his son, in love with*
  Bianca
Gremio and Hortensio, *Bianca's*
  suitors
Petruchio, *Katharina's suitor*
Biondello, Curtis, Grumio,
  Tranio, *servants*
Haberdasher, Pedant, Servants,
  Tailor, Widow

PETRUCHIO Petruchio is desperate to marry money. To get it he becomes a peacetime version of the braggart soldier beloved of farce, swaggering, bullying, making monstrous and provocative remarks. Everything he does is against expectation. He woos Baptista's 'wrong' daughter – to win a bet. He mocks the wedding by dressing in rags and refusing to feast or dance. He claims that his wife is tender and gracious when her behaviour declares the opposite. Saying that he loves her, he illtreats her unmercifully; calling her his soul, his 'better part', he still treats her like an object and not a person.

The main point of all this is entertainment, a contest of outrageousness between Petruchio and Kate. They are like two children seeing who can be naughtier – and Petruchio wins easily.

But the play is not about the breaking of Kate's spirit, and he is not just her 'tamer': her complicity in what happens is essential. Petruchio's behaviour is like a mirror, showing her two conflicting images. His actions are as boorish and intolerable as she was when the play began. But his words are often gentle and loving – an alternative way to deal with people, and one which she devastatingly adopts in the final scene.

In the double act between Kate and Petruchio, he plays an ironical role throughout, constantly switching from bully to wooer and back again, and waiting till the final act before stripping off the mask and showing true feeling (by kissing her). The irony between the part he plays and his true nature is central to the play. *The Taming of the Shrew* is not about individuals, but about the way a relationship develops from war to love. However knock-about Kate and Petruchio's relationship may seem on the surface, she is 'taming' him just as he is 'taming' her, and the union which begins as a conjunction of opposites ends as a harmonious, love-driven partnership of equals.

KATE At the start of the play, Kate is a standard farce virago, bullying her father and sister, shouting at servants, using physical violence on would-be suitors. The part is funny but shallow, and the reasons for her behaviour are never explored. She is strong-willed, funny and sparky – but why do these qualities come out as shrewishness? Is she the man-hater some productions make her, a self-tormentor or simply driven to distraction by the fools all round her?

As Kate is subjected to Petruchio's 'taming', she appears to change entirely, from loud to soft, from harsh to gentle, from hatred of the world and its ways to love. And once again, we wonder why. Petruchio's impersonation of tyranny has a declared objective. But the reasons the play offers for Kate's submission are physical, not emotional. His behaviour leaves her exhausted and hungry, and the only way to get what she wants is to agree with everything he says. Does this mean that she, too, is playing games?

Several Shakespeare comedies show couples, apparently incompatible, who begin by fighting but finally reveal the love we saw they had for each other from the start. *The Taming of the Shrew* shows the farce equivalent of such a relationship. The last scene, and Kate's speech of submission in it, bring the whole matter to a head. No hint of collusion between her and Petruchio, no ironical common stand against the zanies who surround them, is visible on the page. But given what we have seen of them so far, and the way their relationship has changed and deepened, it is hard to believe that Shakespeare's ending is as simple as it seems.

BAPTISTA, BIANCA, GREMIO AND HORTENSIO In the original cast-list, Gremio is called 'pantaloon', the capering fool from *commedia dell'arte*. This description has encouraged hundreds of productions in *commedia* style, setting Kate and Petruchio in the midst of a slapstick, carnival whirl in which Baptista is a stock dodderer, Hortensio an amorous fop, Bianca a simpering young girl and so on. Italian *commedia* companies toured England in the 1580s, and may have performed in lordly households exactly as the Players of the Induction here perform for Sly. But there is no real evidence that *The Taming of the Shrew* was intended as *commedia*.

TRANIO A witty, upwardly-mobile servant, Tranio is given a heaven-sent opportunity to fulfil his ambitions when he disguises himself as Lucentio to woo Bianca: he becomes his own master.

☞ *About the play*

Superficially, *The Taming of the Shrew* seems no more than the 'Christmas gambol or tumbling-trick' Sly takes it to be, the kind of farce any competent dramatist could knock up in a week or so. But the Induction establishes a framework of identity-questioning, metamorphosis and masquerade which crucially changes the meaning of everything that follows. When the beggar Sly becomes a lord – simply because he is persuaded that he *is* one, persuaded that white is black – and the pageboy is made his lady, appearance becomes reality, metamorphosis rules and the world is turned upside down before our eyes.

This theme is worked out in the main play not only when some of the farce-characters assume fictional identities (Latin teacher, music master), but also in the central relationship. Neither Petruchio nor Kate are ever, entirely, what they seem. Petruchio, playing an arrogant bully, is actually desperate (for cash, and then for Kate) and vulnerable. He is high-spirited, quick-witted, audacious – and depressive. A professed anti-romanticist, he falls in love. For her part, Kate at first behaves like a man in woman's clothes (a gift to the boy player), tormenting Bianca, cheeking her father, battering her tutors – and then, after giving Petruchio as good as she gets in invective and slapstick violence, discovers the femininity in herself and uses it, clinchingly, to conclude the action.

Throughout their relationship, Kate and Petruchio are a kind of rough-house Beatrice and Benedick, and the play is concerned not just with the roles they play to one another but with the reasons for those roles. They try constantly to confuse each other, and their methods are reminiscent less of love-play than brain-washing, a comical dehumanization by physical torture. They rely on confusion, illogicality and discomfort to produce disorienta-tion. At the wedding, Petruchio behaves as unlike a groom as possible; Kate then reverses expectation even more spectacularly by behaving *exactly* like the stereotype of a true and loving wife. Her final speech wins them not only the relationship they have been working for, but also a substantial bet. We know that what began as a marriage of convenience has turned into a love-match, but we can also be sure, because of what we have seen, that these words are by no means likely to be Kate's last in this rela-tionship of equals. The final human truth is that, in a good-spirited and friendly way, individuality can be subordinated to the good of the whole, but only by choice and not by force.

If the basic structure of Shakespeare's plot, and many of its details, belong to farce, the spin he puts on it carries it into differ-ent worlds entirely. For example, the motor of the action is not Petruchio, the man (who would dominate a normal farce), but Kate, the woman. By charging her character with erotic power, Shakespeare points up not only the ambivalences in human nature which are signalled in the Induction (rich includes poor, poor rich, male female and so on), but also the collision, fundamental to all farce, between desire for money and lust for sex. On the surface, knockabout comedy rules, but the complex, intriguing and equivocal characterization which underlies it makes this a subtler and far more more disturbing play.

☞ *In performance*

Although the play was well-liked in Shakespeare's day – popular enough for his successor John Fletcher to write a sequel in 1611, *The Woman's Prize*, or *The Tamer Tamed*, in which Petruchio's second wife treats him exactly as he treats Katharine in Shakespeare's play – it was then supplanted for two hundred years by adaptations, including John Lacy's *Sauny the Scot* (1667) and David Garrick's *Catherine and Petruchio* (1754), each of which retained popularity for over eighty years. Shakespeare's text was retored to the stage in 1844 and has been a favourite ever since. Famous Kates have included Ada Rehan – perhaps the best-remembered Shrew of all – Edith Evans, Peggy Ashcroft, Vanessa Redgrave and Fiona Shaw. Famous Petruchios have included Ralph Richardson, Peter O'Toole and (on television) John Cleese. Alfred Lunt and Lynn Fontanne played Petruchio and Kate as a stormy double-act on stage in the mid-1930s, and two other husband-and-wife teams, Douglas Fairbanks Jr and Mary Pickford and Richard Burton and Elizabeth Taylor, repeated the trick on film. In the nineteenth century Herman Goetz's operatic version held the stage for decades, and a century later Cole Porter's *Kiss Me, Kate* counterpointed offstage and onstage quarrels and 'tamings' to delirious effect.

> PETRUCHIO She shall watch all night
> And if she chance to nod I'll rail and brawl
> And with the clamour keep her still awake.
> This is the way to kill a wife with kindness. [IV, i]

The Tempest

Original.

 Story of the play

Twelve years before the action of the play, Antonio, the wicked brother of Prospero, Duke of Milan, took advantage of his brother's preoccupation with magic arts to organize a coup and exile him from his dukedom. Ever since then, Prospero and his daughter Miranda (an infant at the time of the banishment) have lived on an enchanted island, with no companions but the supernatural spirit Ariel, child of air, and the monster Caliban, earthy child of the witch Sycorax (who ruled until Prospero arrived). Now, as the play begins, Prospero discovers that Antonio is at sea near the island, with his henchmen King Alonso of Naples and Alonso's brother Sebastian. He sends a magic storm which lands them on the island and separates them from their ship and sailors.

Prospero makes Ariel torment the new arrivals, setting them to plot against each other, organizing a banquet which vanishes as soon as they try to eat, disguising himself as a spirit of revenge and telling Alonso that his son Ferdinand has been drowned to punish Alonso's wickedness. Ariel also bemuses Caliban, who has made a plot with Antonio's drunken butler Stephano and Alonso's jester Trinculo to oust Prospero and make Stephano ruler of the island. The three of them stagger about the island in a drunken haze, falling into middens and horseponds and bewailing their lot.

Ferdinand has not drowned, but has been enslaved by Prospero. He is in love with Miranda, and she with him. The sight of their innocent, honest affection moves Prospero to arrange a bethrothal masque of supernatural spirits for them, but he discovers Caliban's conspiracy and breaks it off. The conspirators meantime break into Prospero's cell and try on his clothes, only to be attacked by spirits in the form of guard-dogs. Ariel pleads with Prospero to show mercy to the unhappy mortals, and pity at last thaws Prospero's revengeful heart. He gives up his magic, sets Ariel free, pardons all the visitors, receives back his dukedom and returns to Milan in the new spirit of enlightenment and generosity of spirit which the play's events have wrought in him.

🦪 Characters

Alonso, *King of Naples*
Sebastian, *his brother*
Ferdinand, *his son*
Prospero, *the rightful Duke of Milan*
Miranda, *his daughter*
Antonio, *his brother and usurper*
Gonzalo, *an honest old counsellor*
Caliban, *a savage and deformed slave*

Ariel, *an airy spirit*
Trinculo, *a jester*
Stephano, *a drunken butler*
Adrian (*a lord*), **Boatswain,** **Francisco** (*a lord*), **Gods and Spirits** (*in the Masque*), **Mariners, Shipmaster, Spirits**

PROSPERO One of the play's central preoccupations is Prospero's recognition of fallibility in himself, and thence in all humanity. At the start he is little more than a cold-hearted necromancer. During his years as Duke of Milan he neglected his duties for the study of magic, and was eventually banished for it. Throughout his time on the island, with no human company but that of the growing child Miranda, he has used his 'art' to control everything around him, from the weather to the supernatural spirits Ariel and Caliban. The only thing he has been unable to control is his own human emotion, and as the years have passed he has developed twin obsessions: concern for Miranda's happiness, and hatred of those who dismissed him from Milan. Now Fate simultaneously gives him the opportunity to punish the usurpers and the challenge that Miranda is a grown girl able to make her own decisions about the future. To deal with the situation, he must come to terms with his own nature and the magic powers which have sustained his entire adult life.

At first, Prospero is reluctant to accept the need for change at all. We see him raising a supernatural storm, despotically threatening Ariel and cowing Caliban, enslaving Ferdinand and refusing to admit the possibility that Miranda has grown away from the need for his protection. But gradually the simple force of her love for Ferdinand softens him, and as he comes to accept it, his rage even against Antonio and Alonso diminishes. He begins to pay attention to Ariel's persistent pleas for freedom, and to the paradox that even Ariel, a supernatural spirit, feels pity for the human condition. As this 'sea-change' – something immeasurably slow but irreversible – takes place in him, he is less and less fulfilled by his 'rough magic' (a metaphor, perhaps for the 'divine right' of kings); he finally abandons it entirely and is accepted as the worldly-wise, kindly ruler he has become.

MIRANDA As an infant, Miranda was banished to a remote island. In the ensuing fifteen years she has seen no humans but her father, and no other living being except Caliban. (Ariel is invisible.) It is hardly surprising that when she sees Antonio, Alonso and their courtiers she bursts out 'O brave new world / That hath such people in it!' and is overwhelmed by Ferdinand. Her innocence represents the natural force of love, and when Prospero watches her playing chess with Ferdinand, he is emotionally changed – the process of education completed intellectually by Ariel.

FERDINAND The young prince of Naples is noble, pure and honest. Just as Miranda has grown up to be totally unlike her father, so he is utterly different from Alonso. With Miranda, he represents the innocent goodness of nature: they have no need of the moral healing of Prospero's magic island. He is not changed by Prospero, but (with Miranda and Ariel) is part of the process which changes *him*.

ARIEL Ariel was imprisoned by Sycorax, the witch who ruled the island before Prospero came. Prospero set him free, but then fastened him with new bonds, the prison of gratitude, and although Ariel accepts this cheerfully, his longing is to be entirely free. He is the agent of Prospero's 'rough magic', bringing enchantment to Miranda and Ferdinand, confusion to the villains and slapstick indignity to Caliban, Stephano and Trinculo. But he is not malicious. His mischief is harmless and he is subject to human emotions. He has compassion for his victims, and in the end even Prospero learns from it: *Ariel*: 'Your charm so strongly works 'em / That if you now behold them your affections / Would become tender.' *Prospero*: 'Dost thou think so, spirit?' *Ariel*: 'Mine would, sir, an I were human'. He is, as his name informs us, a being of lightness and insubstantiality, and changes his shape at will, disguising himself as a sea nymph, a will-o'-the-wisp, a goddess. He sings several songs, including 'Where the bee sucks' and 'Full fadom five', and stage-manages the masques and other musical entertainments.

CALIBAN Caliban, the child of a witch and a sea-monster, personifies earthiness as Ariel stands for air. But he is not entirely soulless: for example, even if he can find no words to describe the supernatural music, he is aware that 'the island is full of noises'. Nevertheless, he is predominantly comic, not serious, and whereas Miranda's glimpse of the first new human beings on the island for twelve years fills her with rapturous wonder, his awe is principally for Stephano's drunken pomposity and his store of drink. He plots energetically to make Stephano Miranda's husband and ruler of the island instead of Prospero, and his comeuppance is suitably doleful when the plan fails and the first hangover arrives: 'What a thrice double ass / Was I to take this drunkard for a god / And worship this dull fool'.

ANTONIO Although in the greater scheme of things it may have been right for Antonio to drive Prospero from Milan, his personal motives were envy, ambition and malice. A splendidly two-dimensional villain, he shouts at the Boatswain during the storm as if he is the voice of the weather made flesh ('Hang, cur, hang, you whoreson, insolent noisemaker'), plots to murder the sleeping Alonso and is stopped only by Prospero's magic, and in the end gives way and restores Prospero's dukedom with a very bad grace indeed. He is one of the few people on the island unchanged by its magic, and one imagines that if he goes back to Milan with Prospero, Prospero should mind his back.

STEPHANO Two things persuade Trinculo and Caliban that Stephano will be a better ruler of the island than Prospero: his butler's dignity and his secret hoard of wine, both of which have survived the shipwreck. He spends most of the play gathering the rags of his position about him and making himself a sozzled caricature of regality; lines like 'For my part, the sea cannot drown me. I swam, ere I could recover the shore, five and thirty leagues off and on. By this light, thou shalt be my lieutenant, monster, or my standard' are typical.

TRINCULO Drink makes Caliban pugnacious and Stephano pompous, and it makes Alonso's jester melancholy. He spends the play following his companions through horseponds and middens on their farcical quest to overthrow Prospero and make Stephano king in his place. Even so, and for all his drunken grumbling, enough shreds of sharp-tongued wit remain to remind us of his former profession – 'The folly of this island! They say there's but five upon this isle. We are three of them. If th'other two be brained like us, the state totters.'

☞ *About the play*

The Tempest is often spoken of as the great dramatist's farewell to his art, and Prospero is seen as heavily autobiographical. The notion is romantic, attractive and just about textually justifiable: 'this rough magic / I here abjure'; 'deeper than did ever plummet sound / I'll drown my book'. But Prospero's powers are not simply metaphors for art. His struggle with and final renunciation of his 'art' (magic) is, in part, a political allegory. Society is collapsing and must be reformed; only when just order is restored can he resign his powers.

The Tempest begins with the sinking of the galley of the King of Naples, a ship of state whose internal corruption is embodied both in 'high' figures (Antonio, Sebastian) and 'low' ones (Stephano, Trinculo). The storm separates these characters – and such morally 'good' but impotent ones as Ferdinand, Gonzalo, Francisco and Adrian – from their ship (that is, their state) and throws them into a 'brave new world' where they must reinvent society, and within it, themselves. People react to the island according to their own moral perception. Some see Paradise, others Hell. Antonio and Sebastian operate at their former machiavellian level, plotting in the shadows to bring about Alonso's death. Trinculo and Stephano use the resources they find on the island (a 'magic' store of wine, Caliban's local knowledge) to help preposterous schemes of self-advancement. By contrast, Gonzalo dreams of an ideal society on such an island, a place where 'All things in common Nature should produce . . . / To feed my innocent people.'

Such dreams were not just playwright's fancy. Thirty years before the play was written, the Elizabethans had begun exploring their own 'brave new world': the Americas. Expeditions, like those of Sir Walter Ralegh in the 1580s, had braved the Atlantic – in those days, a journey like our setting out to colonize the Moon – to create communities in the 'new-found land'. Such adventures had philosophical rationale as well as the brute search for gold. Intellectuals claimed that true moral innocence was to be found in places uncorrupted by the lusts and intrigues of 'advanced' human society. The 'new world' was, literally, Utopia, Eden before the Fall, and explorers could learn from it and its people. Two years before *The Tempest*, a boatload of colonists had been shipwrecked on a 'magic' Caribbean island (Bermuda), and found it Paradise. Accounts of this adventure were best-sellers when Shakespeare began his play.

Unlike Bermuda, Shakespeare's island already has a ruler from the 'old world': Prospero himself. He is not an Edenic figure. He governs not by philosophy but by magic, and he is a tyrant who must also undergo a 'sea-change' to a new moral condition. The agent of change is his slave Ariel, the supernatural spirit who makes Alonso, Antonio and Sebastian confront their own sin, uses the lusts of the drunken would-be revolutionaries to lure them into the mud, and forces Prospero himself to confront his tyranny and admit the possibility of mercy.

Set against all the political and philosophical machinations is the radiant love of Alonso's son Ferdinand and Prospero's daughter Miranda. Prospero is at first reluctant to accept it, believing that Ferdinand is still tainted with his father's guilt, the 'beast in man'. But the innocent dignity of the couple's romance – symbolized first by Ferdinand's labours and then by his playing chess with Miranda, their souls in harmony – triggers change in him and, in fairy-tale style, makes a bridge between the warring brothers.

A generation after *The Tempest* was written, England was to prove, with the execution of Charles I, two of Shakespeare's persistent themes: that absolute monarchs do not have magic powers and that moral self-reinvention is all but impossible. But artists exist to show us visions, and it is one of the attractions of *The Tempest* that its landscapes of social, psychological and moral potential are wider than the confines of a single narrow island, however magical.

☞ In performance

Richard Burbage probably played Prospero at the play's first known performance, at court on 1 November 1611, the culmination of a career which had run in tandem with Shakespeare's since he created Richard in *Henry VI* some twenty years before.

In 1667 John Dryden and William Davenant reworked the play as *The Enchanted Island*, a semi-operatic version which held the stage for a century and a half. Spectacle was often lavish: 60 children took part in Garrick's 1756 production, and the stage effects in Kean's 1857 production required no fewer than 140 technicians. The true text was restored to the theatre by Frank Benson in the 1900s, and in the century which followed the play was regularly performed: John Gielgud, for example, the most admired Prospero of the century, played the part in four separate productions.

STEFANO (*Sings*)
    Flout 'em and cout 'em
    And scout 'em and flout 'em
    Thought is free. [III, iii]

Timon of Athens

☞ Sources

An anonymous farce, *Timon*, was circulating at the same time as Shakespeare's play; scholars are unsure whether this used Shakespeare or he used it. The story is touched on in two Greek sources: briefly in Plutarch, *Lives* (which Shakespeare was reading for *Antony and Cleopatra* at the same period), and in Lucian's satire *Timon the Misanthrope*. William Painter also gave a moralistic account of Timon's life in his 1566 short-story collection *Palace of Pleasure*.

☞ Story of the play

Timon is a rich and generous Athenian. His friends, servants and acquaintances have only to ask for money, and he gives it gladly. He holds banquets at which he is surrounded by well-wishers; only the cynical philosopher Apemantus has doubts about the depth of all these people's affection, and Timon's steward Flavius is anxious that Timon's cash reserves are almost gone.

Timon's creditors ask for payment, and he has no money left. One after another, he asks his friends for help, and they refuse. Timon's one loyal friend, Alcibiades, is exiled from Athens for asking the Senate to spare the life of a man who has killed someone in a drunken brawl. Timon invites his fair-weather friends to a last banquet, serves hot water in bowls and throws it at them.

Timon goes to live as a hermit in a cave by the sea. Digging for roots on the shore, he finds hidden treasure. He gives it away: to whores, three bandits who find him as he is digging, to Alcibiades to pay the army he is leading against the Senators of Athens, and the rest to Flavius to reward his loyalty. Apemantus mocks Timon's change of state, and the two have an argument and throw stones at one another.

Time passes. Timon thrashes a poet and painter who try to

flatter him, and rejects the Senators' request to help them against Alcibiades. Alcibiades wins his war against the Senators, but says that he will rule justly, punishing only those who opposed him or showed Timon no mercy. A soldier brings news that Timon is dead and that, to the end, his hatred of the human race was unabated.

🖙 Characters

Timon
Alcibiades, *his true friend*
Ventidius, *his false friend*
Lucius, Lucullus, Sempronius,
 flatterers
Apemantus, *a churlish philosopher*
Phrynia, Timandra, *whores*
Flavius, *Timon's steward*

Amazons, Attendants, Bandits,
 Cupid, Fool, Jeweller, Lords,
 Merchant, Mercer (*fabric-
 merchant*), Old Athenian, Page,
 Painter, Poet, Senators,
 Servants, Soldiers, Three
 Strangers

TIMON Timon, like Lear, has no understanding of love or friendship. He mistakes flatterers for intimates and fails to recognize those who truly care for him. He squanders everything he has on a mirage, and regrets it. In the grand sense, these are tragic flaws and a tragic action from which there can be no recovery.

None the less, as a character Timon lacks a crucial tragic dimension which makes Lear great. We feel sorry for Timon, but his plight never touches our souls as Lear's does. He is not redeemed by his suffering. There are few 'lessons' for human nature or behaviour in what he is or does – or if there are, they are the harsh preaching of a morality play rather than the devastating invitations to reflection which great tragedy can offer.

This iciness in the play may come from the central fact that what Timon squanders is not a living thing but money, soulless and inert. A miser's obsession is pathetic rather than moving because the object of his or her affection is inanimate; Timon, the wastrel, is the mirror image of the miser from the old morality plays, and his 'virtue' is a reflection of the miser's 'vice'.

At times, Timon's language does give him Lear-like grandeur – an example is his savage curse on Athens and the Athenians as he goes into exile: 'O thou wall / That girdlest in these wolves, dive in the earth / And fence not Athens! Matrons, turn incontinent! / Obedience fail in children! Slaves and fools / Pluck the grave, wrinkled senate from the bench / And minister in their steads!' But then, given a second chance at redemption when he finds buried treasure and could learn and grow from what he has suffered, he simply descends even further into the pit of his own disgust, giving the gold to bandits, whores, and finally to his loyal steward Flavius on condition that he hates the world and becomes a second Timon.

At the end of *King Lear*, the king's painfully-acquired new understanding gives his death both tragic resonance and moral dignity. Lacking any similar understanding, Timon simply changes from one kind of allegorical monster (Folly) into another (Hatred). In the end he crawls into a cave and dies – an end whose pointlessness crowns the symphony of discord that has been his entire existence.

APEMANTUS Apemantus belongs to the Cynic school of philosophy. These people held that all the conventional bonds of human society – from personal friendship to the rule of law, from generosity to love – were a hollow sham, and that the only way to cope with life was to be true entirely to oneself. They affected a rude, noisy way of speaking, standing at street-corners and heckling passers-by: hence their name ('cynic', in Greek, means 'dog-like'). In the play, Apemantus begins by denouncing both Timon and the false friends who sponge on him, then drops out of the action until Timon has exiled himself from Athens, when he returns to sneer at him further. Their dialogue in this scene is typical, and it and Apemantus's presence generally go a long way to explaining the bilious impression which the play so often seems to make. (*Timon*: 'I'll beat thee, but I should infect my hands.' *Apemantus*: 'I would my tongue could rot them off.' *Timon*: 'Away, thou issue of a mangy dog ...' *Apemantus*: 'Would thou would burst.' *Timon*: 'Away, thou tedious rogue! I am sorry I shall lose a stone by thee.' (*Throws a stone at him*) *Apemantus*: 'Beast!' *Timon*: 'Slave!' *Apemantus*: 'Toad!')

ALCIBIADES Alcibiades is a military commander and Timon's only true friend. He would have loaned Timon money when he needed it, except that he (Alcibiades) was in exile at the time. He is a warm, impulsive man, loyal to people rather than ideals, and this sets him at odds with the Athenian senate, when he tries to defend before them a friend who has killed a man in a brawl. He responds to exile by marching on Athens, but when he captures it he refuses to harm the ordinary people, merely punishing his own specific enemies. His story parallels Timon's, and his true generosity and forgiving nature make a striking contrast with Timon's blinkered and obsessive view of human relationships.

FLAVIUS Apart from Alcibiades, Timon's steward is the only person to show qualities of true human warmth and sympathy. He is aghast at the way Timon is squandering his wealth, and distressed when things go wrong for him – 'I bleed inwardly for my lord' – but has neither the means nor the rank to offer him assistance. He goes to visit him in exile – 'O you gods / Is yond despis'd and ruinous man my lord?' – and Timon offers him the gold he has just discovered. But Flavius refuses his conditions, that he turn misanthrope and miser, and Timon sends him packing ('If thou hatest / Curses, stay not. Fly, whilst thou are blest and free. / Ne'er see thou man, and let me ne'er see thee.') None the less, he is still concerned for his master, and brings two senators in a (vain) attempt to persuade him back to Athens. The part is small, but Flavius' generous-heartedness and human dignity pointedly contrast with the attitudes of almost everyone else in the play.

SENATORS The Senators are old, foolish and slaves to precedent. They refuse to help Timon in his predicament, banish Alcibiades for insulting them when they reject his plea to pardon his friend, panic when Alcibiades attacks the city and try desperately to persuade Timon to return from exile and lead the Athenian people against him. When the city is under siege they stand on the battlements and beg for mercy, claiming that 'We were not all unkind, nor all deserve / The common stroke of war'. Shakespeare's depictions of the fatuity, arrogance and moral obsolescence of the old ruling class were often biting, but none more etched in acid than his picture of these dodderers.

BANDITS The Bandits (perhaps played by a trio of Shakespeare's comedians) happen to be walking along the shore as Timon digs up a hoard of gold. He offers it to them (claiming that they are the only honest men in the world, since they wholeheartedly engage in their profession, and enjoy it), and they take the money but miss the point entirely, saying that their banditry is forced on them and that they will give it up 'as soon as there is peace in Athens'. In short, Timon misunderstands their nature as he does everyone else's.

☞ About the play

Timon of Athens is thought to have been written hard on the heels of *Othello*, *King Lear* and *Macbeth*. Its companions are *Antony and Cleopatra* and *Coriolanus*, and the germ of it may have lain in Shakespeare's research for these classical projects. His thoughts were already moving towards a new theatrical style, that of such 'romances' as *Pericles* or *The Winter's Tale*; some see *Timon of Athens* as a transitional work, romance-like in form but centring, like the tragedies, on the suffering of a single emblematic individual.

Timon himself is in a long line of Shakespearean characters whose disenchantment with themselves, their society or the human race at large leads them to try to refocus their lives by changing their companions or circumstances. In comedies the change involves a move from everyday reality to a world of genial, anarchic magic, as when the lovers in *A Midsummer Night's Dream* or the courtiers in *As You Like It* find themselves in the forests of fairy tale. In other plays the change has profound moral or philosophical implications: examples are the Duke's masquerade in *Measure for Measure* and *King Lear* battling his demons on the blasted heath.

In all these plays, the change succeeds, and the characters ultimately find the happiness or understanding they look for. In *Timon of Athens*, by contrast, the change entirely fails. Timon's double move – from philanthropy to misanthropy and from city to seashore – leads him not to redemption but to self-torment and a bleak and pointless death. The play is an unblinking exposition of human harshness. Its world is that of revenge tragedy, unremitting horror depicted in language of icy grandeur; the difference is that the nightmares it shows are not physical rapes, poisonings and beheadings but psychological ravishment. Perceptions, not muscles, are sliced and scraped before our eyes. The play's parodies reinforce the point. Money (gold) is buried in the ground, in true romance style, but digging it up is described as a kind of mother-rape. The meals, and Timon's betrayal at them, bleakly suggest Christ's Last Supper.

Timon of Athens is a bumpily-written play. Timon is a character of grand psychological and philosophical potential – one critic called him 'this still-born twin of Lear' – but that potential is never fully realized. There are moments when his rows with Apemantus lacerate our hearts and ears in the same way as the arguments between Lear, his Fool and Edgar as 'poor Tom'; at other times they seem no more than bilious rant. The verse can soar (as when the Merchant describes Timon, before his fall, as 'a most incomparable man, breathed as it were / To an untirable and continuate goodness'), and it can also fall headlong (as when the Steward addresses him, after his fall, as 'My dearest lord, blessed to be most accursed / Rich only to be wretched, thy great fortunes / Are made thy chief afflictions'). Common people, usually in Shakespeare the embodiments of human good sense and decency, are either parasites and predators or are baffled and dispossessed by what happens.

In the past, scholars explained all this by saying that *Timon of Athens* is either Shakespeare's revision of someone else's text or the completion by another writer of a Shakespearean draft – with the implication that the 'good' bits are Shakespeare's and the 'bad' bits his collaborator's. Others surmise that Shakespeare may have suffered a kind of creative breakdown during the writing, or may have exhausted this particular dramatic mode in the three preceding tragedies. There is no evidence for any such assumptions, and they patronize Shakespeare as both a creative and practical artist. *Timon of Athens* may be a portrait of human nature painted entirely in black, or it may share the death's-head irony of the revenge style, elusive on the page but easy to discover in the theatre. Either way, it sets out its view of the dark side of the human race with unsettling efficiency – and who is to say that this is not precisely what Shakespeare, at the peak of his creative life, set out to do?

In performance

Although *Timon of Athens* was published in the First Folio of Shakespeare's plays in 1623, so far as is known it was never performed in his lifetime. The first authenticated production of the unadulterated text took place as late as 1851. In between, the play was known in bastardized versions by Thomas Shadwell (1678) and Richard Cumberland (1771), both of whom pointed up the musical and farcical elements of the story.

Even in the twentieth century, the play remained on the fringes of the repertory. Among the few notable productions were those by Barry Jackson (1947), Michael Langham (1963–4), Peter Brook (1974) and Trevor Nunn (1991).

APEMANTUS O you gods, what a number of men eats Timon, and he sees 'em not. It grieves me to see so many dip their meat in one man's blood, and all the madness is, he cheers them up too. [I, ii]

TIMON
Gold? Yellow, glittering, precious gold?
No, gods, I am no idle votarist.
Roots, you clear heavens. Thus much of this will make
Black white, foul fair, wrong right
Base noble, old young, coward valiant.
Ha! you gods, why this? What this, you gods? Why this
Will lug your priests and servants from your sides
Pluck stout men's pillows from below their heads.
This yellow slave
Will knit and break religions, bless the accursed
Make the hoar leprosy adored, place thieves
And give them title, knee and approbation
With senators on the bench. [IV, iii]

Titus Andronicus

☞ *Sources*

Original, but influenced by Seneca's Roman tragedies and by two blood-and-thunder plays popular in 1580s London, Marlowe's *The Jew of Malta* and Kyd's *The Spanish Tragedy*.

☞ *Story of the play*

After a victorious campaign against the Goths, the Roman general Titus Andronicus brings home their queen Tamora and her three sons, as prisoners of war. He sacrifices Tamora's eldest son Alarbus to placate the ghosts of those of his own sons who have died in battle. Encouraged by Titus's brother Marcus, the Roman people offer Titus the throne, but he recommends instead Saturninus, the late emperor's elder son. Saturninus asks to marry Titus's daughter Lavinia, but his brother Bassianus, her lover, kidnaps her. Saturninus immediately accuses him of raping her and marries Tamora – and this makes it possible for Tamora to plan revenge on Titus for sacrificing Alarbus.

The rest of the play is a chain of murder and revenge. Tamora's sons Demetrius and Chiron (helped by her scheming lover Aaron) kill Bassianus and rape Lavinia, removing her tongue and hands to stop her incriminating them. They arrange for two of Titus's surviving sons, Quintus and Martius, to fall into a pit where Bassianus's body is lying; Quintus and Martius are arrested for his murder. Titus begs Saturninus to spare his sons, and is told that if he sends his brother's hand, and his own hand, his sons will be returned to him. He sends the hands – and receives back his sons' severed heads.

Lucius, Titus's eldest son, deserts to the Goths to gather an avenging army. Lavinia, meanwhile, finds a way to tell Titus who raped her, and Titus plots revenge on Demetrius and Chiron. Aaron finds out about this, but has to escape from Rome because

Demetrius and Chiron have ordered the death of his and
Tamora's bastard child. He is captured and tells all he knows.
Titus invites Tamora, Saturninus and Lucius to a banquet, serves
Demetrius and Chiron baked in a pie, stabs Lavinia dead (to end
her shame) and murders Tamora. Saturninus kills Titus and
Lucius kills Saturninus. Lucius, by now the only living,
unmaimed member of the royal family, is elected emperor. He
orders state funerals for Titus, Saturninus and Lavinia, throws out
the corpses of the others as carrion and orders that Aaron be
starved to death.

☞ Characters

Saturninus *and* Bassianus, *sons of the late emperor*	Alarbus, Chiron, Demetrius, *her sons*
Titus Andronicus	Aaron the Moor, *her lover*
Marcus, *his brother*	Aemilius, Caius, Publius,
Lavinia, *his daughter*	Sempronius, Valentine, *noble*
Lucius, Martius, Mutius,	*Romans*
Quintus, *his sons*	Attendants, Captain, Clown,
Young Lucius, *Lucius's son*	Goths, Messenger, Romans,
Tamora, *queen of the Goths*	Senators, Soldiers, Tribunes

AARON Aaron is the most theatrically-developed character in
Titus Andronicus, and one of the first of Shakespeare's self-
delighting, ironical villains. (The Greek word *eiron*, origin of
'irony', literally means 'dissembler'.) He bides his time until his
mistress Tamora has married Saturninus, and then announces
himself in a typically extravagant, gloriously worded soliloquy:
'Away with slavish weeds and servile thoughts! / I will be bright,
and shine in pearl and gold / To wait upon this new-made emp-
ress . . . / This goddess, this Semiramis, this nymph, / This
siren . . .'

Aaron continues his relationship with the audience, stepping
aside from the play to revel in his malevolence and the horrors he
is planning. Just for the fun of it, he makes himself the agent of
Tamora's vengeance, organizing the rape of Lavinia, the death of
Bassianus, the framing of Quintus and Marcus for murder, their

deaths and the amputation of Titus's hand. When he is forced to confess at the end of the play (bizarrely, from the top of a ladder), he glories in his evil: 'Even now I curse the day – and yet I think / Few come within the compass of my curse – / Wherein I did not some notorious ill / As kill a man, or else devise his death / Ravish a maid or plot the way to do it / Accuse some innocent and forswear myself . . . / Set fire on barns and haystacks in the night . . . / Oft have I digged up dead men from their graves / And set them upright at their dear friends' doors . . .'

As that catalogue suggests, Aaron is almost a comic character, and his cocky swagger in the midst of all the blood and guts is an important element in establishing the play's elusive tone. Shakespeare gives him one touch of redeeming humanity, his love for his infant son. When Tamora, the boy's mother, sends him to Aaron with orders to kill him, Aaron defends the child with uncharacteristic affection ('This, myself / The vigour and picture of my youth / This before all the world I do prefer / This maugre all the world will I keep safe . . .'), before arranging for him to be smuggled to safety. His Act Five confession on the ladder is made to save the baby's life a second time.

Paternal love is the one chink of human feeling Aaron allows himself. As he is led away to die, snarling defiance, he ends the play with the same comic malignity as he has always shown: 'I am no baby, I, that with base prayers / I should repent the evils I have done. / Ten thousand worse than ever yet I did / Would I perform, if I might have my will. / If one good deed in all my life I did / I do repent it from my very soul.' The play's Romans, with their turgid rhetoric and tormented self-justification, are no match for such seductive villainy. It is almost as if they are the frame for Aaron's story, rather than he for theirs.

TITUS Titus's predicament holds the seeds of tragedy. His participation in violence is a tragic flaw, and he shows his deepest humanity in his concern for his family. Some see him as a prototype of other, grander heroes: a suffering colossus, driven mad by an inability to cope with the malevolence of Fate. At times his despair reaches Lear-like heights. But he is trapped in a sequence of events whose surreal pointlessness *is* their point. He is a noble soul caught in black farce, and there is no redemption.

LAVINIA When Lavinia first appears, she is so sweet and innocent that we can be sure she is intended for some terrible fate. Sure enough, she is raped and mutilated, and spends the rest of her time (until her father kills her) gibbering and shrieking about the stage, handless and tongueless, trying to find some way to name her attackers. Depending on the style of the production, she is either nightmare fleshed or a spectacular black-comic turn.

CHIRON AND DEMETRIUS Tamora's sons always appear together and are indistinguishable in speech and character. They murder Bassianus (and have Titus's sons Quintus and Martius arrested and executed for the crime), rape and mutilate Lavinia, attack Aaron's baby son and are finally themselves butchered and baked in a pie. They are a magnificently sinister double act, the Rosencrantz and Guildenstern of horror.

LUCIUS Titus's eldest son opens the play with murder – 'Give me the proudest prisoner of the Goths / That we may hew his limbs, and on a pile / *Ad manes fratrum* sacrifice his flesh' – and ends it with another, ordering Aaron's execution. It could be argued that both are judicial actions, in keeping with the picture he presents throughout of being untouched by the evil which taints every other Roman in the play. Acclaimed Emperor at the end of Act Five, he makes a ringing declaration of honest and fair intent: 'Thanks, gentle Romans: may I govern so / To heal Rome's harms and wipe away her woe. / But gentle people, give me aim awhile / For nature puts me to a heavy task. / Stand all aloof. But uncle, draw you near / To shed obsequious tears upon this trunk. / O, take this warm kiss on thy pale cold lips.' (That 'warm kiss' is the first truly human touch in the entire action.)

Some modern directors and actors, considering Lucius's family and surroundings and the tone of the play itself, make him as unscrupulous and devious as every other character. In Shakespeare's time, by contrast, he was almost certainly played as straight as the lines suggest: a noble and heroic stripling.

MARCUS ANDRONICUS Titus's brother, 'gentle Marcus', 'thou reverend man of Rome', stands apart from the butchery all round him. His interests lie elsewhere – 'I have dogs, my lord / Will rouse the proudest panther in the chase / And climb the highest promontory top' – and he is genuinely appalled by what is happening: 'Now let hot Etna cool in Sicily / And be my heart an ever-burning hell! / These miseries are more than may be borne'. But he is no politician, and although he briefly takes command at the end of the play, he is relieved and happy to hand power over to his nephew Lucius.

YOUNG LUCIUS Young Lucius is a child, Titus's grandson. The story of Tereus and Philomela in his school text of Ovid's *Metamorphoses* suggests to his mutilated aunt Lavinia a way to tell who attacked her. At the end of the play he plays a key part of the new tone of honesty and reconciliation which (ironically or otherwise) takes over from the bloodshed. ('O grandsire, grandsire, even with all my heart / Would I were dead, so you did live again. / O lord, I cannot speak to him for weeping. / My tears will choke me if I ope my mouth.')

🖙 *About the play*

At the beginning of his career, learning his trade by practising it, Shakespeare wrote plays in each of the genres popular at the time: history (*Henry VI*), romance (*The Two Gentlemen of Verona*), farce (*The Taming of the Shrew*) and comedy of wit (*Love's Labour's Lost*). In each of these he stretched and developed the style he found, laying foundations for the work of his artistic maturity. *Titus Andronicus* belongs to a fifth genre, the revenge play, as popular in 1590s London as films of extreme violence became four centuries later.

Revenge plays were written to a formula as precise as that of a Hollywood Western. At the beginning of the action a serious wrong was done, and the play charted the characters' machiavellian and macabre progress towards revenge. The predominant tone was surreal. Events included mutilation, rape, madness, murder and the appearance of ghosts and spectres. The props were as ghoulish as the action: one skull, used as a poison-cup in *The Revenger's Tragedy*, did sterling service for twenty years, and was greeted by the audience like an old friend on each new appearance.

Above all, revenge plays used particularly ornate, stylized language. The characters set out their schemes or shared their emotions with the audience in soliloquies, discussed the issues in speeches as intricate as law-court oratory, and indulged in fanciful similes and allusions to Greek and Roman myth. Violent revenge needed to be spectacular to work, and *Titus Andronicus* is spectacularly violent.

Once the pattern of violence is accepted, the play's more intriguing logic becomes apparent. Tucked between the 'slasher' episodes are vignettes of powerful family tragedies. Titus's decision to avenge his sons by human sacrifice leads to the corruption or destruction of his entire family, and drives him personally to madness and despairing rage against injustice, the emperor and the gods themselves. At times this is philosophical, even playfully intellectual (for example when he shoots arrows at Heaven); at other times his tears are like Job's, 'falling on stones, watering no plants'; then, at the end, when his last cathartic act of vengeance leads ironically to his own death, Shakespeare rounds off his story, in a beautiful stroke, with a reference to him as father. His son Lucius says to his grandson, 'Come hither, boy, come and learn of us / To melt in showers. Thy grandsire loved thee well. / Many a time he danced thee on his knee / Sung thee asleep, his loving breast thy pillow.'

The second family tragedy involves Tamora. The revenge cycle is started by the sacrifice of her eldest son in the first scene, and Shakespeare is initially keen to show her as wronged, to ask who is more barbaric, Romans or 'barbarians'. Later, when she has become as brutal as her own surviving sons, ruthless both in revenge and in ambition, Shakespeare still manages to sustain our ambivalence towards her – and then trumps even this by giving the archetypal villain Aaron ferocious paternal love for his baby son.

If the play has a weakness, it is not so much bloodthirstiness as Shakespeare's somewhat over-eager display of his own virtuosity. The disjunction between comedy, brutality and the poise of the verse can seem too studied. There is neither political analysis nor the later Shakespearean interest in counterpointing the misdeeds of the powerful with the everyday struggles of common people. The mature plays plumb emotional depths and examine the complex truths of family ties and friendship in ways unimagined here. But Shakespeare had to start somewhere, and in this robust box-office hit he reveals flashes of true genius in both scenic vision and mastery of dramatic language. *Titus Andronicus* could be by no one else.

☞ *In performance*

Ben Jonson, never a man to mince words where rivals' successes were concerned, said in 1614 that anyone who admired *Titus Andronicus* had lost touch with a quarter of a century's development in theatre taste: the implication is that *Titus* was still being played a generation after it was written. That, however, was virtually the end of its stage life for three centuries. It surfaced briefly in the early eighteenth century (in an adaptation by Edward Ravenscroft), again in the 1850s (in a version by the American actor Ira Aldridge), and again in 1923 (when Shakespeare's text was restored). Otherwise, the story is silence until a handful of productions in the second half of the twentieth century, notably Peter Brook's in 1955, starring Laurence Olivier, Deborah Warner's in 1987 and Silviu Purcharete's in 1997. But the play remains on the margins of Shakespeare's output, so much so that some authorities throw in the towel and say that he had very little hand in it.

TITUS

  Why, foolish Lucius, dost thou not perceive
  That Rome is but a wilderness of tigers? [III, i]

Troilus and Cressida

☞ Sources

Geoffrey Chaucer, *Troilus and Criseyde*; Homer, *Iliad*; William Caxton, *The Recuyell of the Histories of Troy*.

☞ Story of the play

For ten years, the Greek army has been encamped outside the walls of Troy. The siege is getting nowhere, the war is stalemate – and the reason is that the Greek commanders, egged on by the sardonic Ulysses and the scurrilous Thersites, are at one another's throats. In particular, Agamemnon has stolen a prisoner of war from Achilles, and Achilles is sulking and refuses to fight. In Troy, Prince Troilus tells the silky courtier Pandarus that he is in love with Cressida (daughter of the Trojan Calchas who has deserted to the Greeks), and that she loves him.

The Trojan prince Hector challenges any Greek to single combat, and the Greek lords suggest that they hold a lottery and fix it for Ajax to win, so making Achilles jealous and provoking him back to battle. The Greeks tell the Trojans that they will lift the siege if the Trojans hand over the Greek princess Helen, whose elopement with Paris of Troy began the war. The Trojans debate this. Hector and Cassandra urge acceptance, but Paris insists that the war continue, and Troilus supports him.

Calchas asks the Greeks to bring his daughter Cressida to the Greek camp, exchanging her for the captured Trojan Antenor. Diomedes effects the exchange, and Cressida is welcomed into the Greek camp. Ajax now accepts Hector's challenge, but Hector refuses to fight because they are distantly related. To Achilles' fury, the Greeks fête Ajax as a hero.

Ulysses brings Troilus to where he can eavesdrop on Cressida flirting with Diomedes, and Troilus vows to kill Diomedes. He rampages through the Greek army, but although he duels with

Diomedes, neither is hurt. The fighting becomes general, and Hector kills Achilles' friend Patroclus. This finally brings Achilles back into the battle, and he and his soldiers treacherously surround Hector and kill him. Troilus takes news to Troy that the war is continuing, as hopelessly as before, and that Achilles has tied Hector's corpse to his horse's tail and is dragging it through the dust. The play ends in the same chaos and disillusion as when it started.

☞ Characters

GREEKS

Agamemnon, *commander in chief*
Menelaus, *his brother*
Helen, *Menelaus' wife, living with Paris in Troy*
Achilles, Ajax, Diomedes, Nestor, Patroclus, Ulysses, *commanders*
Thersites, *a deformed and scurrilous common soldier*

Margarelon, Paris, Troilus, *his sons*
Cassandra, *his daughter, a prophetess*
Aeneas, Antenor, *commanders*
Calchas, *a priest who has defected to the Greeks*
Cressida, *his daughter*
Pandarus, *her uncle*
Alexander, *her servant*

TROJANS
King Priam
Deiphobus, Hector, Helenus,

OTHERS
Prologue
Attendants, Servants, Soldiers

TROILUS In the midst of the sterility and impotence that is the Trojan War, Troilus suddenly finds himself romantically in love, and expresses it to Pandarus in language of heroic dash and gush: 'I tell thee, I am mad / In Cressid's love. Thou answerest "She is fair" / Pourest in the open ulcer of my heart / Her eyes, her hair, her cheek, her gait, her voice . . .' The play shows his journey to disillusion, first with Cressida herself – his romantic passion sours to lust ('I am giddy, expectation whirls me round / . . . what will it be / When that the watery palate tastes indeed / Love's thrice-repured Nature? Death, I fear me / Swooning destruction . . .'), then to despair ('O Cressid! O false Cressid! False, false, false!') – and finally to fury at the whole pointless enterprise of the war, when he projects his passion from his beloved to the fighting and ends with as much energetic, futile rhetoric as he began ('You vile abominable tents / Thus proudly pight upon our Phrygian plains / Let Titan rise as early as he dare / I'll through and through you . . . / Hope of revenge shall hide our inward woe').

CRESSIDA We first see Troilus as a romantic hero; immediately afterwards Cressida expresses her fascination with the Greeks in the plain below and indulges in frivolous badinage with her bawdy uncle Pandarus. Some are led by this to think that she is a cheat and deceiver from the start, a companion character to Helen whose wiles brought about the war in the first place. Later in the play, Ulysses bluntly calls her 'a daughter of the game', a harlot. Others, by contrast, see her as an innocent, doomed because of her own playful nature but also, more importantly, caught up in the greater tragedy of the war itself. Like Troy, she is fated to fall, and all her glitter and brightness cannot prevent but merely postpone the moment.

ACHILLES Achilles personifies the arrogance of genius. The noblest of all the Greek heroes, he withdraws from the fighting from pique (he is insulted by Agamemnon), and returns for an equally selfish reason (fury that his friend Patroclus should be killed by Hector). He is roused to undignified rage when he finds that the Greeks are giving honour to the fool Ajax and not to him. The end of his feud with Hector is not a clean, honourable duel, but treachery (his men surround the unarmed Hector and stab him in the back): in this all-tainting conflict, even the mightiest are corrupted.

AGAMEMNON The Greek commander-in-chief is a hollow man, a walking uniform. He speaks orotund, ceremonious verse, linguistic bravado replacing the dignity and authority we might expect from a true leader of men. His opening remarks are typical, taking an enormously long time to say nothing at all: 'Princes, / What grief hath set the jaundice on your cheeks? / The ample proposition that hope makes / In all designs begun on earth below / Fails in the promised largeness. Checks and disasters / Grow in the veins of action highest reared. / As knots . . .' – and so on for thirty lines.

DIOMEDES Diomedes, the young Greek officer who fetches Cressida (and Troilus) from Troy to the Greek camp, makes his cynical view of Cressida and his intentions towards her perfectly clear as soon as Troilus puts her in his charge. Troilus tells him to 'use her well' or have his throat cut; Diomedes answers 'O, be not moved, lord Troilus . . . / . . . when I am hence / I'll answer to my lust, and know you, lord / I'll nothing do on charge. To her own worth / She shall be prized'. We next see him talking cheerful nothings with Cressida, in a scene which repeats the tone of her bright shallowness with Pandarus right at the start of the play, but which Troilus (brought by Ulysses to eavesdrop) mistakes for genuine flirting and seduction – and which turns into precisely that, as if Troilus's mistake has willed it to happen. Finally we see him in a furious but inconclusive duel with Troilus: it erupts twice on stage and each time they go off still fighting.

HECTOR Priam's heir, crown prince of Troy, Hector at first seems to have all the qualities of a wise and noble ruler. In council, he suggests ending the war by returning Helen to the Greeks ('She is not worth what she doth cost / The holding'), and speaks sage-sounding generalities ('. . . To persist / In doing wrong extenuates not wrong / But makes it much more heavy'). But the war infects him with the same fatal moral futility as everyone else, and this leads him to go against his better judgement (when he lets Paris and Troilus persuade him to keep Helen in Troy), to a challenge of pure bravado against the Greeks (one, he claims, which 'will strike amazement to their drowsy spirits'), and finally to an ignominious death, cornered on the battlefield and hacked to pieces.

ULYSSES Ulysses is the sanest of the Greek lords. He is clear about the waste that is the war, and has a sure plan to end it: persuading Achilles, by whatever means, back into the fighting. But neither his common sense nor his smooth-tongued eloquence ('Thank the heavens, lord, thou art of sweet composure. / Praise him that got thee, she that gave thee suck. / Famed be thy tutor, and thy parts of nature / Thrice-famed, beyond all erudition . . .') have any effect, and in the end even he sinks into despair, utterly cynical for all its fine expression: 'O, let not virtue seek / Remuneration for the thing it was / For beauty, wit / High birth, vigour of bone, desert in service / Love, friendship, charity, are subjects all / To envious and caluminating time'.

THERSITES Thersites is a mean-minded, rancorous cynic, a 'bitter clown' who serves Ajax and Achilles as jester and sneers insults at his masters and everyone else. Although his wit earns him regular thrashings, his view of the war (as 'too much blood and too little brain') and its causes ('all [its] argument is a cuckold and a whore – a good quarrel to draw emulous factions and bleed to death upon . . .') is accurate, and he sets the action of the play, and all those involved in it, in a framework of clear moral disapproval.

PANDARUS Cressida's uncle has given his name to pandars, those who take money to bring people together for sex. But this is not his character in the play. He is a pliant, amoral man, a wit and a singer, and brings Troilus and Cressida together more to divert himself than out of moral conviction (of which he has none) or for cash (which he does not demand). His ceaseless flow of jokes and the style in which he speaks (and sings) the play's epilogue suggest that the part may have been written for the comedian Robert Armin.

About the play

In *Troilus and Cressida* Shakespeare follows in the footsteps of such ancient Greek dramatists as Sophocles and Euripides, taking one episode from a well-known myth-story and developing it to draw out specific philosophical and ethical ideas. The story in this case is a single moment from the huge myth-cycle about the Trojan War, and the underlying theme is passion – in war, sex and self-image, corrupted in each case by human pomposity and misunderstanding.

The basic story, a favourite in late medieval Europe and brought to England by Chaucer in his *Troilus and Criseyde*, centres on Troilus's passion for Cressida, his ecstasy when she appears to share his love and his despair when she transfers her affection to the Greek Diomedes. In Chaucer's version the events of the war itself are of little importance: the struggle between Greeks and Trojans is merely the setting for the love-affair, as the Montague-Capulet quarrel provides the background in *Romeo and Juliet*, essential to create tragedy for the main characters but irrelevant in detail. Shakespeare's play retains this simplicity: the scenes involving Troilus and Cressida and those close to them (for example Pandarus) could be isolated from the rest of the action and performed as a cathartic drama on their own.

The war, however, is there and cannot be ignored. It began when the Greeks sent a huge expedition to topple Troy and win back Helen, who had abandoned Menelaus, her Greek husband, for the Trojan prince Paris. The fighting involved famous heroes on both sides: King Priam and his son Hector for the Trojans and in the Greek camp Achilles, Agamemnon, Diomedes and Ulysses. The war lasted for ten years, largely because the Greek commanders squabbled among themselves, and ended only when Achilles killed Hector and the Greeks filled a Wooden Horse with soldiers and tricked the Trojans into dragging it into the centre of their city. From the time of Homer (whose *Iliad* dates from about the eighth-century BC), writers tended to treat the Trojan War as a monumental mixture of epic and tragedy, human dignity constantly tripping up on vainglory and futility. The trick of the Wooden Horse and the destruction of Priam's city are the ironical starting-point for Western civilization: the Fall of Troy is the myth which explains why nothing ever lasts. Troy is the site of relativism, a place where such 'absolute' values as honour and duty collapse into sand. As Shakespeare's Thersites sourly reminds us, the war was fought over a harlot; it took the noblest heroes ever known, men like Hector, Achilles, Ajax and Ulysses, made them brawl like bored schoolboys and subjected them to painful defeats and ignominious deaths; it was ended not nobly but by treachery. In such a world, even Cressida, the embodiment of purity and the object of courtly love, turns out to be faithless and becomes a byword for falseness.

At the end of Chaucer's sweeter, more equivocal examination of the same story, Troilus goes up to Heaven, looks down on the battlefield and smiles. Shakespeare gives us no such consolation. He makes use both of the *Iliad*'s epic grandeur (in Chapman's famous translation) and of the irony and cynicism with which Homer undercuts that grandeur. He consistently changes the focus of his play, one minute concentrating on the intimacy of the affair between Troilus and Cressida (and the personal passions and agonies which sustain it) and the next pulling back to show us the wider picture of commanders planning and undertaking ever more pointless skirmishes in a war which seems to have neither purpose nor any end in sight. Each perspective colours the other – and Shakespeare provides yet a third, the jaundiced view of human striving articulated by Ulysses, Thersites and Pandarus. The contributions of these three characters – Ulysses' wit, Thersites' caustic bawdy, Pandarus' self-interested shamelessness – have led some critics to call *Troilus and Cressida* a 'comedy'. If so, it is the comedy of Hieronymus Bosch, of Death capering in plague-pits at the Day of Judgement, and its bleak hilarity continually takes such qualities as dignity (Priam), nobility (Hector), passion (Troilus) and innocence (Cressida) – and curdles them.

In performance

After Shakespeare's lifetime, *Troilus and Cressida* was not performed until 1907. In the twentieth century it was given some extraordinary interpretations (a Hollywood spectacular version in the Boboli Gardens, Florence in 1949, a nineteenth-century Ruritanian version at the Old Vic in 1956, a US Civil War version at Stratford, Connecticut in 1957, a post-nuclear, beach-set version at the Citizen's Theatre, Glasgow in 1972), but also in more orthodox and more satisfyingly-spoken accounts (notably by the RSC – where it is practically a repertory piece – in 1948, 1954, 1968, 1976, 1985, 1989 and 1997).

Twelfth Night

📖 Sources

For the Viola/Sebastian/Orsino/Olivia plot, Shakespeare drew on a romantic short story in Mateo Bandello, *Stories* (1554), also the inspiration for *Much Ado About Nothing*. The Malvolio/Sir Toby/Sir Andrew plot is original.

📖 Story of the play

Olivia, an heiress of Illyria, is mourning for her brother. She refuses to let Duke Orsino pay court to her, and her steward Malvolio rebukes her uncle Sir Toby Belch for carousing into the night with his cronies Sir Andrew Aguecheek (a fool he is tricking out of his money by pretending that he will persuade Olivia to marry him), Fabian and Feste the clown. Meanwhile, a ship is wrecked in a storm, and the young noblewoman Viola is separated from her twin brother Sebastian. Thinking him dead, she disguises herself as a man ('Cesario') and goes to serve Orsino as his page. Orsino sends 'Cesario' to Olivia to plead his suit, and Olivia is attracted to 'Cesario'.

Angry with Malvolio, Sir Toby and the others forge a letter from Olivia saying that she loves him and wants him to woo her cross-gartered and in yellow stockings. Thinking that his dreams have come true, Malvolio does so and is locked up as a madman. Sir Andrew, jealous of Olivia's growing relationship with 'Cesario', reluctantly challenges him to a duel. Viola, already confused by the effect her boy's disguise is having on Olivia, fights with just as much reluctance, and is amazed when Antonio, the ship's captain, bursts in and breaks up the duel, calling her 'Sebastian' and asking for help in a forthcoming court action.

Everyone now mistakes the real Sebastian for 'Cesario'. He fights Sir Toby and Sir Andrew and is amazed when Olivia flirts with him. Mocked by Sir Toby and the others in his prison,

Malvolio begs Feste to deliver an abject letter to Olivia. Everyone still takes 'Cesario' for Sebastian, and confusion reaches its height when a priest tells 'him' that he has just married Olivia. Only when Sebastian and Viola are both on stage can the knots be untangled. Brother and sister are reunited, Olivia pardons Malvolio (who sweeps off stage vowing revenge 'on the whole pack of you'), Sir Andrew decides to go home, the Duke agrees to marry Viola, and Feste rounds the whole play off with a song.

☞ Characters

Duke Orsino *of Illyria*	**Fabian,** *an upper servant*
Countess Olivia	**Viola**
Malvolio, *her steward*	**Sebastian,** *her twin brother*
Sir Toby Belch, *her uncle*	**Antonio,** *a sea captain, his friend*
Sir Andrew Aguecheek, *her*	**Attendants, Captain, Lords**
suitor	(*including* **Curio** and **Valentine**),
Feste, *her jester*	**Musicians, Officers, Priest,**
Maria, *her chambermaid*	**Sailors**

VIOLA Viola's boy's disguise is an emotional catalyst for every-one else in the story. Both Orsino and Olivia are captivated by 'Cesario', and this genuine feeling (albeit for a shadow) allows them to escape from the false emotions (Orsino's melancholy yearning for Olivia; her over-extended mourning for her father) in which they have been trapped. Each is rewarded with a 'real' equivalent of 'Cesario': Olivia with Sebastian, Orsino with the undisguised Viola. The presence of 'Cesario', a potentially power-ful rival for Sir Andrew with Olivia, similarly adds impetus to the sub-plot. Even so minor a character as Antonio is affected by the arrival on stage of 'Cesario' and his uncanny likeness to Sebastian.

For Viola herself, 'Cesario' becomes an emotional prison – something which eventually happens to all Shakespeare's heroines who adopt male disguise. For all her wit and light-heartedness, she is a serious person, and her disguise traps her in a masquerade which moves from romp to psychological torment (as 'Cesario' she can never be emotionally honest) and finally to farce (when she duels with Sir Andrew). She becomes less and less able to extricate herself from the situation of her disguise, and the result is that when her 'lost' true brother appears and frees her from the burden of being 'Cesario', the emotional release is overwhelming, all-enabling and exhilarating to behold.

FESTE A professional Fool, aware of human frailty and the transience of happiness, Feste masks his knowledge (at least in the dialogue scenes) by taking part in games and masquerades and by mocking the other characters. His lines – for example when he disguises himself as Sir Topas and preaches at Malvolio – can be vindictive and heartless. But *Twelfth Night* is comedy, not tragedy, and Shakespeare makes Feste the guardian of its ironical and autumnal qualities by letting him woo the audience directly, taking us into the players' confidence about what is happening and framing the action with three wistful and elegiac songs, 'O Mistress Mine,' 'Come Away Death' and 'When That I Was and a Little Tiny Boy'. Feste is one of the briefest of Shakespeare's major roles, but he steers the play.

OLIVIA Olivia's character is both the double and the opposite of Viola's. Like Viola, she begins the play in an assumed role (mourner), and the action shows her evolving from this to happiness thanks to the discovery and admission of her true emotional identity. But where Viola is hot she is cool, where Viola is impassioned she is restrained, where Viola engages with the farce-characters (however reluctantly), she recoils from them. These differences, set against the characters' emotional similarity and complicity, give their scenes together a philosophical energy to match the irony of seeing how their various kinds of role-playing (by the characters in the action; by the actors playing the roles of people playing impersonations) will succeed.

MALVOLIO In the comedy ensemble, Malvolio is the humour-less, oppressive stooge whose comeuppance is the consummation for which everyone devoutly wishes and which is made even more delicious by his self-deluding, literal-minded pomposity. He is also a bridge between the two modes of the play, comedy and farce. The role-playing into which he is gulled is a farcical mirror of that chosen for themselves by Viola, Orsino and Olivia – and it is as much against his nature. But while they are emotionally liberated by what they do, and their stories end happily, he remains trapped by his own dour character and ends the play in as much misery and confusion as he began it.

SIR ANDREW AGUECHEEK Lanky, flea-brained and lugubrious, Sir Andrew has a remarkably short fuse. Maria sums him up exactly, saying that he is 'a great quarreller, and, but that he hath the gift of a coward . . . ,' 'tis thought among the prudent he would quickly have the gift of a grave.'

SIR TOBY BELCH Olivia's roistering uncle is shameless (conning Sir Andrew out of his cash), rude ('Sneck up!') and a quarrelsome, self-important drunk ('Dost think, because thou are virtuous, there shall be no more cakes and ale?') Because he is a dissolute aristocrat, he is sometimes played as a kind of cut-price Falstaff, but he is more like Bottom, one member (perhaps the leading member) of a group of comedians playing company knockabout. He belongs entirely to the world of farce; his only connection with the comedy world is with the disguised Viola, and he misunderstands and attacks 'Cesario' throughout.

☞ About the play

Twelfth Night was written at the same time as *Hamlet* and *Troilus and Cressida*, and shares themes with them: death, eroticism, identity. Its focus, however, could hardly be more different. Where the other two plays centre on futility and frustration, *Twelfth Night* is ultimately optimistic and energetic; where their movement circles round cruelty, pain and loss, *Twelfth Night* is a progress towards discovery, fulfilment and happiness. These qualities, coupled with irresistible comic momentum and the exquisite sad music of the verse, make it one of Shakespeare's most consummate works. If all his other plays vanished overnight, *Twelfth Night* would still show us everything about the scope and generosity of his genius and the quality of his achievement.

Like *Hamlet*, *Twelfth Night* is haunted by death. In *Hamlet* the haunting, and the deaths, are literal; in this play the only real deaths (those of Olivia's father and brother) happen before the action starts, and our concern is more with the effects of mourning, or the apprehension of sorrow, on people's minds. Olivia's mourning colours everything which happens in her house – and the colouring is what matters, not the deaths which caused it. Viola and Sebastian are each in mourning for a loss (the supposed death of their twin) which is an illusion. Orsino, in the throes of unrequited love, morbidly longs for a death brought about by an excess of melancholy music in which 'The appetite may sicken and so die'. Feste uses the aesthetics of death as a way of describing emotion: 'Come away, come away, Death / And in sad cypress let me be laid'. A recurring metaphor for death is the sea: both are simultaneously terrifying and comforting, both renew life even as they end it. Such ideas give the play a far more complex attitude to mortality than the traditional comedy moral of the 'triumph of love'. The cloying, dark indulgences of Christmas celebration, the death-throes of the old year, are essential preliminaries to the birth of the new year's positive energies. The play's title is not an accident.

The narrative of *Twelfth Night* is driven by tried and trusted dramatic mechanisms, the farce mechanisms of impersonation and mistaken identity and the comedy mechanism of unrequited love. They are tightly entwined, farce pace bracing the love-pangs and rhapsodic passion humanizing the farce. The two characters at the centre of the action, Viola and Malvolio, are involved in both farce and comedy, and what happens to them satisfyingly mirrors their characters, the failure of Malvolio's impersonation increasing his anguish, the success of Viola's bringing the joy she longs for. Shakespeare uses prose to enhance the hard, 'masculine' energy of the farce-scenes, verse for the more pliant, 'feminine' mood of the romantic scenes, and clinchingly brings them together at the final scene, allowing Malvolio's unsatisfied fury to darken the otherwise sunny, even conventional, romantic ending.

If *Twelfth Night* replaces the close-focus, dark eroticism of *Troilus and Cressida* with a whirl of sexual charades and longings

(Orsino's, Malvolio's and Aguecheek's love for Olivia, Orsino's and Olivia's love for 'Cesario', even Antonio's love for Sebastian, an emotion whose true nature is never disclosed), it also takes the destructive, sterile play of ambition which cancers the Greek and Trojan lords and replaces it with robust class-comedy. In this, too, Malvolio is a central figure. In a society dominated by aristocrats who are self-indulgent (Orsino; Olivia), raucous (Sir Toby) or vacuous (Sir Andrew), and by upwardly-mobile, quick-witted servants like Maria and Fabian, Malvolio is a fish entirely out of water. He is a steward who longs to be his lady's husband and lover, in the circumstances an unfulfillable ambition. His social and sexual frustration leads him to treat other characters with a disdain which is not so much Puritanism (a quality often imported into the part, but hardly suggested in the text) as a kind of alienation: from the world, from his office (he was, we are told, formerly an efficient and trusted steward) and finally, when he thinks himself mad, even from himself. None of the other characters understands him, and his final threat to be 'revenged on the whole pack of you' takes on an ominous energy in a society which, so far from pitying him or punishing him, treats him as mere irrelevance.

A final contrast with *Troilus and Cressida* is between two characters who both take part in and step aside from the main action, offering (apparently) objective commentary: Thersites and Feste. Thersites's wit is sour, malevolent and sterile. People constantly try to quench him, as if he were a stinking bonfire: he is beaten and derided. Feste's character – and the mood of the play which it embodies – are significantly different. For all his foolery, he often seems like the only grown-up at a children's party: aware from experience that there are 'tears in things', that joy and sorrow are inseparable in human life and that this is the lesson we all must learn by living it, since 'Youth's a stuff will not endure'. The last verse of his closing song exactly captures the mood of elegiac, ironical and wistful insouciance which is one of his main contributions to this most complex play: 'A great while ago the world began / With a hey, ho, the wind and the rain / But that's all one, our play is done / And we'll strive to please you every day.'

☞ In performance

Some scholars think that Queen Elizabeth commissioned *Twelfth Night* for a gala production before a visiting Italian grandee (Valentino Orsino) on Twelfth Night (6 January) 1601, but apart from the coincidence of the name Orsino, there is no evidence. The first known performance took place on 2 February 1602, when Richard Burbage played Malvolio and Robert Armin played Feste. The play has been popular ever since, often in versions incorporating scenes and songs from other plays, but since 1900 usually in Shakespeare's unadulterated text. Notable Violas have included Garrick's mistress Peg Woffington in the eighteenth-century, Hannah Pritchard, Ada Rehan and Ellen Terry in the nineteenth century, and Helen Hayes, Edith Evans, Peggy Ashcroft, Vivien Leigh, Katharine Hepburn and Judi Dench in the twentieth. Among the male stars who have had particular success in the play are Henry Irving, Herbert Beerbohm Tree and Laurence Olivier (Malvolio), Thomas Betterton and Ralph Richardson (Sir Toby) and Paul Scofield (Sir Andrew).

Twelfth Night is one of the few Shakespeare plays whose original music surivives: Feste's songs, set by Thomas Morley. Frederick Reynolds wrote an operatic version of the play in 1820, a patchwork involving two dozen songs from other Shakespeare plays. Sixty years later Smetana wrote an opera (*Viola*) which marries Shakespeare's story to rhythms and melodies inspired by Bohemian folk-song. There have been four *Twelfth Night* films, silent in 1910, in Russian in 1955 (doubling Viola and Sebastian), in German in 1955 and in (disappointingly spoken) English in 1996.

VIOLA

> My father had a daughter loved a man
> As it might be perhaps, were I a woman
> I should your lordship. [II, iv]

The Two Gentlemen of Verona

🖝 Sources

The main plot comes from the story 'Titus and Gisippus' in Giovanni Boccaccio, *The Decameron*. Launce and Speed are Shakespeare's own invention.

🖝 Story of the play

Valentine decides to move from Verona to Milan to seek his fortune. His friend Proteus decides to stay in Verona, to be near his beloved Julia. Valentine's servant Speed delivers a love-letter from Proteus to Julia. Proud and disdainful, she tears the letter up, then lovingly reassembles it. She writes back to Proteus – but he has just been told by his father that he, too, must go to Milan. Proteus and Julia part, and as soon as Proteus and his servant Launce have left, accompanied by Launce's dog Crab, she disguises herself as a boy and hurries after them.

In Milan, Proteus finds that Valentine is in love with the Duke's daughter Silvia. Because the Duke has another husband (Thurio) in mind for her, she and Valentine plan to elope. Proteus, enraptured by Silvia, sets out to win her for himself. He tells the Duke about the elopement, and the Duke banishes Valentine – who is kidnapped by a band of outlaws and made their leader. Proteus arranges for Thurio to serenade Silvia ('Who is Silvia?'), but then starts courting her himself. Julia, disguised as the boy 'Sebastian' and now employed as Proteus' page, overhears, and is even more broken-hearted when Proteus sends him / her to Silvia with a ring and a declaration of love. Silvia tells 'Sebastian' how sorry she is for Julia.

Silvia escapes to the forest in the care of the old knight Sir Eglamour, and the Duke, Thurio, Proteus and 'Sebastian' follow her with soldiers. She is captured by the outlaws. Proteus rescues her and asks the Duke to reward him by letting him marry her. But

Valentine (who has discovered everything) scolds him and forces him to feel true shame. 'Sebastian' faints, and Proteus realizes that she was Julia, and his true love, all the time. Thurio refuses to fight Valentine for Silvia, and the Duke agrees to let her marry Valentine. The lovers are reunited, the Duke pardons the outlaws, and everyone lives happily ever after.

Characters

Valentine
Speed, *his servant*
Proteus
Antonio, *his father*
Launce, *his servant*
Julia, *loved by Proteus*
Lucetta, *her servant*

Silvia, *loved by Valentine*
Duke of Milan, *her father*
Thurio, *also in love with Silvia*
Host, Musicians, Outlaws,
Panthino (*servant*), **Sir**
Eglamour (*knight*)

VALENTINE Valentine is adolescent passion and emotion personified. At the start of the play he is determined to leave home and see the world. Next minute, in Milan, he is headlong in love, writes a gushy poem – 'My thoughts do harbour with my Silvia nightly; / And slaves they are to me that send them flying. / O could their master come and go as lightly / Himself would lodge where senseless they are lying' – plots an elopement, and when he is banished by the girl's father, plunges into the blackest depths of melancholy: 'And why not death, rather than living torment? / To die is to be banished from myself / And Silvia is myself . . .'. Exiled to the forest, he revels in it because 'Here I can sit, unseen of any / And to the nightingale's complaining notes / Tune my distress and record my woes'.

The roller-coaster ride continues. Valentine is captured by outlaws, elected their chief, kidnaps everyone in sight, rails at Proteus for betraying their friendship ('Thou friend of an ill fashion . . . / . . . Treacherous man / Thou hast beguiled my hopes!'), threatens to fight Thurio for Silvia ('Thurio, give back, or else embrace thy death') – and when he finally wins her, tells her father in a line of superb, throwaway understatement, 'The gift hath made me happy'. Even among the crowd of amorous young men in Shakespeare he stands supreme, and few are so persistently, affectionately sent up by their creator.

SILVIA Silvia is Valentine's soul-partner. Breathless with love, she plays heady, risky games with her own affection, giving him back the letter he himself has written 'to an unknown beloved', flirting with Thurio in front of him, planning an elopement. When Valentine is banished, she hurries after him. She is captured by outlaws ('O Valentine, this I endure for thee!'), three separate suitors squabble over her, and finally, wordlessly, she collapses into the arms of her true beloved.

PROTEUS Proteus is a youth who has no idea what it means to be grown up. He is happy-go-lucky, blind to other people's feelings and has no idea how badly he is behaving. At first, we think – and perhaps he does, too – that he loves Julia devotedly, but when his father sends him away to Milan he says goodbye to her as casually as if he had never had any feelings whatsoever: 'O, how this spring of love resembleth / The uncertain glory of an April day / Which now shows all the beauty of the sun / And by and by a cloud takes all away.' In Milan, mistaking Valentine and Silvia's love for flirting, he breaks up the affair and starts courting her himself. Then, when Valentine confronts him in the wood and he is brought up short with his behaviour, he collapses instantly into remorse ('My shame and guilt confounds me. / Forgive me, Valentine. If hearty sorrow / Be a sufficient ransom for offence / I tender't here. I do as truly offer / As e'er I did commit') – and then realizes, as if thunderstruck, that he has really been in love with Julia all the time: 'O Heaven, were man / But constant, he were perfect! . . . / What is in Silvia's face, but I may spy / More fresh in Julia's with a constant eye?'

JULIA Julia is the most serious of the four young lovers, and the first to be transformed by love (in the scene where she tears up Proteus' letter and then desperately reassembles the pieces). Broken-hearted when Proteus leaves for Milan, she disguises herself and follows him. Now it is her boy's disguise which prevents her from declaring herself. Events move out of her control – and then, in a fairy-tale transformation in the wood, the scales fall from Proteus' eyes and she is able to watch, and stage-manage, his realization that she is not his pageboy but Julia, and that he has loved her from the very start.

LAUNCE AND SPEED The servants respectively of Proteus and Valentine, they are sharply distinguished. Launce, a lugubrious youth, constantly dreams of his ideal beloved: a girl with 'more hair than wit and more faults than hairs', but who will also, perhaps fortunately, possess 'more wealth than faults'. Until she comes along, he takes morose pleasure in his mongrel Crab, 'the sourest-natured dog that lives'. Speed, like Dromio of Syracuse in *The Comedy of Errors*, is in love with language, but he also has his priorities straight: if cheek and wit get in the way of food and comfort, he forgets them fast.

☞ About the play

The Two Gentlemen of Verona is early, and is overshadowed by Shakespeare's first real masterpiece, *The Comedy of Errors*. But although it lacks the richness and depth of his mature work, the play does sketch in many of his favourite themes and motifs, and has excellences of its own: clarity of construction, charming characters, an easy and unselfconscious style.

The genre is Italian romance, of the kind Shakespeare favoured throughout his career. Its ingredients are fine-feeling aristocrats and sharp-witted servants, insensitive fathers and independently-minded children, serenades, elopements and good-hearted outlaws. The plot follows formal romance structure, but the quality of the writing is less stilted than that suggests and has characteristic Shakespearean humanity and wit.

At the play's heart is the love-quartet of Valentine, Silvia, Proteus and Julia. Each of them, struck by the first grand passion of his or her life, is affected in a different way. In a later play (*The Winter's Tale*, for example) Proteus' behaviour might have been the catalyst for darker passions; here it is part of the insouciance of youth, a heedlessness of other people's feelings which can even allow him melodramatically to threaten rape unless he gets his way. Valentine's love makes him think seriously for the first time in his life; Silvia rebels against her father; Julia disguises herself as a pageboy and runs after her beloved.

This disguise, the young women's running to the forest and Valentine's coronation as King of the Outlaws take the play into that transcendental, alternative moral universe in which so many of Shakespeare's comedies are set: a place where city formality is replaced by country easiness, where power is not fought for but freely given, where love and courtesy overcome all discomfort. The characters (and we with them) are given a glimpse of how people could behave with each other in a better world, the truth of what has happened is finally revealed and the pain is resolved. The ending is both romantic and symbolic. As a result of their actions, the lovers grow up, escape from their parents' tutelage and take charge of their own lives and happiness, both individually and together.

This romantic story could easily have tumbled into sentimentality. Shakespeare avoids the trap by sharp characterization and amiable irony (romantic gush has seldom seemed at once so ecstatic and so silly), and above all by his brilliant use of the servants. Their parts have a comic energy which transcends the genre (*commedia dell'arte*) to which they belong, and are full of hints at glories to come in later work. Speed, for example, in what seems like a simple insistence that it's time for dinner, sets out the play's entire dialectical structure: 'Ay but hearken sir: though the chameleon Love can feed on the air, I am one that am nourished by my victuals, and would fain have meat. O be not like your mistress: be moved, be moved.' Contrasting perspectives are essential for any three-dimensional, realistic view of the world – and in this comedy, as so often in Shakespeare, those perspectives depend on class.

It is in Launce's relationship to his dog Crab that Shakespeare really comes into his own. The Crab scene has all the appearance of a comic 'turn' (perhaps devised by the original actor and his dog) which Shakespeare sews into both the plot and the underlying philosophy of his play. Launce, forced to go to Milan with his master Proteus, complains that Crab cares nothing at all for the misery this causes. Since Crab is a dog, nothing else can be expected of him, and so Launce's complaint can only be comic. But the episode leaves a more profound question in our minds: why do animals which *are* blessed with souls and imagination, namely human beings, behave just as insensitively, as if *they* were dogs? In its gentle way, related to the main characters' behaviour to one another, this scene prefigures a major Shakespearean theme: the human race's terrifying potential for cruelty.

☞ *In performance*

No performances are known until David Garrick's production of 1762, in a version tricked out with songs and new dialogue. Frederick Reynolds made a musical version in 1821 – one of his freshest, most charming Shakespeare adaptations, and with excellent new comedy for Launce and Speed. The play was revived half a dozen times in the twentieth century, most notably (as a musical) by Joseph Papp in 1971 and (straight) by Jack Shepherd in London in 1996, when it was the first play produced in the New Globe Theatre, restored on the site of Shakespeare's original.

> LAUNCE I think my dog Crab be the sourest-natured dog that
> lives. My mother weeping, my father wailing, my sister
> crying, our maid howling, our cat wringing her hands, and
> all our house in a great perplexity, yet did not this cruel-
> hearted cur shed one tear. He is a stone, a very pebble-
> stone, and has no more pity in him than a dog. [II, iii]

The Two Noble Kinsmen

☞ Sources

Chaucer, *The Knight's Tale*. Some episodes (the mad scenes, the gaol scenes) were influenced by earlier Shakespeare plays, and the Schoolmaster and rustics who entertain at the aristocratic wedding were imported bodily from Francis Beaumont's 1613 *Masque of the Inner Temple and Gray's Inn*.

☞ Story of the play

Palamon and his cousin and friend Arcite are Thebans, courtiers of their uncle, the villainous King Creon. They take a vow that their friendship and loyalty to each other will last until death. King Theseus of Athens leads an army against Thebes, defeats Creon and takes Palamon and Arcite back to Athens as prisoners of war. While they are awaiting sentence they both catch sight from their prison window of Princess Emilia, Theseus' sister-in-law. Both fall headlong in love with her, and their friendship turns to rivalry.

Theseus sentences Arcite to banishment, but he returns to Athens in disguise and enters Emilia's service. Palamon is sentenced to prison, but the Gaoler's Daughter falls in love with him and helps him to escape. She begins to pine for him, goes mad for love and follows him, raving, into the forest.

In the forest Palamon and Arcite meet each other, quarrel over Emilia, and are about to fight a duel when they are interrupted by Theseus and his hunting party. He orders their execution, but when Emilia and Queen Hippolyta beg for mercy, he pardons them on condition that they fight a formal duel in one month's time, the winner to marry Emilia and the loser to be executed.

The month passes. A Wooer is encouraged to win the Gaoler's Daughter (and restore her wits) by dressing himself as Palamon. This plan succeeds. Palamon and Arcite meet and fight. Arcite wins, but is then crushed to death when his horse falls on top of him. With his last breath he makes up his quarrel with Palamon and bequeaths him Emilia's hand. The Duke spares Palamon's life and the wedding ceremonies begin – not just for Palamon and Emilia, but also for the Wooer and the Gaoler's Daughter, now fully restored to sanity.

🐾 Characters

Palamon, Arcite, *nephews of King Creon of Thebes*
Theseus, *Duke of Athens*
Hippolyta, *his bride*
Emilia, *her sister*
Pirithous, *Theseus' friend*
Valerius, *a Theban*
Gaoler
His Daughter
Her Wooer
Hymen, *god of weddings*

Boy, Countrymen (*morris-dancers*), Country Wenches, Doctor, Executioner, Bavian (*Fool in the morris-dance*), Guard, Herald, Gaoler's Brother, Maids, Nymphs, Schoolmaster, Six Knights, Taborer (Drummer), Three Queens, Wooer *of the Gaoler's Daughter*

PALAMON High-spirited but shallow, Palamon lives his life on the knife-edge of his own emotions. Everything is instant and absolute; he allows no compromise. Until both he and Arcite fall in love with the same woman, he thinks them inseparable ('Is there record of any two that loved / Better than we do, Arcite?'); as soon as they *do* fall in love, he snarls (*Arcite*: 'Heigh-ho.' *Palamon*: 'For Emily, upon my life! Fool / Away with this strained mirth! . . . Base cousin . . .'). Imprisoned by Theseus, he takes the first opportunity to escape, lurks in the forest and challenges Arcite to a duel for Emilia – and when he loses, he accepts the penalty of death with impassioned bravado: 'Adieu: and let my life be now as short / As my leavetaking.' The next events of the plot – the horse crushing Arcite, Arcite handing him Emilia and dying, Theseus pardoning him and allowing the marriage – leave him emotionally breathless ('O cousin . . . / . . . that nought could buy / Dear love but loss of dear love!'). He is the hero of a knightly fairy tale, and his guilelessness and good luck are the most appealing things about him.

ARCITE Arcite is a swashbuckling romantic hero to whom vows of honour, disguises and derring-do are more precious than life itself. He fights his own dear cousin for the girl they both love, wins, is crushed by a horse and hands her over all in an instant, dying as flamboyantly and elegantly as he lived. He has one of the best speeches in the play, the Act Five invocation to Mars, the Roman god of battle: 'Thou mighty one, that with thy power hast turned / Green Neptune into purple, whose approach / Comets prewarn, whose havoc in vast field / Unearthed skulls proclaim, whose breath blows down / The teeming Ceres' foison . . .'

EMILIA Like her sister Hippolyta, Emilia is an Amazon, a warrior-princess who worships the hunting-goddess Diana. Her collapse into emotion when she discovers that she is loved – and not by one man, but by two – is one of the most unexpected and warmest-hearted moments in the play, and Shakespeare gives her a moving scene when she compares the pictures of her two suitors, so that she can choose between them and end their quarrel. ('Two such handsome men / Shall never fall for me. Their weeping mothers / Following the dead cold ashes of their sons / Shall never curse my cruelty . . .')

GAOLER'S DAUGHTER The Gaoler's Daughter, who arranges Palamon's escape from prison and then goes mad with unrequited love for her social better, is the most Jacobean character in the play. Her hand-wringing and moping seem to come from masque rather than drama, and her lines read less like authentic Shakespeare than some talented assistant's memory of that similar but better imagined suffering heroine, Ophelia in *Hamlet*: 'Give me your hand . . . I can tell your fortune. / You are a fool. Tell ten. I have posed him. Buzz. / Friend, you must eat no white bread . . .' The size of the part, out of all proportion to its importance in the plot, suggests a 'turn' specifically aimed to win audience applause.

SCHOOLMASTER The Schoolmaster is a distant reminiscence of Quince in *A Midsummer Night's Dream* and Holofernes in *Love's Labour's Lost*, devising and rehearsing an entertainment to perform at court. Unlike his predecessors, however, he is in charge not of actors but dancers, and all the lines are his. His best moment comes when he introduces the dance at court, in a wonderful display of pointless erudition: 'Dainty Duke, whose doughty dismal fame / From Dis to Daedalus, from post to pillar, / Is blown abroad, help me, thy poor well-willer / And with thy twinkling eyes look right and straight / Upon this mighty "Moor" of mickle weight / "Ice" now comes in, which being glued together / Makes "Morris", and the cause that we come hither . . .' He may also speak the prologue and epilogue.

DANCERS The Dancers, including Friz, Maudlin, 'little Luce with the white legs', 'bouncing Barbary' and 'freckled Nell that never failed her master' open the play in the masque of Hymen, and are later rehearsed by the schoolmaster for the morris dance before the court. 'Swim with your bodies / And carry it sweetly and deliverly', he urges them, with characteristically over-the-top enthusiasm.

About the play

The Two Noble Kinsmen was Shakespeare's last dramatic work, and scholars are divided about how much of it he wrote. Some think that it is all his, others that he had no hand in it at all, others again that he collaborated with the up-and-coming John Fletcher, contributing characters, plot-ideas and a number of scenes, notably in Acts One and Five. The play is in a loose verse style (so loose that some think it was written partly in prose, which was then chopped up on the page to look like verse), and its character-drawing veers widely – even in the same characters – between the complex Shakespearean model and the more fluid, masque-like style favoured by Fletcher in his other work. It lacks the kind of poetic density so evident in, say, *Cymbeline*, and the reader can be shocked to find that the most lucid scenes are usually attributed to Shakespeare's partner.

'Explanations' of the play are all speculation, but fascinating. Did Shakespeare leave unfinished drafts when he retired from the theatre and moved back to Stratford – drafts which were later amplified by Fletcher? Did the two men discuss their work, and divide the writing between them (as seems to have happened with *Henry VIII*)? Did Shakespeare intend a fully original play, in the mood and style of such late romances as *Pericles* and *The Winter's Tale*, only to abandon it for reasons we can hardly even guess at? The play feels too caught in its narrow Jacobean romance genre to speak to modern readers directly. But for all its lurches in dramatic and poetic level, it has haunting glimpses of late-Shakespearean glory, and hardly deserves its almost total absence from the stage.

☞ *In performance*

A reference in Jonson's *Bartholomew Fair* suggests that the play was performed in 1613 (the Dancers and Schoolmaster probably repeating their parts from the Beaumont masque of the same year), and it stayed for some time in the repertoire of Shakespeare's company. William Davenant rewrote it in 1664, removing the mad scenes and retitling it *The Rivals*. It then dropped out of sight until the twentieth century, when it was revived at the Old Vic in 1928 and at the RSC in 1986. These major productions, and a few smaller-scale appearances, apart, the play remains better known on the page than on the stage.

PALAMON   O cousin Arcite
    Where is Thebes now? Where is our noble country?
    Where are our friends and kindreds? Never more
    Must we behold those comforts, never see
    The hardy youths strive for the games of honour
    Hung with the painted favours of their ladies
    Like tall ships under sail. Then start amongst 'em
    And as an east wind, leave 'em all behind us
    Like lazy clouds, while Palamon and Arcite
    Even in the wagging of a wanton leg
    Outstripped the people's praises . . . [II, i]

The Winter's Tale

👉 Source

Robert Greene, *Pandosto*, a romantic 'novel' published in 1588 and reprinted in 1607. Shakespeare changed the tone and style of this original, provided a new ending (the statue coming to life) and added Autolycus, Antigonus, Paulina and the rustics.

👉 Story of the play

Polixenes, king of Bohemia, visits his old friend King Leontes of Sicilia. He is so affable with Hermione, Leontes' queen, that Leontes thinks they are lovers and that Polixenes is the father of Hermione's unborn child. He plots to poison Polixenes, but Polixenes escapes and hurries home to Bohemia. Leontes accuses Hermione of adultery, and sends messengers to the Delphic Oracle to ask for proof. Hermione gives birth to a baby, and Leontes orders it to be taken to a remote place and left to die.

The messengers bring word from Delphi that Hermione is innocent. But Leontes refuses to accept the oracle, and is punished when his son Mamillius dies of grief. Hermione collapses, and her lady-in-waiting Paulina tells Leontes that he has caused her death, and takes her to sanctuary. Leontes vows never to marry again until he finds a wife as loyal as Hermione.

Antigonus, Paulina's husband, exposes Hermione's baby (now named Perdita) on the wild seashore of Bohemia, where he himself is chased by a bear and eaten. A shepherd brings her up as his own daughter. Sixteen years pass, during which both Perdita and Polixenes' son Florizel, prince of Bohemia, grow up. Polixenes begins to wonder why Florizel is spending so much time in the country, visiting the old shepherd, and goes in disguise with his lords to investigate. They arrive during a sheep-shearing festival, and Polixenes finds that his son has been posing as a shepherd, Doricles, and is about to be betrothed to Perdita. He forbids the match, but Florizel changes clothes with the trickster Autolycus and elopes with Perdita to Sicilia.

In Sicilia, Leontes welcomes the young couple. Polixenes, who has learned the truth from the old shepherd, arrives in hot pursuit. Perdita is revealed to be Leontes' long-lost daughter, and Polixenes agrees to her engagement with Florizel. They all go to Paulina's house, to a chapel containing a 'statue' of Hermione. Leontes kisses the 'statue', full of love for the wife he has mourned for sixteen years – and it comes to life in his arms.

☞ Characters

Leontes, *King of Sicilia*
Hermione, *his queen*
Perdita, *their daughter*
Mamillius, *their son*
Polixenes, *King of Bohemia*
Florizel, *his son*
Autolycus, *rogue*
Dorcas, Mopsa, *shepherdesses*
Shepherd, *thought to be Perdita's father*

Clown, *his son*
Antigonus, Archidamus, Camillo, Cleomenes, Dion, *lords*
Paulina, *Antigonus' wife*
Attendants (*including* Emilia), Gaoler, Gentlemen, Ladies, Mariner, Officers, Servants, Shepherds, Shepherdesses, Time (*as chorus*)

LEONTES At the start of the play, Leontes, Polixenes and Hermione are exchanging light, friendly conversation when Leontes suddenly has a fit before our eyes ('I have *tremor cordis* on me. My heart dances. / But not for joy, not joy'). In the space between two speeches he goes mad ('I'fecks! / Why that's my bawcock. What, hast smutched thy nose? / They say it is a copy of mine. Come, captain / We must be neat') and convinces himself that because Polixenes has kissed Hermione's hand they must be lovers. ('Is whispering nothing? / Is leaning cheek to cheek? Is meeting noses? / Kissing with inside lip? Stopping the career of laughter / With a sigh? . . . Horsing foot on foot? / Skulking in corners? Wishing clocks more swift? . . .') He insults Hermione ('O thou thing!'), puts her on trial against all advice, and dismisses Apollo when the god declares him wrong ('There is no truth at all i' the oracle. / The sessions shall proceed'). At once, and again in the space of a few lines, he is punished by the death of his son and (as he thinks) of his wife, and becomes as wretched as he was once implacable, bowing to Paulina's reproaches ('Go on, go on: / Thou canst not speak too much: I have deserv'd / All tongues to talk their bitterest') and promising penance ('Once a day I'll visit / The chapel where they lie, and tears shed there / Shall be my recreation . . . Come, and lead me / To these sorrows').

After such spectacular domination of the first three acts, Leontes disappears from the play until Perdita and Florizel come to Sicilia in Act Five. Sixteen years of grieving soften his madness but do not cure his grief. He receives Florizel with a kind of exhausted sorrow for his wrongs to the boy's father Polixenes. We do not see his recognition scene with Perdita (it is reported by a group of gentlemen) – and the reason is that Shakespeare is reserving his true redemption, the miracle that restores him to sanity and happiness, for the moment when Hermione's 'statue' comes to life before his eyes.

HERMIONE Leontes' young queen makes light, affectionate conversation with her husband and Polixenes ('Come, I'll question you / Of my lord's tricks and yours when you were boys. / You were pretty lordings then?'), and we also see her in a touching scene with Mamillius, when the boy tells her a bedtime story. Her humanity, and her dignity in the face of Leontes' jealousy ('Sir, you speak a language that I understand not. / My life stands in the level of your demand, which I'll lay down.'), win our hearts and prepare us for the transcendental moment in the final act when her 'statue' comes to life and she is reunited with her husband and long-lost daughter.

PAULINA Hermione's lady-in-waiting takes enormous risks. She falsely tells Leontes that his actions have killed Hermione, and fakes withering scorn to do so: 'What studied torments, tyrant, hast for me? / What wheels, racks, fires? What flaying, boiling / In leads or oils? . . . The queen, the queen / The sweetest, dear'st creature's dead'. She hides Hermione in her own house for sixteen years, until Leontes has paid his full penance. She stage-manages the last-act miracle of the 'statue' coming to life ('Music, awake her! Strike! / 'Tis time. Descend. Be stone no more. Approach. / Strike all that look upon with marvel. Come'), and finally presents Hermione with her long-lost daughter ('Turn, good lady: / Our Perdita is found'). In a play of whirling events and chaotic feelings, her steadfast humanity is an important emotional and dramatic anchor.

POLIXENES In Act One Polixenes is a pleasant, witty young man, the close friend whom Leontes accuses of seducing his wife Hermione. Prudently leaving Sicilia before Leontes has him killed, he drops out of the action until Act Four. By then, sixteen years later, he has become a concerned father, sternly trying to prevent his son marrying a commoner. Even so, his way of discovering what is happening (going in disguise to the shearing festival) retains some of the gamesomeness of his earlier self – he is not quite the unbending patriarch he plays.

CAMILLO Camillo arranges Polixenes' escape from Sicilia, and later stage-manages the happy outcome of Florizel and Perdita's romance. He is bluff, sincere and honest, a male equivalent of Paulina, and in the very last speech of the play, Leontes arranges for him to marry her.

CLEOMENES AND DION Like a benign Sicilian Rosencrantz and Guildenstern, Cleomenes and Dion only ever appear together, an inseparable and interchangeable couple. Leontes sends them to consult the Delphic Oracle, and they bring back word that the god declares Hermione innocent and Leontes a tyrant. Instead of letting them merely leave the stage and return with this news, Shakespeare lavishes his art on them in a glorious six-speech scene in which they enthuse, tourist-like, on everything they see: *Cleomenes*: 'The climate's delicate, the air most sweet . . .' *Dion*: 'I shall report / . . . the celestial habits / . . . And the reverence / Of the grave wearers.' *Cleomenes*: 'But of all, the burst / And the ear-deafening voice o' the oracle . . .'

AUTOLYCUS In ancient myth, Autolycus was a shapechanger, able to become anything he chose. In the play his namesake is a conman, using his skill at impersonation to fool everyone he meets and rob them. When the Clown is passing, he pretends to have been attacked by bandits and writhes in fake agony while he picks his rescuer's pocket. At the shearing festival he pretends to be a pedlar, charms the rustics into buying a trayful of trinkets and steals anything he can lay his hands on. When he changes clothes with Prince Florizel, it is as if he becomes an aristocrat on the spot. He is a fine singer and dancer, one of the most disarming rogues in Shakespeare, and his cheerful amorality warms up the play.

PERDITA Perdita is a true fairy-tale heroine. She is beautiful: 'the prettiest . . . lass that ever / Ran upon the greensward'; 'the most peerless piece of earth . . . / That e'er the sun shone bright on'. She falls in love with a handsome prince. Thinking herself a shepherd's daughter, then a foundling, she finally discovers that she was a princess all the time, and is restored to her long-lost parents. The part is small, but she lights up the stage whenever she appears.

SHEPHERD AND CLOWN The Shepherd and his son the Clown are, with Autolycus, the chief comic characters, and play several scenes together. Their characters recur, in different circumstances and under different names, in play after play, so much so that one imagines them a popular and standard 'turn'. The Shepherd is a gullible bumbler, bemused by what happens (and taking every word Autolycus says as literal truth) but good-hearted and honest. His son is a gawky yokel, who comes into his own at the shearing festival, dancing, singing and courting his beloved Mopsa.

☞ About the play

Written towards the end of Shakespeare's career, this play is the apotheosis of a fascination with Italian romance which had inspired his work since *The Two Gentlemen of Verona* some thirty years before. This kind of fiction, enormously popular in Elizabethan England, is perhaps best described as 'fairy tales for grown-ups'. The stories take ordinary, 'real' people to dream-countries, magic places where they have adventures with pirates, outlaws, exotic wild animals and supernatural beings. Extravagant coincidences and bizarre events (a woman saved in a trunk from shipwreck; a man eaten by a bear; a statue coming to life) are everyday occurrences. The characters include anguished parents, young lovers, comic rustics, kind old lords and melodramatic villains. The stories begin with separation (wives from husbands, children from parents), often include disguise and mistaken identity, involve reunion and reconciliation, and end in marriages. The interest is as much in the intriguing, even preposterous, sequence of events which make up the plot – a kind of literary comic strip – as in depth of characterization or likeness to reality.

In his earlier work, Shakespeare tended to take the elements from these romances he needed for particular comedies, reworking them and stitching them into stories of other kinds (the plots of *Twelfth Night* and *As You Like It* are typical). *The Winter's Tale* uses the form without alterations or omissions. It is picaresque and self-consciously artificial – at one point, even, Old Father Time arrives to announce that sixteen years have passed since the preceding scene. But it is unified by two of Shakespeare's greatest recurring themes, balance and reconciliation.

The play is constructed like two facing pages from an open book, so that the second half contrasts with and completes the first. The first part is set indoors in Sicilia, and is dark, tragic and powered by Leontes' guilty, irrational jealousy. The second part is set outdoors in Bohemia, is light, comic and powered by Perdita's innocent awakening to adulthood and love. The last scene brings all the main characters together (even the supposedly dead Hermione, miraculously restored to life before our eyes) and effects reconciliation by bathing the emotions and tensions of the first half in the sunshine of the second.

This unusual structure is unified by the alchemy of Shakespeare's poetry and by the way the main characters grow and change as the plot develops. However bizarre and arbitrary their adventures, their reactions are always those of 'real' people. Wonder-struck, they relate what happens to their own previous behaviour: they respond and learn. As often in Shakespeare's comedies, the process of growth involves age renewing itself by coming into contact with youth, city with countryside, courtiers with commoners and sterile rationality with the healing super-abundance of Nature. When Leontes, after long years of suffering caused by his own insane beliefs and actions, reaches the end of his self-imposed penance and is restored to the wife, friend and child he thinks he has lost, the emotional effect matches any of the grim cath-arsis of tragedy – and the reason is that Shakespeare, by stirring grace and redemption into traditional romance, reinvents the genre.

🖙 In performance

After its first known performance, at the Globe Theatre on 15 May 1611, the play was revived for a generation, then vanished until 1741, when two simultaneous productions were mounted in London. In 1756 David Garrick starred in his own *Florizel and Perdita*, a pantomime-like play with music, set in Bohemia, cen-tring on Perdita and much expanding the comedy of Autolycus; this and a couple of similar pieces by others eclipsed *The Winter's Tale* for the rest of the century. In the nineteenth century, Shake-speare's original was restored, notable performances including William Macready and Johnston Forbes-Robinson as Leontes (respectively, 1823 and 1887) and the eight-year-old Ellen Terry making her stage début as the child Mamillius (1856).

Although the play has not often been seen in the twentieth century, several revivals were memorable: the 1945 Theatre Guild production in New York, centring on Hermione and Paulina, Peter Brook's 1951 version starring John Gielgud, two RSC pro-ductions (1969, in which Bohemia became a hippy, flower-power land of dreams and Judi Dench doubled Hermione and Perdita, and 1992, in which John Nettles played Leontes as a kind of scowling philosopher-prince), and Théâtre de Complicité's 1994 version, combining physical inventiveness and other-worldly radi-ance. The play was featured in the opening season of the New Globe Theatre in 1997. Laurence Harvey starred in a 1966 film, notable alike for his cadaverous looks and his fine verse-speaking.